SIMPLY THE BEST

Insights and Strategies from Great Hockey Coaches

Ryan Walter played more than 1,000 games over 15 seasons in the NHL. Drafted second overall by the Washington Capitals in 1978, Ryan became the youngest NHL captain in his second of four seasons, went on to win a Stanley Cup during his nine seasons with the Montreal Canadiens and finished his career as an assistant captain with his hometown team, the Vancouver Canucks. He captained Team Canada in the World Junior tournament, played in the NHL All-Star game and for Team Canada in four World Championships, was a vice-president of the NHLPA and was honoured as NHL Man of the Year.

Ryan is both an inspiring motivational speaker and an interactive leadership coach whose mission is to inspire the hungry spirit. He has a Master of Arts in Leadership/Business, co-founded two start-up companies, and is the author of two books. *Off the Bench and Into the Game,* now updated and expanded, has sold over 20,000 copies worldwide and is available at www.ryanwalter.com along with Ryan's original board game *Trade Deadline Hockey.* Ryan is a television hockey analyst, an expert advisor and actor in the movie *Miracle* and the reality-TV series *Making the Cut,* and parodies himself on screen in *Being Ian.* **Book Ryan to inspire your corporation or team at 1-866-728-3603 or www.ryanwalter.com.**

Mike Johnston holds a master's degree in Coaching Science. He began his head coaching career at Camrose Lutheran College in 1982 and then moved to the University of New Brunswick, where he compiled three consecutive first-place finishes and two McAdam Division titles from 1989 to 1994. He won the Saint-John *Telegraph-Journal* Coach of the Year award in 1993, and was named 3M Coach of the Year in 1994.

Mike guided Canada to two World Junior Championships as an assistant coach and won three Spengler Cup gold medals coaching the Team Canada Selects. He won bronze and silver medals with Canada's National Team at the 1995 and 1996 World Championships and a gold medal in 1997. After four seasons as assistant coach with the Canadian National Team, he became head coach and GM in 1998 as well as assistant coach for Team Canada at the 1998 Winter Olympics. He was invited to coach in the 2007 World Championship where Canada again won gold.

As associate coach from 1999 to 2006, Mike played a major developmental role in the Vancouver Canucks' consecutive 100-points-plus seasons and subsequent Northwest Division championship in 2004. He joined the LA Kings coaching staff in 2006.

SIMPLY THE BEST

Insights and Strategies from Great Hockey Coaches

Mike Johnston and Ryan Walter

Heritage
House

Heritage House Publishing Company Ltd.
#108 – 17665 66A Avenue
Surrey, BC V3S 2A7
www.heritagehouse.ca

Heritage House Publishing Company Ltd.
PO Box 468
Custer, WA
98240-0468

Library and Archives Canada Cataloguing in Publication

Johnston, Mike, 1957–
Simply the best: insights and strategies from great hockey coaches / Mike
Johnston and Ryan Walter.—2nd ed.

ISBN 978-1-894974-37-0

1. Hockey—Coaching. 2. Hockey coaches. 3. Success. 4. Motivation (Psychology). I.
Walter, Ryan, 1958–   II. Title.

GV848.25.J64 2007   796.962'07'7   C2007-906178-8

Cover design: Frances Hunter
Cover photo of Pat Quinn and Shane Doan: Andy Clark/REUTERS

Printed in Canada

Heritage House acknowledges the financial support for its publishing program from the
Government of Canada through the Book Publishing Industry Development Program
(BPIDP), Canada Council for the Arts, and the province of British Columbia through
the British Columbia Arts Council and the Book Publishing Tax Credit.

BRITISH
COLUMBIA
ARTS COUNCIL

This book has been produced on 100% post-consumer recycled paper, processed chlorine free and
printed with vegetable-based dyes.

Foreword

I often pass the time flying home on team charters with movies, a discussion of the night's game, or a meal and some much-needed sleep, but one evening two years ago Ryan Walter and I had a chance to sit together and talk about our goals and interests. Ryan was just completing his first book, *Off the Bench and Into the Game*. For several years I had wanted to write a book that would document the qualities that made great coaches unique. I commented that I had never read a book on Scotty Bowman or Clare Drake, two coaches who, because of their incredible achievements, should have dozens of writers clamouring to find out what makes them tick. Ryan also mentioned that one of the coaches he had always respected, Roger Neilson, was at that time sick with cancer. To Ryan's knowledge no one had ever talked to Roger in depth about his amazing career and how he functioned in a coaching environment. So at 30,000 feet the project was born, with the plan to talk to great coaches at various levels in an interview format and attempt to draw out what really motivates and makes them unique.

After much debate we decided to stick with the sport of hockey and focus on 12 great Canadian coaches. Because we left it open to coaches who had experienced success at the junior, university, or professional level it became a very difficult list to narrow down. Our final list included 35 coaches, and not knowing how many would participate, we decided simply to approach them one at a time. Remarkably, all but two of the first 14 agreed to be interviewed, so our list was cut off and the process began.

As always with undertakings like this there are people behind the scenes without whom the project would not have been possible. Both of our wives, Myrna and Jenni, not only kept us on track but also handled the majority of the administrative work and deserve a lot of credit for the final product. Finally, we would like to once again thank the 12 coaches who have made this book what it is, for their patience and openness.

We are all essentially coaches, whether coaching our own children, a youth sports team, the project team at work, students in a classroom, or our employees in a major corporation. Great coaches have to be able to provide direction and vision, stay on a firm path while also recognizing when change is needed, motivate, maximize the potential of their people, and deal with adversity. As you will see, our selected coaches' techniques, strategies, and personalities are all quite varied, but deep down there is something there that allows them to be successful while others struggle to attain a similar pinnacle.

We have chosen to define "successful coaches" for the purpose of this book as those who have influenced the game of hockey with their strategies, approach, and team accomplishments. We recognize that sometimes your greatest achievements in coaching go unnoticed because they are measured by the influence you have on individuals. Often the highest compliment for a coach comes in that brief moment when you meet one of your "former players" while walking down the street or at a function and he thanks you for the impact you have had on his life.

We hope the information provided in this book will inspire you and, in turn, those you coach.

Mike Johnston and Ryan Walter
August 2004

Contents

Pat Quinn

Player, coach, GM, lawyer, even president—Pat Quinn has done it all, and more, in his celebrated connection to the game of hockey. Born in Hamilton, Ontario, Pat started his NHL career as a defenceman with the Toronto Maple Leafs from 1968 to '70, and went on to play for the Vancouver Canucks from 1970 to '72 and the Atlanta Flames from 1972 to '76. He channelled his well-known work ethic into his education and earned a bachelor of arts from York University while he was an NHL player, and later a law degree from Widener University, Delaware School of Law.

He became the Philadelphia Flyers' head coach during the 1978–79 season, and the following year set an NHL record by going undefeated for 35 straight games. The record still stands, and at the time earned him the Jack Adams Trophy as the NHL's top coach. The Flyers won the Campbell Conference title that year and finished with the best record in the NHL at 48–12–20. Pat stayed with the Flyers until 1982 and joined the LA Kings as head coach from 1984 to '87.

When Pat Quinn joined the Vancouver Canucks in 1990 as president, GM, and alternate governor, and head coach as of January 31, 1991, they had just completed 11 consecutive losing seasons. Under Pat Quinn in 1991–92, the Canucks had their first 40-plus win season in franchise history, and Pat won the Jack Adams Trophy for the second time, one of only three coaches to win this award with two different teams. The Canucks won more than 40 games each of the following two seasons and advanced to the Stanley Cup final in 1994, losing to the New York Rangers in Game 7.

Pat Quinn became head coach of the Toronto Maple Leafs in the 1998–99 season and immediately coached them to their first post-season win since 1996 and their first appearance in the Conference finals since 1994. He was runner-up for the Jack Adams Trophy and became the "winningest" active coach during this time. He led Toronto both to the playoffs and to a .500 or better road record for five consecutive seasons. He also helped them in 1999–2000 to win their first regular-season division title since 1962–63, and to set a new club record for most overall wins (45), road wins (22), and points (100) in a season. He was the fourth coach in Leaf history to attain 400 wins and became the third to be coach and GM simultaneously, from 1999 to 2003. Quinn holds third place in all-time coaching wins and fourth place in all-time games coached for the Toronto Maple Leafs.

Pat Quinn's credentials are equally as illustrious in international hockey. He coached Team Canada in 1986 at the World Championships and was part of Team Canada's management team at the 1996 World Cup, the 1997 World Championships, where Canada won gold, and the 1998 World Championships. He coached Team Canada to Olympic gold in 2002 and to World Cup victory in 2004 for the first time in 10 years.

The husband of Sandra, father of daughters Valerie and Kalli, and grandfather of three, Pat Quinn coached his 1000th NHL game on October 25, 2001, and became the seventh coach in NHL history to reach 500 wins on December 6, 2001. He was a head coach at the All-Star games in 1987, 2000, 2002, and 2004, and has coached two teams in the Stanley Cup final (Philadelphia in 1980 and Vancouver in 1994). He was named the *Hockey News* coach of the year in 1980 and 1992, the *Sporting News* coach of the year in 1980 and 1992, and the *Hockey News* Executive of the Year in 1992. In addition, Pat was instrumental in establishing Hockey Canada's B.C. Centre of Excellence, is the honorary coach of Hockey Canada's coaching program and is a member of the committee that determines admission into the Hockey Hall of Fame. He was inducted into the Hamilton Gallery of Distinction in 2003. The boy from Hamilton, who became a powerhouse behind the bench, could well have followed the advice he gave to the Convocation of Social Sciences on June 6, 2006, when McMaster University granted him an honorary Doctor of Laws degree: "Follow your dreams, listen to your heart, and obey your passion."

The Interview

What started you down the coaching road?

We were talking earlier about preparation for the end, and none of us wanted that end to come because there is joy in playing. Even though there are tough times and things you don't like about the playing side, for the most part when you get up in the morning you look forward to going down to the rink. It's a pretty nice way to go through life, but it ends because you get older, although none of us really get old.

I always thought my parents were the ones who drove me. They figured that I was a lucky guy if I was able to earn a living at something that I really enjoyed, and they were right, but they always wanted me to prepare through education for the day when I wasn't going to be able to have that enjoyment anymore. I can remember when we were younger and spent months digging out the basement because of a new city bylaw, that my dad constantly reminded me to get an education so that I could hire somebody to do this job next time. Consequently, I went to school a long time. When other guys were taking the summers off, I had to get a job, and I wanted to go to school at the same time, so I just kept at it. There are penalties you pay for that. You're away from your family in the summer as well as the winter, but it was something I was determined to do.

I still wasn't ready for the day hockey stopped. Suddenly I was without a playing job. I really hadn't thought about coaching. I had watched my coaches through the 14 years I was a pro and remember thinking they didn't seem to be enjoying the job. I tried instead to get into law school at Emory University in Atlanta, but I was too late for the exams. If I wanted to go to law school I had a year to put in someplace. I tried to buy into a business, and that didn't work, but in the meantime I was asked to be an assistant coach in Philadelphia. They had lost their coach to cancer, and they were very diligent about asking me. I told them no at the start, but they kept coming back. Finally in mid-August we had a family meeting and decided to try it for one year to see how it went, and then the next year I would go to law school anyway. In that first coaching job I had the opportunity to observe and work with Fred Shero, and he somehow whetted an appetite for coaching I hadn't known was there.

What drives you and keeps you going as a coach?

It's always a desire to win. Winning has been a pleasure. I've had the privilege of winning quite often in my life. **In a bigger sense a winner is a guy who shows up and gives his best, prepares hard to have success at the end of the day, and feels like what he does makes a difference to someone, especially to the person inside.**

Coaching has given me the opportunity to stay around a game that was fun for me as a player. I've been really lucky my whole life, even when things didn't go well. I've lost two jobs now, one as a coach in Philadelphia and then one as a GM in Vancouver, and each time someone wanted to hire me again. Even when I thought, that's it, I've had a good run and I'll try something else, I was given the opportunity to stay in the game.

The game itself motivates me, and, most important, the people. I've been around some marvellous people throughout my entire playing career. I've played for them, I've played with them, and now I try to work for them. **I am driven by the desire to somehow be able to help someone be the best they can be. That is really important to me.** At the end of the day most of us don't win, in the sense of winning a championship. We have 30 teams in the NHL now, and only one is going to win; that's it. You strive for that. That's the end of the road, the goal, but it's how you go about getting there that matters. The things you do, how you influence and relate to other people, and your importance to the guys you work with, are all there in this job. It's almost like a teacher. You're not going to influence everybody, but if you can help the guys you are working with just one iota to be the best they can be, to have self-satisfaction, you are building those inner strengths in a person. You can write down what your goals are, what satisfies you, and if it's money in your pocket, they don't mean a lot. That's one common thread I still feel today. **Today's players make 50 times what I made as a player, but that doesn't matter to them; they want to win. That's the common thread.** It's still there and, yes, we might be more material today than I remember we were then, but the common thread is they want to mean something to themselves or their teammates and at the end of the day feel important.

Do you believe that coaches have a responsibility to motivate?

It's hard over a long period of time. A lot of people think of motivation in terms of Knute Rockne walking in and giving the "rah, rah" speech. I think there's a time and place for that encouraging speech to get the emotions going, but it doesn't last long. You have to help someone identify what they want to achieve and create an environment where they can have that happen. The support mechanisms for the players are around them in the dressing room. I'm not in it so I'm there to support it and to give some guidelines and a framework, but motivation has to come from the heart. You have to feel it somehow. **I don't know if you can teach it, but you can ask for it when you ask people to be dependable. You need to be able to look across the room and say, "I expect you to do the job because I'm going to do mine for you."** That becomes more important than the coach coming in and giving the big speech.

It's something that works from within. You take pride in your own work, and it does start with the "I." **Everyone says there's no "I" in team, but there is. It's a big "I," but that "I" has to be one that now builds. You have to have self-esteem. You have to be proud of your work. You have to be able to look in the mirror and say, "I am accountable. I am the one who can work with these guys to accomplish a common goal."** Then it becomes a "you." You are going to be with me or you're going to be against me. Next it becomes "we," and we are trying to work toward what the team wants to accomplish. What we really want to accomplish is: "I want to be really good at my work." What's my work? Coaches help define what the work is.

It's nice to want to be a guy who everybody else says is a good player, but if they say about me, "This guy cares about what he does," my teammates know that they're going to get the best from me even if I might not be a really good player. How does a coach develop that? First of all you have to describe it, and then the players have to feel it. It becomes part of their life, part of their makeup, and then they take all of their physical tools and go onto the ice. All those intangibles make it work. I try to work in a general sense on those intangibles that they can control. Some things you can't control. If God gave you bad feet, you've got bad feet, but you can still play this game.

Motivation is how you play. It's an environment where you can help them to recognize what is important. **Of course, I'm not going to tell them what's important; they have to establish that themselves. At the end of the day we want to win, but that's the destination, and the journey's way more important.**

How important is building trust?

I don't think you get great teamwork unless there's trust. If we all talked about the things that are important to us in the team sense, "trust" would be one of the key words. If any of my teammates say, "You know what? I can trust Pat," that's way more valuable to me than "Pat's going to score the winning goal for us." I don't know if I'm going to score the winning goal, but I do know you can trust me, and I want to feel the same way about you. If we can trust each other, then we can do a lot together even if we don't win. That is fulfillment. That is motivation. That helps you to be a bigger person. After all, the game is something we've decided we want to do because we like to win, but more important, whether you work in an office or factory or whatever, you want to take pride in the product. If it takes a few guys to put that product together, you want to know that when you put your work in, someone else is going to do their part too. At the end of the day they look over and say, "Look at that car. It's a beauty. I put the wheels on, but Joe did the engine." I think trust is one of the most important elements of who I am. **When anybody measures me as a person it will be as a hockey guy because that's what identifies me, but I would also like to be known as a guy who is trustworthy.**

How powerful or motivating is the fear of losing?

Part of the fear in our game is the fear of losing. **While I was preparing to go to the 2002 Olympics I read the remarks of the coaches and managers who had been in Nagano in '98, and some of them felt that the fear of losing was so powerful that they fulfilled that fear.** A mechanically good team went out on the ice and was afraid that they were going to lose, afraid of the criticism in Canada. We saw it in our first game of the Olympics in Salt Lake City. We were bums right off the bat, so we tried to talk about that element right away. That was something I addressed in our very first meeting in Calgary, that if the element of fear takes over we won't achieve what we want to achieve. So as a motivating factor I think it works the other way.

There are players who respond to the fear "you're going to get sent down," "you're going to lose," or "you're going to be thought of as a loser," but I really don't think of it in terms of motivating someone. I think of it in terms of the player who can't perform because he's afraid. I think it's a debilitating factor that you have to help the player through. He has to understand what's going on so that he can go out and function.

So did you actually push the guys towards the vision of winning as opposed to focussing on "what if we lose"?

I just put it out on the table. I honestly didn't know how to handle it. I'd read the reports from Marc Crawford and Bobby Clarke, both great hockey people and high achievers, which talked about it affecting the '98 Olympic team. I was bothered the whole summer about how I would approach this because I knew it was going to be there. The idea that in Canada we only go for the gold medal is baloney. You go there to do the best job you can. When we didn't win the gold medal in '98 it just astounded me that we were considered failures. I knew we had the same group and it would be the same pressure. Even though the big stars knew how to play, I wondered how they were going to respond to this. In '98 the big stars somehow couldn't get it done, but should they have done it? I don't know. There were six good teams there, and maybe they shouldn't have been expected to win, but in your own heart you've got to win. That's why you go. That's what you want to accomplish, but if fear is in the way, you give away time and space because you don't want to be near the action; you pull away.

Fear of the unknown is a powerful element in our game, and it goes along with expectations as teams develop. I think the Vancouver team has faced this: They've had a couple of years where they have been getting better, but you've got to learn how to win when you're expected to win. If you're entering the playoffs and everybody says, "Look at them in first place. They're a marvellous team," that other team is going to come in and say, "We've got something to say about that." Now you become afraid because you're supposed to win, and that fear is a powerful thing. All the good teams had to learn it, Detroit, the Islanders, the great Oiler teams, the Montreal teams, they all had to learn how to perform and win when the pressure was on. It's a learning process. Nobody can just walk in and say, "Here's how you do it, guys." You've got to lose, you've got to battle, you've got to feel the pain, and then you've got to rise up and come back again.

Do you win at all costs?

It depends on what "at all costs" means. Would I do everything in my power within the rules that I live by to win? Yeah, you bet, if that's "at all costs," but if I go beyond my own rules, beyond what I believe is right, if I don't treat people right or if I violate my own code of ethics, then I don't want to be out there. It's not that important to win if I'm cheating myself.

What are your thoughts on confidence and on the significance of self-talk and body language?

I think body language and self-talk are really important and revealing. I used to watch a young Trevor Linden in Vancouver come to the bench like it was the end of the world, and I'd say, "Wake up. If you're afraid of mistakes, don't show the rest of the world." Davey Keon was not much older than me when I first started playing in Toronto, but he was very accomplished at a young age. One night I came back to the bench and banged my stick after a shift that I didn't like. Dave told me, "If you do that again, I'm going to give you the stick. You don't show 20,000 people that you're unhappy with yourself, and you don't show the other bench either." It made a lot of sense to me.

With regard to confidence, it's the chicken and egg thing: Does a coach give a player confidence, or does a player give confidence that he can do the job to the coach? You're always wondering that. When I meet with players one-on-one the player often says, "You don't believe in me," or "You don't play me enough," or "I should have more ice time." That's the self-talk. I try to say to the player, "Look, I do believe in you, and you're going to get quality ice time." I am a coach who uses 20 players all the time. I give second chances. I haven't been the guy with the short rope. Other coaches do it, and they do it successfully. They use fear—the fear of "I'm pulling your ice time"—to try to get a better performance. It's not something I've tried to do, although there are nights when I have wanted to.

You don't treat everybody the same. You can't; it's just not possible. You're not the same to me as you are to your teammates, and you have to develop your own self-worth. I can help you do some things, like building your self-esteem. I can help you through practice. We do segmental practice, so to speak, where you break a team skill or an individual skill down into small parts, and then you work on the small parts. You get good at the small parts, and then when you build the whole package you become able to take those small parts into the whole and become even better.

When we practise, every drill is designed to fit into a system of play so that the players don't have to think about what our system is. The system doesn't matter; it will look after itself if you're able to do the fundamentals. The player needs to understand what he has to do when he's the first man. We all love the word "system," but systems are a guideline, that's all. We want the players to think and play when they are out there. This game is transitional, so when there's transition you need to have some thought. If you're just a robot, then you go where robots go: over by the boards. We see guys coaching 10 year olds saying, "You've got to be here. Don't cross this line." That's not the game of hockey. The game of hockey is meant to express an art. It is much more complex. **Yes, you have to do some simple things in the game once in awhile, but it can be so beautiful if it's played with a brain and all of the physical tools that some of these great athletes have.** These kids are better athletes than I was. All of them are terrific athletes, maybe not better players than I was because they may not know how to use their tools well, but better athletes who can make this a beautiful game. I think we are coaching kids to be robots with the emphasis on system. That's not what hockey is. Can you win with a strong system? If you lose the puck, your guys line up and go 1–2–2 or trap or whatever you want. Sure, you can win with that. Is it nice? Is it fun to watch? Is it fun to play? No, I think we're missing the boat, really.

How do you lead a player who has lost his confidence?

You have to talk about it first. Some people have the inner strength to be able to deal with those emotion things, one of which is confidence. You can either feel the success you are having or know you're not having it and wonder why. You have to understand why things change. For example, when Markus Naslund first came to Vancouver, he displayed that fragile confidence that a lot of the Swedes have where one bad shift and, boy, they lose their sense of where they are. **I believe when we start our life in hockey it's a long-term picture, and one shift is not going to make or break us. We always call it a game of mistakes. If you're determined not to make a mistake, it usually means you're trying not to do anything; you're trying to hide.** You don't want to hide in this game; it is too much fun to hide from, even though guys still do it. Hiding alone defeats self-esteem. When Naslund came he had no confidence whatsoever, for whatever reason; maybe his former coach didn't like him, I don't know. When I see this I try to put the players in situations where they can succeed. I try to find out how I can help, and it might have to be in practice.

I have observed, by closely watching Pavel Bure and others, that when elite players are not scoring they start moving to places where they think something will happen, where the puck is going to come to them. They start playing the game on the outside, which only makes the problem worse. They end up doing the checking job for the opposition. They are generally standing someplace waiting for something to happen instead of being inside and making something happen. The good scorers get on the inside. Most of these players don't understand why they are not scoring. They can still boom the shot, but when they get the puck they have no room to move, no space, no speed, nothing; they're just there, and when that happens they are doing the job of the checker, going to spots where they check themselves. Half the time the puck is not going to come there, and now the team is shorthanded and gets scored against, and that makes it worse. Now they can't even keep it out of their own net.

Confidence is one of those things you need to build on, where you have small successes. It works the same way for teams and individuals. **To succeed you have to do little things right. You have to want to do the things that winners do. A lot of people who don't win won't do those little things.** Some of them mean discipline and some of them mean work and some of them mean sacrifice. If you don't want to do them, then you're not going to get the success because success doesn't come just because you want it. I know a thousand hockey players who want success, but they don't want to do the things it takes to get it. It's like all of us dreaming, I wish I had been born to a rich daddy.

Give us some examples of what you've done to find an angle to get players to the next level.

I've never believed this is a gimmicky game, and I've never wanted to gimmick the players; yet I know that I have a responsibility to help them move along. Part of it is setting those expectations and then moving along in a general way toward the improvement that a player can make by understanding that he has to do certain things. Some coaches I know have been very successful at finding the angle that's going to do it. They have the little carrots, as they call them; I'm not sure I have any. I want to be able to respect this guy, and I want him to respect me for the way I deal with him. There's no little angle. An angle to me is squeezing something or tricking somebody, so I don't think my personal approach would ever be angling to get guys to do anything.

What is your responsibility prior to the game to get your team ready to play?

I always felt my responsibility was to try to get them prepared on game day: to give them information, as much information as possible, about the opposition and about ourselves. The focus, though, is often too much on the opposition and not enough on us. You have to know what the other team is trying, who their top players are, and how they perform on the ice, but the big thing is preparing our team to respond to our own feelings and goals. **If we focus on us then we'll be all right. That's the most important part because you can't control them, but you can control yourself.** I have always found that particularly when things aren't going well, that's when you really try to get them to refocus on themselves and what our team is trying to do and the elements of our game that are important for success. There's often a lot of repetition, but that is where the focus should be. All teams have those ups and downs, even if they are a top team. You might not lose because of it, but you can tell your play is off.

Sometimes I present negative stuff and explain, "This is why this is happening," or put it up on the board, and they have to buy it, they have to trust me. I know everybody wants to win, and it's my job to say, "If you want to win, here's how to do it." I am prepared, though, to never have all the answers. I wish I did. Even though I don't have all the answers, they know I'm not going to b.s. them. I'm going to try to find out how I can help them because that's the biggest job a coach has. **I'm there to help these guys be the best they can be. That means a lot of things, like being a good person, caring about their teammates and family. You carry out all of those things both on and off the ice.** You are who you are both on and off the ice. Some guys take on a whole new aura on the ice. A lot of the scrappers I've known over the years are the nicest guys in the world off the ice, but you put them on the ice and they do what they have to do. That's the persona that you can take on because that's what you need to have the success you want. We can identify where we want to go, but we have to figure out how we are going to get there. **Is this bus going the right way, and are we all on it? You've got some kids hanging off and some wanting to get off. The coach is trying to get everyone on the bus. If you have some skill, terrific, you're lucky, but you're luckier if you have will.** That's the motivation part, the self-motivation, the challenge, and you hope you provide a framework in which they want to challenge themselves and feel good about what they're doing. Recognition for good work done builds self-esteem, "my contribution to my team." That is something that people really work for. Everyone wants that feeling inside.

Do you have a process where you set that vision of the bus going in the direction of the goal and establish a way to measure it?

We do, but I'm not a formula sort of person. I think formulas are for bookworms. You usually can't address the issues of teamwork or team-building by pulling some formula out of page five in a book. It doesn't work. Hockey teams are living organisms, and they change all the time. The personalities change; desires and needs change. You're in there in that mix trying to make sure that everything is going the right way. Some guys get out of whack and start bitching, "I'm only getting 12 minutes," and you've got to remind them of what we are trying to accomplish. When guys suddenly think that they are way more important than their team, you've got to tell them they're not. They have to accept the vision of where we want to go.

I've learned from a lot of management books that you have to have vision. You have to know what you're trying to accomplish. Thirty teams say they want to win the Cup this year, but only one will. There might be 10 that have a real good chance and another 20 that are just trying to get by. **You have to identify where you are and set up a plan to convince your players that this is how we're going to get to the end of the line. "We have the assets to do it here, but now we're going to have to pull it together.** Here's the plan; here's how we're going to do it; here's our style of play; here's how we're going to treat each other; here's how the respect gets built up." It obviously doesn't happen in just one day. **A team is an organism that you have to work on every day, much like a family.** If someone in your family has the sniffles and doesn't want to go to school, you address it. As a parent you cannot let those things become unimportant because they are part of your family getting on the bus. "Here's where we're going: I want you all happy. Happiness is an important thing for a family, but in the meantime I want you to be ready to go out into the world when you become an adult, and I want to protect you while you're home."

People don't grow unless they feel safe, so we want to create an environment where they feel safe. There are many threats in the game, coming from both outside and within. The trade deadline is threatening and scary and preoccupies players. They can't think about their work because they're worried about "What if I go somewhere? What if I go to a team that's not good?" We are challenged all the time; that's the business. That's where the coaches come in. You help people meet those challenges and try to keep everybody together. Somehow we've got to go on the ice and win a game despite the distractions that are always going on. That's the mental discipline that you can't really teach. You have to help guys through it, help them find out about themselves, and then the player has to come up with some answers: "Here's how I do it: I can block this off. I can not worry about that. Yes it all matters to me, but I'm going on the ice."

It sounds corny when everybody talks about winning one shift at a time, but that's what it is: You win a shift at a time. I tell lots of guys to play, rest, refocus, and play. Those are the four things that I talk about during the game. If you go out there and don't play well and the other guy is good, then you come back in, collect your thoughts for a second, and refocus because you don't want the same thing to happen again. You quickly identify your assets in your mind's eye. You decide to use your strengths next time and hopefully will be more successful.

What has been the identity of most of the teams you have coached?

A lot of people like to think that they know what that identity is and identify a coach with a certain style. They say I go for big teams, and some consider Toronto to be a goon team. I've never wanted to have that sort of team, but I do want guys to stick up for themselves, play strong, and create that safety net. When I was in Vancouver the league kept saying they were going to go for speed, so I decided to put together a team that could skate, stickhandle, shoot, and play this game with beauty. We got to the playoffs and got the snot beaten out of us. Yes, we could stickhandle, but unfortunately the other team didn't want to let us. I realized that doesn't work and that the league speaks with forked tongue.

I like character in people, and I want the kind of team that can compete in whatever game is going to be played. In the late '90s we went through the whole trap mentality that I played through in the '60s, but it's become so negative to the creation of the things we like in the game. I like good plays, good offence, and hits that take people off their feet. It's pretty hard to get through the traffic now. You've got to really have teamwork and patience, but it slows the game down. The trap is designed to slow the game down. I'd like to see the game speed up. I don't know how we do it, but that's the kind of team I'd like to have, a team that can play any way you want them to play. If you want to play rough tonight, we're here; if you want to play with more open ice, we're here. **We want the opposition to know that when Toronto or Quinn's team comes in, that we're going to compete.**

"Compete" is one of the most important words we have in our business. If you want to compete you set the will to "go" and put it together with your skill set. You're going to do it, and you're going to do it against this guy, and you're going to do it all night long. The opponent's going to look up and say, "Oh, no, here they come again." Never say die. Never accept that you're not good. I hate when guys walk around with poor body language. You can bet some nights I'm not going to be worth a darn and the other team will be terrific. I can deal with that as long as we competed. If there was one word I would like to hear people say, it's that Quinn's teams compete. I would walk around with a big chest if people said that.

In today's environment of high salaries, can you swing players' focus away from themselves and more toward the good of the team?

The biggest change in our game is the materialism that has developed. I have always believed the common thread in hockey is that guys want to feel good about what they do. I started my coaching career in the '70s. This is basically my fourth decade in the coaching ranks and that's the one thing that's still the same. These guys want to feel good about what they do. **Sure, they make a lot more money than they ever dreamed of, and, yes, at 12 years old they're getting agents and the parents are driving them, but I still think there's good value in these young men, and it's part of my job to dust them off and polish them up and bring those things forward because that is really the key to whether or not you succeed.** The values that one has in life—do you care, are you trustworthy, do you care about your teammates—are the things that teams must have to go forward. At the end of the day it's good if you want to get a million bucks or whatever, but if you do the job you will get the money. It just works out, so let's focus on doing the job. That's the approach you have to take.

How do you attempt to establish a tradition of excellence in an organization?

You try to establish expectations for the players: what they're capable of, how they can grow, both individually and as a team. I have a kind of evaluation tool, sort of a ledger. On one side I see the physical abilities of the players and the team. Here are our physical abilities, the tools that we have to use to get what we want. We want to win; we want to be better; we want to be good people; we want to be known; we want to make money. Those things are all part of it. So now you break it down. On the left side of the ledger, as I look at it in my mind's eye, are the physical things, and on the right side are all those intangible things. As a coach I'm trying to build the right side. I don't know how much I can influence the left side, but we can skate a little bit better, and maybe we can handle the puck a little bit better. We practise those things every day, but as that side gets a little better just by repetition, it's the other side I have to pay attention to as a coach. That side is what makes it all tick. Do we have character on our team? Do we have that level of confidence that you need to ride through tough times? Do we have the support group around us when everything seems to be falling apart? **You try to build that environment of interdependence.** Even though players and coaches change often now, you are still trying to work on that side because that's what sets the level of excellence.

You can strive for excellence, but you can't always achieve it. **I distinguish between excellent hockey and hockey excellence. Excellent hockey is just something you see once in awhile. Hockey excellence is doing the good things all the time.** You're playing the game right, you're in transition, you're competing, and you approach it with a professional attitude. It's your name, it's your print: "I'm Pat Quinn, and this is how I play," and you want that stamp to be something that's good.

That's the self-challenge and the team challenge. You talk about peers! They're looking across the room, and they want you to be good too, because if you're good, they're going to be good. There are lots of individual goals in that common goal. It's when those individual goals smother the common goal that you've got to be careful. I become insufferable when some players become more important than the team. **Yes, some players are better than others and more important to the success of the team, but it still has to be team-oriented. It's not all about them.**

When I first came to Vancouver and walked into that dressing room, I sensed right away that we had four or five guys who never got blamed for anything. They hadn't won in five or six years, but these guys never got blamed. They were the stars. They acted like stars and the other guys were dog dirt, chopped liver. I thought, they're not chopped liver; they're part of my team. Maybe they only play three shifts a night, but they've got to feel that those three shifts matter. It's not the coach who makes it happen; it's the guys who are in the leadership. The guys who are better players have to respect the other players. **It's like a play. At the end of the performance we want the people in the audience to say, "Bravo." You've got to play your part. I might be the star, maybe I've got the lead role, but I'm not going to treat you like dog dirt.** There were five good ones on that team and the rest were dog dirt. **I thought, no wonder they don't win anything, they can't win, the players in the dressing room won't let them win.**

Why do so few organizations reach that level of excellence?

There's such pressure to win in our game today that ownership doesn't have the stability necessary to build that repetitive framework that sets high standards. Owners who have big investments are coming in and telling you to get a different coach or asking, "What's the matter with this?" That in itself breeds a company with a "save your own ass when the pressure's on and look out for number one" attitude. When that happens, your teamwork is gone. You are looking out for number one, and you can get undermined in so many ways.

If the player can go to the general manager and the GM undermines the coach, you might as well let the coach go because that authority to handle and help the player has to be there. In the military if a private is able to go to the general, then you might as well get rid of the other guys in command. Then nothing will ever get built because it will always be about the private. The owners nowadays are kind of like that; you see them interfering everywhere. In the old days we had one owner, one company, or one guy who was identifiable, but there are very few of those anymore. Now we have the suits, the formula guys who know better. They know how to run the organization because they did it over there with the Widget Factory.

The bottom line for me is people. People make it work and they need respect, they need to be disciplined, they need to be told, "Here's what we're trying to do," they need to be pulled together, and they need to be supported. All of those things are important in developing a team. **If you're going to undermine people in the positions they are in, then you haven't got a chance. If you're going to let someone be more important than the group in their own minds, even though we know obviously some guys are better, then you haven't got a chance. We're not all treated the same, but we all should be treated with respect.**

Too often we don't have time to wait for people to put things together, and consequently good people get booted out the door. I run into people who say, "Boy, I wish you were back in Vancouver," but it's like when your dad sends you out the door with, "Bye, son, you're on your own. Get on with your life." You're on your way, and you can't go back home. Sometimes it's wrong. You can end up with people who don't share the vision, nor do they have the time, and two years later they're out. How do you then build anything when the workers always have the excuse of "Hey, it's not my fault"? You can sense it when a coach is going to get it. They've already hung him out to dry, so the players don't have to take any blame, and then it starts to disintegrate. **They say the coach loses his room, that the players stop listening. Well, they don't stop listening. They start listening to the other squeaky wheel or the undermining of this guy or their ability to hide because they don't have to be accountable. When you don't have to be accountable you can be smart as hell.** That happens in organizations. You undermine and blow good men away just because that strength isn't there. If you look at all the excellent organizations and their hierarchy, it starts right at the top, and they are solid all the way down. The players know what their expectations are, they know they have to be accountable to everybody, and so they follow suit.

How do you define success?

I think success is in the eye of the beholder. You have to identify what you are capable of doing. There aren't any guarantees to have the one success we all get measured by: the Stanley Cup. That is the Holy Grail, the crowning glory. Some teams are going to have it and a whole lot aren't. That's our desire, but real success is that process you're working on, living up to your expectations on the way there. To win a Cup now, you have to be injury-free. It's harder today than it's ever been. You have to go four rounds and it's mentally difficult. It's like a war. I hate when I say it's like going to war! It's not like going to war. We don't really know what going to war is. **Success is living the principles that you value, and if you win the Cup, that's terrific.** If you don't win it why should you feel bad about it? You've done your best. It's still a process, and you have to feel good about that process. You've gone with the process. You've challenged yourself. As I mentioned earlier about the Salt Lake City Olympics, we weren't there just for the gold. We were there to feel good about ourselves, to compete at our best. If someone's judging you and says you're a failure because you didn't win the gold, they're way off base. It's not about the gold. The gold's the big reward, the ultimate dream, the Holy Grail. You might get it, but there's a good chance you won't. Be good in the process.

What did all your successful teams have in common?

That drive that we call motivation, that internal drive, that willingness to compete. I was on a team in Philadelphia that went undefeated for 35 games. Everyone said, "What a marvellous team!" and it was a marvellous team, but it didn't have those great names on it. We had the three Bs on defence playing a regular shift. I get asked all the time, "Who are the three Bs?" Nobody knows. We had a solid team without great individuals. They were great individuals in a lot of ways, but they weren't terrific players and had no thoughts about making the Hall of Fame, but for three and a half months they were marvellous.

Success is when you look around and don't have to accept that you can't succeed. Success is setting some standards and trying to move to those standards. The standards are easy in our game. I always tell our guys that we're on a journey, and at the end of the journey is the Stanley Cup, but we're not going to get there unless we're dealing with the potholes along the way. It is the process that brings about the results, and if we pay attention to the process we can achieve a lot of things. If someone says, "I failed. I didn't get the goal," you don't have to accept that. They didn't fail, because their success is defined in some different way, by who they are and what they do and how they approach the game. Look in the mirror at the end of the day and say, "I gave my best, and that's what God wanted me to do. That's what I wanted me to do. I gave my best." That's what pushes men along.

How do you handle pressure?

You have to identify it. You have to know that it's there. Toronto, for example, is a tough place to work. You can't have a bad practice. A lot of guys don't want to play there because they don't want that scrutiny; yet it can be turned into a positive to help you push along. If you have trouble getting ready for anything, Toronto will help you change that. Mind you, our job should help you change that, because it's fun.

Then again a lot of days it's not fun. Earlier in the year, and it's happened with a few teams I've been on, you could tell the guys didn't want to go to the rink. Nothing was going right for them. They weren't happy about their work or the pressure, and of course the media in Toronto was on them. Those talk shows are outrageous; they really are. You want to run away and hide, but you can't. You've just got to face up to it. "We're having a little tough time here, so what are we going to do? Are we just going to take it, are we going to be robots, or we can do something about it?" Hopefully you have a plan to get through. The plan is the one thing, and the willingness to put it to work is the other.

Coaches can usually get the players' attention during tough times because the guys need help, but when it's going well they don't need you. They really don't. You truly are a gate opener; you just say, "Next." **In the tough times the players need you. That's when you've got to be steady** and reliable and appear confident, even though you're like the duck paddling like hell underneath. **Adversity comes in all of our lives. It's distracting, it's distasteful, but it's real.** Somehow you have to find a plan that will work to get beyond it.

What was your worst moment, and how did you recover from it?

I've had some tough times in life, like recently losing my younger brother and my dad. Those are big losses but that's what happens and everyone faces it. In my occupation my worst moment was the first time I got fired. I couldn't understand it. People usually get fired for bad performance or bad results, but I wasn't having bad results. I started to question why I was fired. Was I a bad person or was I screwing up these players, or what the heck was it? I struggled with that for a little bit because I hadn't seen it coming, for one thing, and when it happened I couldn't understand it. I'm not a dumb guy, but I just couldn't get it. My family was young at the time, and they took it hard too because that was the first time that something had publicly happened to their family.

Emotion can pull your guts right out sometimes. You can go around and feel your guts and look at them lying on the table, but it doesn't do you any good. You've got to stuff them back in and get going again. I dealt with it and took the opportunity to go to law school. I had tremendous parents, and in all the tough times they were there. They were steady. They were rocks. If things aren't going well, remember tomorrow is going to happen. As long as you get up and you've got a pulse in the morning, that's good.

How do you help your team deal with adversity?

Sometimes you can prepare for adversity ahead of time. The knowledge that it happens to all of us helps you deal with it. You can seal yourself emotionally. When emotions take over, bad things generally happen because you're not analyzing the situation. Many of the Canadian teams who went overseas, especially earlier on when our pros first started to play against the Europeans and the Russians, got a thousand penalties. Then we allowed that to be an excuse. We got stiffed, we got screwed, and all of a sudden we had an excuse not to win. You can't let that happen because there are no excuses.

Right now I'm upset with the officiating and how we get treated. People say you get special favour in Toronto, but in reality it works the opposite way. Yet all my bitching just hurts us more, really. When I get upset with what's going on, I'm not a good example for the guys, because then I speak about it and then I'm giving our guys an excuse. You need a plan to get around the adversity, and you have to exercise that plan. Everybody has to go along with it; it's that bus idea.

What types of players are the most challenging to coach?

The players who are full of themselves and, on the other side, the guy who really doesn't believe in himself; both are projects. You try to get them to work within a framework, but if they don't, then you should move them, regardless of how talented they are. I see the incredible things that happened with Naslund, who went from a timid little guy who didn't want the puck, didn't want to play, wanted to hide, to one of the best players in the game right now. It would be wonderful to talk to him about what he believes happened to him along the way, because as a coach you don't always know why there are big changes. Naslund's was such a dramatic change. He's marvellous, he's courageous, he's brilliant, he's just about everything you like to see in a player, and he's confident and humble. I'll bet he's a really nice person. **The most difficult player for me to coach is the hot dog, the guy who needs to be treated better than everybody else, because he ruins teamwork. He has to be above everybody else.** He doesn't want to be in the bus. He wants to be around it, on it sometimes, but not at other times. The team is secondary to the player, and that makes him hard to deal with.

How do you deal with confrontation?

I'm not a procrastinator, but when I see a situation I usually try to talk my way through it. **I'm not afraid of confrontation, but it should not come in a public way in front of everybody else. It should only come between the people who are directly involved.** Regardless of whether it's a confrontation among teammates or the coaching staff or how it occurs, because it can happen in many ways, it's still two concepts of what's right, and they clash. You can't let it become a disease. I've been lucky. The guys haven't challenged me publicly very much in my career. Maybe they think I'll backhand them one in the head or something.

How does the dressing room environment influence team success?

Strong leadership is really important, and expectations need to be properly set so people strive to meet those expectations. In the dressing room you need to have guys who can show the way and guys who can help you along the way. You need good leaders and good followers. The followers need to understand that one day they will become leaders too. There are bad leaders as well. They're the ones who pull the guys aside and say, "The coach is stupid. You should be playing tonight," and exert peer pressure. **Freddie Shero told me, "I've got 18 guys in there. Six like me and six don't like me. My job as a coach is to keep the six who don't give a damn away from the six who don't like me."** You need those guys in the room to be the conscience of the group, to know what's right and show the way and care for their teammates. That's what leaders do.

Do you call them the glue guys, or do you have another special word for them?

I've heard all those words, and they're terrific. They're very descriptive. The glue is important. It holds those guys who are on the fringe. There are always guys on the fringe. They want to be there to make their living, but they really don't want to pay the price. Teams have to pay a price to win so the glue guys can bring them in or say, "If you're not in you're going to be out." They don't run and tell the coach—I don't like rats—but you find out. You see it.

What qualities do you look for when you're selecting your captains and your leaders?

It doesn't hurt if he's a terrific player, but I don't think your captain has to be your best player. He has to be a guy who's reliable, he has to be disciplined, and he has to be an example for the other guys who may be more talented than him. **Talent alone doesn't win in this business. There are a lot of talented people who have done squat with the beautiful talent they have.** They have to be empathetic and show that they care about their teammates because that's a characteristic that great teams have. Caring about their teammates is where that bond of trust gets started.

The captain also has to be wise because he's really the liaison between management, the coaching staff, and the players. Sometimes the coaches need to be advised of things, whether the guys are upset with something or they feel they're staying at a bad hotel. There has to be that communication. A lot of guys are afraid to speak to the coaches because that's the way they were brought up, so the captain is the voice of the team and he has to be the barometer in the room. Sometimes your practices are too hard, and so you need that feedback. I remember when I first started I ran two-hour practices until finally the captain of the team, Mel Bridgeman, came up to me and said, "We're working too hard, especially on game day." I was going an hour the morning of the game. I was a young coach thinking I was doing the right thing and that I needed the teaching time. Your leaders and captains are very important. They're not going to b.s. you; they talk to you because it's their team. **I want the captains to feel that they are the shepherds and it's their team. Am I going to let them run it all the time? No, it's still an autocracy, not a democracy, but they'll have a say. It's important for them to have a say.**

Are you a philosopher coach, Pat? Do you teach your players life lessons within this game?

I think that's important. On the right side of the ledger I was describing earlier you have to have life lessons, the intangibles. I think they're so important to our whole being. You put who you are in a competitive situation, and it's important to develop all those things. In fact, that's where coaches need to spend most of their time. **Anybody can set up a nice practice and do drills, but it's how you do the drills and what you want to accomplish which is helping your players to feel good about themselves.** You have to prepare to practise because your practices are the rehearsal to win. All coaches who have enjoyed some success have probably paid more attention to that side of the ledger than anything else.

In what ways have you changed your coaching/leadership style over the years?

I probably do fewer one-on-one meetings than I did years ago. I don't know why they are diminishing, but that is what's happened. I've always told the players that my door is open if they have something they want to talk about. I've always been a generalist. I'll generalize in the dressing room by speaking to the players in that general meeting about what my expectations are for them. Some get it and some don't. Then maybe I have to pull them in if I want to talk to them individually. I try to talk to them individually during the general meeting, and I hope some others are picking up on the message as well. I don't think much else has changed with my approach. Maybe that's why it has pretty much worked over the decades, because it's a straightforward attempt to use an honest approach with people who want to achieve. **They know I care about them. I care about how they feel about themselves, and I care about them succeeding in their own way. I think they know that, and that's the common thread that hasn't changed over the years.** Maybe some other things have changed, but I always took pride in my practices and the mechanics of the game. I've always tried to prepare the information for them so they have it available, but I still think it's the way you deal with people that's the most important thing.

Do you trust your instincts and go with your gut feeling?

Yes, sometimes when I'm on the bench I'll make a change that I feel is important. I'll flop a winger or put a guy out for a faceoff or dress a certain guy. One of the hard things is picking the right guys, only dressing 20 out of a roster of 23. How do you handle your goaltenders and keep them involved, especially if you have a dominant one and a guy who's more of a backup? **I think there's a lot of hunch in there, but a hunch is probably the accumulation of knowledge that you have suddenly popping out. A lot of times hunches are based on your own years of being in those situations and making decisions.**

Do your principles of success spill over into other areas of your life?

I would say yes and no. I'm a pretty boring person. Hockey has been my life. I have loved it. My family's been involved with it all the way, and they've been the perfect hockey family. When I get up in the morning I know where I'm going and I know what I want to do. I'm very lucky and happy because I'm doing something that I would say is my life. I've had lots of kicks in the teeth, but that doesn't matter. Does it carry over to other parts of my life? Sure. A lot of the characteristics that we have talked about define the person, and that will show up in your work. **It's about who you are as a person, so I hope that whatever I've learned through hockey, from my family and my parents and all those values that I have, have made me a good person because that's important to me.** Coaching was an opportunity that I didn't dream about and didn't think I wanted to do, but the satisfaction for me comes when I see guys become the best they can be. That sounds so corny, but if I can help them do that I'm a happy guy. If we win at the end of the day, terrific, but it's not the most important thing, because you're winning just by being a better guy.

Ken Hitchcock

A native of Edmonton, Alberta, Ken Hitchcock started his winning ways behind the bench in AAA Midget hockey and has never looked back. During his 10 years coaching at the minor hockey level he posted a remarkable 575–69 record and was recognized as Sherwood Park Minor Hockey Coach of the Year in 1982–83 and the Alberta Minor Hockey Association Coach of the Year the next season. Following his success in Sherwood Park, Ken was hired by the Kamloops Blazers of the Western Hockey League, where he recorded a .291-115-15 record over six seasons, won two WHL championships in 1986 and 1990, and never had a losing season. He was named WHL Coach of the Year in 1987 and 1990, and Canadian Major Junior Coach of the Year in 1990 after the Blazers won the WHL title and finished third at the Memorial Cup.

Hitchcock then moved on to the professional ranks, where every team that he has coached for a full season has made the playoffs every season. Prior to obtaining his first NHL head coaching job, Ken spent three seasons as an assistant coach of the Philadelphia Flyers and three as head coach of the Kalamazoo Wings, Dallas's IHL affiliate team. While there, he was selected to coach at the IHL All-Star event in both 1994 and 1995.

Hitchcock coached the Dallas Stars for parts of seven seasons from 1995 to 2002, compiling a 277–166–60 record and a .610 winning percentage. In his first full season with Dallas, 1996–97, he coached the team to a first-place finish in the Central Division, no small feat considering Dallas had finished at the bottom the previous season. This distinguished Dallas as the ninth team in NHL history to go from last to first place in a single season, and their 38-point increase tied them for fifth best ever. Ken led the Stars to five consecutive Division Championships, two President's Trophies as "the Club finishing the regular season with the best overall record," two Western Conference Championships, and one Stanley Cup championship in 1998-99, followed by another trip to the final the very next season. In 1998–99 the Stars, under Hitchcock, set a team record for most wins in a season (51), most single-season points (114), and the highest winning percentage in a season (.610). Ken Hitchcock holds the Stars' franchise coaching record for most career regular-season wins (277), most career playoff wins (47), highest regular-season winning percentage (.610), and highest playoff winning percentage (.588). In 1998 he was selected to coach the first of three consecutive NHL All-Star Games.

Hitchcock is a winning coach in international hockey as well. He was an assistant coach for Team Canada when they won gold at the 1987 World Junior Championships and for Canada's 2002 men's team at the World Hockey Championship. He won a gold medal as an associate coach with Team Canada at the 2002 Olympic Games in Salt Lake City, Utah, and was an associate coach again when Canada won the World Cup in 2004.

Ken Hitchcock coached at the NHL All-Star game for three straight seasons, from 1997 to 1999, and a fourth time in 2004. He was nominated for the Jack Adams Trophy for three consecutive seasons in 1996–97, 1997–98, and 1998–99 and was named both the *Hockey News* Coach of the Year and the *Sporting News* Coach of the Year in 1996–97. Hitchcock was hired by Philadelphia in 2001 and quickly helped push the Flyers into the elite of the Eastern Conference. In their first season with Hitchcock as their head coach, the Flyers advanced to the Conference Semi-Finals; in their second, they lost to eventual Stanley Cup champions Tampa Bay in game seven of the Conference Finals. In November 2006 Hitchcock became head coach of the Columbus Blue Jackets.

The Interview

How did you move up through the ranks of hockey?

I played until I was 17, but I had gained a lot of weight and I wasn't a good enough player to continue, so I just got out. I didn't come back into the game until the same players I had played with as a kid all of a sudden started to play junior hockey. I ended up getting back together with them in Junior B, and I just hung around the team. Towards the end of my second year on the Junior B team the coach quit, so I ended up coaching the last 10 or 15 games, and I really liked it. Then I coached the Sherwood Park midget team from 1974 until I left for Kamloops in 1984. I coached major junior hockey in Kamloops from '84 to '90.

I was then given the chance to coach in Philadelphia as an assistant coach in 1990. One of the options at the end of my three years was to be the head coach, but I just didn't feel I was ready. I was contemplating going back to junior, even though I really wanted to coach pros, and just as I was about to accept a job in junior, I was offered the head coaching job in Kalamazoo of the International Hockey League. At that time they were the farm team of the Dallas Stars.

What motivates you personally?

I enjoy two things more than anything: I love the challenge of building a team and I love to teach. Those two things take precedence and are paramount in my motivation. I can hardly wait to come to the rink every day to teach, and I can hardly wait to come to the rink to see the type of job I've done. Those two things are the most important and challenging to me.

Do you believe coaches have a responsibility to motivate players?

There's no question that you have to motivate your players. You have to do it, and it isn't just barking and screaming. There are a lot of intricate ways to motivate your players. I think that's your responsibility. **Very few athletes in any sport can come to the rink every day highly motivated. You have to find ways to challenge them, motivate them, and get them excited.** It's a very, very long season and it's a very, very demanding profession.

The biggest motivation for a player is making him feel that, whether he's your best player or the 20th player on your team, every day he is needed and counted on. That's very, very important.

How do you do that if he's your 20th player?

Just make sure every player is challenged to play at his potential. That's a challenge you have to put forward to every player, including a role player who knows he has a responsibility and that he is just as important as your key player. The team building process comes into play when each player feels he has a real value.

How do you shape the vision for your team?

I feel like the coach is a conductor and every piece in that orchestra has a part to play and all of those parts make up a beautiful song. Every part is equally important, and my job is to make them sound and act as one.

Is the fear of losing more motivating to you than the enjoyment of winning?

I remember my losses as a head coach more than I do the wins. I think we need to pause and reflect on our accomplishments. I know, looking back, that I didn't leave myself very much time to enjoy some of the championships in junior and the NHL. There's this fear that if you spend too much time enjoying it you'll get lost, but I think that's wrong, looking back on it. **The next time we win a championship I'm going to spend more time watching people enjoy it.** I think it's a mistake we all make. It's not just the fear of losing; it's the fear of not keeping that competitive edge. I've been lucky enough to go to the finals back to back. We won the Cup in '99, and there was an unbelievable difference in our team's personality the next season. When we came to the rink after we won the Cup it was unbelievable, but when we came to the rink after we lost in 2000 it was like torture getting the players to work again.

I think I'm a much better coach now, having gone through it. Everybody is in such a hurry to get ready for the next year, but you find out there's lots of time to get ready. **You need to enjoy it and take it in and understand the confidence that comes with learning how to prepare to win.** Players don't need all kinds of time to get ready; they need to enjoy it and have fun with it. It's not so much the celebration; it's enjoying it. There are a lot more down times in our business than there are up times.

Are different players motivated in different ways? If so, do you adjust to them?

Definitely. When you come into junior and as you move along, you find out you have to really understand what makes players tick. I think that's a big part of people management. **Players have to be challenged on an ongoing basis. They need to be fully aware of what's going on. You need to hold every player as close to a single standard as you can, but you need to have an individual approach to each one.**

How do you get the "extra" out of each player? How do you get them to go through the wall for you?

I really think that the process takes a lot of time. It's not so much that the player goes through the wall for the coach, but the player needs to give everything that is important to him for the good of the game. That is a process you cannot speed up. **No matter how much you want it, there are certain aspects that have to develop through your team so that the players aren't just willing to commit, but willing to commit gladly.** The player not only wants to make that sacrifice, but also is eager to make it. That goes a long way.

There are so many facets that go into getting that player to go that extra mile. There's the chemistry of the team within the team, friendship and adversity. **You go through tough times together so that you learn about that desperation, that want, and that hunger. Those are all things that take time. You can't build that friendship environment and that camaraderie on your team overnight; it takes time.** That's why you see teams that have won before come back and win again. Look at New Jersey. I'm sure there are a number of hockey teams that think they're as good, but New Jersey has a quality, and that quality is that they just love each other and they're willing to do anything for each other and they always play well at the right time.

Do you concern yourself with a player's self-talk or body language?

It goes back to making that player feel important and having confidence. Confidence is one thing, but then there's confidence without support. A lot of it comes from the way you treat a player with respect. **If you feel that a player can contribute more, then you have to put him in a position where he can succeed.** Even if he doesn't succeed the first time, in the long term it pays dividends. I have learned in coaching that even though the player is not playing his best at the time, if you instill confidence, then he will. It's during those tough times that you stick with people. **When things aren't going as well as they should, good coaches stick with the players.** That's why you see coaches who win on an ongoing basis, no matter what team they're with.

During the day do you listen to self-talk or watch body language?

We have a format now that gives each coach a responsibility to read certain players every day. We touch the players as a staff every day that we're together. That could be saying, "Hello, how are you?" We are very firm believers that if there's a problem, then we'll deal with it and not let anything get in the way. **We also like to move on and not let things evolve, and sometimes that's very hard to do. Sometimes you have to hear things that you don't want to hear.** I feel that if you do that, then the focus is on competition and not on the politics of being on the team.

Do you feel the dressing room environment influences team success?

I think the dressing room environment is everything towards success. If you have a bond and you have chemistry you can accomplish a lot. If you have issues in the locker room, if you're not coming out of the locker room with a commitment toward how you want to play the game of hockey, I don't think that you can accomplish nearly what you want to.

What do you do to influence that?

I think that the leaders have to take over. That's a trust factor that the coaches have to give to the players. It's very, very difficult to motivate all players all the time, but if your leaders are motivated, then the team becomes much easier to work with.

Is the locker-room soapbox speech effective?

On a limited basis, but I think the more you go through things, you learn that there's a place and time to talk on an everyday basis. The biggest thing you have to learn as a coach is to know when they're listening and when they're not. When they're not listening, no matter what you want to say, you're better off not saying a darn thing.

How do you get them to listen?

I think that comes from a lot of experience. I really believe that doing it with humour, doing it with putting people on the spot, and doing it with asking questions before you even start to talk, all evolves. I don't think you should just go out and say blah, blah, blah. Whether you're pointing out something funny about a person or pointing out something about yourself, it makes people feel comfortable, and when people feel comfortable they listen.

Do you ever tell stories, Hitch?

All the time. Stories about what's going on in the league and stories about what's gone on in past history, whether it's revolutionary war stuff, Civil War stuff, or past experiences. I think storytelling is a good quality that a lot of good coaches have. I think they need to tell a story. That keeps people interested. I try to explain why I'm telling it. I say these are similar patterns that happen to us whether they come from other sports teams or history. I just try to make it interesting all the time.

Do you try to find an angle to get your players through to the next level?

No matter what angle I try to use, I don't let people get too comfortable too often. I don't believe in having everything set. I don't believe in having everything cast in stone. **I think that in this day and age people get too comfortable, too quickly, too easily, and I think complacency sets in. I keep it on edge. I would say I keep them not really knowing on an everyday basis exactly what's going to go on.**

What is your leadership style?

My opinion is that leadership is getting players to do exactly what they don't want to do and enjoy it. I really believe in showing the players the value of sacrifice, and I try to show the players the enjoyment of being part of something great. I work very hard at that. Even if it's through other teams' successes in other sports, I try to show the players the value of being a small piece of something that's very, very good. I try to reinforce the value of sacrifice. When I feel a player makes a sacrifice for the team I try to make a big deal out of it.

How important is leadership within the room?

The team can see the natural leaders, who are necessary, but the potential leaders are the most important. They are the people you have to get to. The natural leaders are people you don't have to do very much to. The potential leaders are the people who have the ability to lead and who need that added responsibility. Those are the people you have to spend a lot of time with. They have to have a role; they can't just be your extra players. The team has to know that player is important.

What qualities do you look for in selecting a captain?

The captain has to embody the way you want to play the game, but I also think the captain can evolve. In my view there are very few who are natural captains. They have to evolve as you move along, but there's a quality you're looking for in those players.

How do you deal with team adversity?

I think that's the evolution of coaching. When you first start as a coach, sometimes you hope the problem is going to go away, sometimes you feel like a win or two will correct it, but I have found all that to be wrong. Adversity isn't going away. The only way to deal with it is to deal with it up front and stay ahead of it. Having gone through this, staying ahead of it is very, very important. In order to do that you need to have strong communication with your coaching staff. They have to be willing to listen to the players' complaints, and if you feel like there is smoke, there is always going to be fire, so deal with it while it is smouldering, rather than when the fire is open.

So you'd communicate directly, or do you have a number of ways to deal with it?

It depends on the level of importance. I've included the general manager if it becomes really critical. Generally I try to deal with the problem quickly, immediately, and move on and play the game.

How do you deal with confrontation as a leader?

I try to bring both parties together to talk about it, but I try to get to the bottom of it. I don't like to see those things in a locker room.

How do you deal with a player who has something in his craw regarding you?

I'm relentless in that area. **I'm willing to hear the good, the bad, and the ugly, and I deal with it.** Sometimes I work very hard to dig it out, but other times when I know a player has a problem with me, I will give him the opportunity to bring it out. Once it comes out we start to deal with it. I will not go away until it is solved.

What types of players are the most challenging to you?

The most important challenge for me is having an impact player who buys in and becomes a two-way player.

If we were to interview some of these impact players, how would they describe you?

As demanding, as relentless, as a communicator, and as a teacher, I hope.

How would you challenge an athlete who is performing below his potential?

I would first get into the things that are non-athletic, the personal stuff, to find out what's bothering him, what's preventing him from reaching his potential. I always find that before you can get into the athletic side of things, you have to deal with the non-athletic issues that are involved in preventing that player from performing. I would rather get that out on the table so that we could move on to the competitive side of things.

How do you get the most out of a lazy player?

That's a challenge in coaching. Sometimes you lose those players. I've had players in Dallas that I found to be very, very lazy, but they never felt that they were valued and they felt they never had the coaches' confidence. Those players are maybe 21, 22, or 23, and usually what happens is they end up on maybe their third or fourth team by the time they're 30 and suddenly they see the things that you were talking about. It's very challenging and at times very aggravating trying to get those players to commit.

How close do you like to get to your players?

When you first get into the coaching business your guard is up, and you think that if you get close to your players you won't be able to motivate them at the right time. **There comes a certain time when you feel you can get close to your players and you can have a player/coach relationship and a friendship relationship at the same time.** I'm at that stage in my life right now. I'm confident that I can talk to a player about his family or about personal issues and not have that affect my coaching. I wouldn't have been able to do that early in my career.

What is the identity of a Ken Hitchcock coached team?

The first thing is my evolution as a coach. I grew up in Edmonton during the Oiler heyday, and that's the way I coached. That's the way I coached in junior, and that's the way I coached in Kalamazoo of the IHL. I had a full-court press system, and our teams still hold goal-scoring records in junior and midget that will never, ever be broken. It was pinching my defencemen, it was run and gun, it was a little bit of everything, and I wanted to experience it. I coached that way my first half-season in Dallas and got killed.

In looking back on it, there were teams that had just as much fire power in championship games in championship tournaments, whether it was in the Memorial Cup finals, the Air Canada Cup finals, or the Stanley Cup finals. They had just as much scoring experience and skill, but they were better teams at paying attention to detail. After that half-season in Dallas I changed and I became detailed. Our team still played a strong, positional game, but our attention to detail, which really is just hard work, became very important for me. I felt like our team never got outworked, but if we didn't pay attention to that defensive detail, at the end we broke down.

Have you had trouble or success in obtaining that identity?

I've had trouble with it because it's not an easy way to play. In order to play this way you have to have a strong focus all over the ice. You have to have a strong offensive focus and a strong defensive focus. You have to be able to play a complete game. There's no such thing as being able to play this way just being an offensive player or just a defensive player. We really have high expectations at both ends of the rink, and that's very demanding. There's no easy way.

What did all your successful teams have in common?

The common thread was the attention to detail, whether it was offensively or defensively. I like to see my team play the best hockey possible, and I think at the end of the day the players realize that all that attention to details pays off.

Hitch, you often talk about "the funnel." Was this strategy of play developed for specific times in the game, or is it a broad approach?

It became an approach because teams are very well coached and we had to find different ways to make the other team uncomfortable. **We started to have an offensive mindset where we would look at the ice and ask, "Where are they the most uncomfortable?" It was at the net, so we shot everything at the net.** That was our attitude. We never pass up the shot and never pass up the scoring opportunity from the outside. We are constantly trying to bring the puck to the net as much as possible.

In today's salary scope, how do you keep players focussed on what's good for the team?

That's the biggest challenge in our sport right now, and that's what makes coaches good, in my opinion. Coaches need enough confidence and stubbornness in order to bring that quality of being focussed on "what's good for the team" into the game. We have to be very demanding and make sure there are no grey areas. It doesn't matter what system you play; what sets the good teams apart is having an "all" attitude defensively. Then they can accomplish a lot of things.

What do you do to enhance team cohesion?

I really believe in having fun, whether it's having dinners with the team or leadership bonding sessions. We experiment with all of that stuff. **We try to get the players to do three things: first of all, communicate with each other; secondly, find a goodness in each other; and thirdly,**

make people comfortable in uncomfortable situations. In the beginning they look vulnerable and are vulnerable, and then comfortable after they try these approaches, because now the fear factor is not there. We try to help players take their guard down.

Do you establish a tradition of excellence within an organization, or does it simply evolve?

No, it doesn't evolve. I think you have to set the identity. Your responsibility is to provide the identity of your team, its personality. Decide the way you play. Decide how you want to be thought of. From that standpoint, this is the coach's responsibility. **You constantly have to bring up the team's identity: who you are, how you want to be known, how you want to play the game.**

Why do so few organizations reach that level of excellence?

It's an easy thing to talk about but a very, very difficult thing to accomplish. **Reaching that level of excellence takes a lot of work and a lot of stubbornness. It's relentless pursuit of an identity.** There are a number of times that we falter, and I think it's the coach's responsibility to keep that identity first and foremost in the player's mind. That's the thing that makes you consistent as a hockey player: knowing how you need to play the game to get to that level.

Some people define success as winning championships. How do you define a successful season?

I used to be like that. I found that's fun outwardly, but it doesn't last very long. **You are successful when you see your team act and behave as champions.** That is satisfaction to me. When you are known as a championship-calibre team, that's very important.

What lessons have helped you define your view of success now?

Working with Bob Gainey helped me a lot. I was always the guy who said, "We've got to win the championship," but that was kind of a fantasy. Bob really got me to think in terms of building a team to be a long-term championship team, one win at a time, and to be a long-term championship team to be proud of in years and years to come.

What are you doing during the perfect game?

Basically I am standing and watching and knowing that the players are completely in sync with each other. I am just basically rolling the lines. You know when that's happening and you should just let it flow. You feel that you're not coaching. It feels like the players are in control and you just expect it.

What would be your most memorable coaching experience or your greatest accomplishment?

Obviously the Stanley Cup is very important because we went through it together. We started with a core of 15 guys in 1996 and we built that thing. We lost to Detroit in the conference final in '98, won it in '99, and stayed together in 2000, so there was a four- or five-year run there where the team was totally in sync with the coaches, the players, everybody. That's pretty important. I had coached quite a few of those players in the International league and was at the table when some of the players were drafted. There was a strong bond between everybody.

Do you win at all costs?

No, I don't. I know the rules of hockey very well, but there are some that I just let go and allow the game to be played. I don't ask for stick measurements or things like that. I just play the game.

Do your principles of success spill over into other areas of your life?

They didn't when I first got into the business. That was my personal life. I always did things from a coaching perspective. If I did a good job in coaching, then everything would be OK. I found out later that everything is relevant, and I now believe the two are intertwined and very important. As I got older I found that your image and your reputation become an even more important responsibility as a coach. I guess what I'm saying is that **coaching is one of the most enjoyable jobs a person could have, but it is a job, and who you are is much, much more important than what you do for a living.**

How do you set a vision or mission for the season?

We really spend a lot of time at the end of the season going over what went right and what went wrong. Then we start our following season with a leadership group of seven players. We allow those players to sell that vision in training camp and during the exhibition season. When we cut down to two or three extra players during the exhibition season, then we bring our group tightly together and we really develop an identity. **We do a lot of our selling through our leaders. We allow our leaders to take it back into the locker room, and they trust that we trust them.**

Can you give me an idea of the theme in a certain year?

The year that we won the Cup it was "whatever it takes." It was constantly brought up by the players, mainly because the team was so hungry by the middle of the year that the motivation part of it by the coaches was very limited. We did more teaching and they did the motivating. The players, in my opinion, were harder on themselves than we could ever have been on them, so they were willing to go the distance.

How do you handle pressure?

I find that the more pressure in the situation I'm in, the calmer I am. I feel that I'm not nearly as good a coach when we play teams that are below us in the standings; it's just "another hockey game." I have very limited patience and have a tendency to not stay with the program and make quick changes, probably quicker than I should.

What was your worst hockey moment, and how did you recover from it?

My worst hockey moment was the loss in double overtime in Game 6 of the Stanley Cup finals to New Jersey. I don't think I've ever had a physical feeling like that in my life. I felt physically ill for probably 20 to 30 days, and I couldn't figure out why. I didn't have that understanding of what was going on, and I never felt physically worse in my life. I talked to people who had gone through it, particularly Bob Gainey, who said, "This will be the worst summer of your life and the biggest challenge you'll ever have in your life." There's a pit that gets in your stomach, and it takes a long time and a lot of work to get over it.

Is there a transfer from dealing with players to dealing with your family?

Not really. I think that becomes really difficult because when you're with your family you have to eliminate everything about you that's a coach. You have to deal with your family, just like any aspect of coaching. I'm a step-parent, and there's a big difference from being a parent. I have to walk a fine line. I had to become something other than a hockey coach to my family, and I think that's a real learning experience for me. Every day I try to just be their friend.

How do you handle the responsibilities of a head coach? Do you delegate, or are you hands-on?

I used to do everything, and now I really see the value in trusting coaches. I try to include the coaches in everything and allow them to do things without my watchdog hanging over their shoulders. I just offer my support. They might be responsible for the special teams, for example. I'm really proud to be able to include the coaches in every aspect of the game. There was a period of time when I didn't want to give any of that responsibility up, but now, over the last five or six years, I've really changed that.

Walk us through a typical day, showing how you interact with your coaches.

We start the day at a certain time. We have a non-game-day meeting to discuss the events of the night before and what we want to accomplish at practice. We then have a meeting on players: Which player needs to be touched or talked to? Next we get into problem areas, whether it's a problem with our system or a problem with a player, and then we go on our merry way. The coaches go and work on their special teams, I prepare the practice plan, and then we go on the ice and work together. We always talk for the first five minutes to an hour every day, game day included.

Are you a philosopher coach?

I try to be, and I'm better at it than I was before. I understand that coaching is a long march, not a short sprint. I try to leave every game with a lesson, a lesson of why we won or why we lost.

In what ways have you changed your coaching style over the years?

It has changed dramatically. I'm a lot more confident as a leader than

I was when I first got into the business, which is why I have success on a consistent basis. I see the value in building a team and letting the rest take care of itself. I really value what it takes to build a world championship team, not just wanting to win. There are a lot of aspects that go into that, and I feel that I've been able to listen and learn.

Do you trust your gut feeling to make decisions?

I make gut decisions all the time. I rely a tremendous amount on my gut instincts.

Who has influenced you professionally?

Clare Drake, George Kingston, and Dave King have influenced so many coaches in professional hockey that it's incredible. They have influenced so many of our careers with their teaching methods and their plan to build a team. I would absolutely love to be able to coach coaches.

Marc Crawford

Youth, energy, and success have characterized Marc Crawford's hockey history since his birth in Belleville, Ontario, in 1961. Marc won two Memorial Cups playing major junior hockey with the Cornwall Royals in 1980 and 1981. He capped his junior playing career by being voted to the Memorial Cup All-Star team in 1981. Crawford then spent his entire nine-year professional playing career with the Vancouver Canucks organization, splitting time between the parent club and farm teams in Fredericton and Milwaukee. He was a rookie on the Canucks team that made a run to the Stanley Cup finals to face the New York Islanders in 1982.

After retiring from playing in 1989, he immediately transitioned back to his old team as head coach of the Ontario Hockey League's Cornwall Royals. Following two seasons coaching major junior, Crawford was hired as head coach of the St. John's Maple Leafs, Toronto's minor-league affiliate. There he earned his reputation as a talented young coach, leading the team to the playoffs for three straight seasons, winning two AHL Atlantic Division titles and gaining an appearance in the 1994 Calder Cup championship finals.

In July 1994 he made his debut with the Quebec Nordiques for the lockout-shortened season. Finishing his first year with a 30–13–5 record, Marc Crawford became the youngest coach ever to win the Jack Adams

Trophy for Coach of the Year. The following season the Nordiques moved to Colorado, where the newly named Avalanche finished first in the Pacific Division and went on to win the Stanley Cup, posting series wins over Vancouver, Detroit, Chicago, and Florida along the way. With this victory Marc Crawford became the third-youngest head coach in NHL history to win the Stanley Cup.

Crawford was the head coach for Team Canada in the 1998 Olympic Winter Games in Nagano, Japan, marking the first time NHL players represented their countries in the Olympics. The team finished in fourth place after losing their chance to compete for gold in a dramatic shootout with the eventual winners, the Czech Republic. Crawford also served as an assistant coach with Canada's silver-medal-winning team in the 1996 World Cup of Hockey.

Crawford left the Avalanche in 1998 prior to the start of the season and, after a brief stint as a colour analyst with Hockey Night in Canada, was signed as the head coach of the Vancouver Canucks on January 24, 1999. In 1999–2000, Crawford led a Vancouver Canucks team that had missed the playoffs for two years in a row to its first .500 season in five years, to a playoff berth in 2000–01 for the first time in five years, and to playoff appearances for the next three seasons. He holds the Canucks record for the most wins as a head coach (246) and helped his club to set four new team records in 2002–03, for most points in a season (104), the best road record, the longest winning streak (10 games), and the longest unbeaten streak (14 games). In 2003 Marc Crawford became the first Vancouver Canucks coach to be named head coach in an All-Star game and is currently the third-youngest coach, after Scotty Bowman and Glen Sather, to achieve 400 wins. After narrowly missing out on the division title in 2003 Crawford guided the Canucks to the Northwest Division title in 2004. On May 22, 2006, Marc Crawford was named head coach of the Los Angeles Kings.

The Interview

What motivates you every day?

I believe it's something you develop as you grow up. The competitiveness I have is something that fostered itself from my childhood. Coming from a large family it was all about being an "attention getter." When you performed well, you got attention. I liked the feeling I got when I was complimented, and I believe that's what motivates most people.

So it's the result at the end of the day that drives you?

The result is, I don't want to say inconsequential, but it's not as important as the satisfaction that comes from performing well, and being recognized for performing well. You can string that any way you want if you're a parent or coach. Mentioning to a child that they performed as well as they possibly could have, and really worked hard, is a great compliment to give kids. It's not that I didn't get complimented or praised or loved at home, but I think through sports it was a way of getting a little bit of extra attention that made me feel special.

During a period of time, let's say with the Vancouver Canucks or with the Colorado Avalanche, when everything wasn't going as smoothly as you hoped for the team, what did you do to keep yourself motivated and on top of your game?

I don't think I've ever had a problem with motivation. I believe I have a strong desire to perform well and a strong desire to get the most out of what I have, whether that's personally or, more important, in the profession that I'm in now. **To squeeze as much out of the team you have is what you're paid to do.** When things aren't going well with the team I'm coaching, I'm constantly searching for ways to improve it. **You are constantly searching for ways to get that good feeling back, but you have to realize you only have control over certain things.** You can really push a team's effort, and then tactically you can take care of the cohesiveness of its play. I believe these are the two biggest areas that a coach can control. You can push on leadership and you can push on some other issues, but they are a little bit more complicated and they take up more time, and that's a process that you work through.

Are players different today from the way they were when you played, and do you motivate them differently?

It feels like they are but I don't think that they are that much different. I really don't believe that.

Are their motives similar?

Their professionalism has improved, and I think it's because of the education that's out there, about how to do things, how to play, how to get in shape. I've seen that change pretty dramatically in the last 25 years. From the time I was playing to now, boy, the bar has been raised dramatically. There was a select group of people who were in great condition when I played, but now the bar is much higher, and most players are in at least pretty good condition, and a lot of players are at what we would have called the elite level. They understand the ramifications of performance and non-performance, of competing and not competing, a little bit better than at least I did. I think I was guilty as a player of taking things for granted, and I don't see that as much in today's athlete. I see them being much more directed. There are many more people who provide information about what it takes to compete at a higher level. You've got the European influence now that wasn't there when I started, and most kids are coming through elite minor hockey programs and therefore have some pretty high-level coaching. I can honestly say that I didn't get exposed to high-level coaching until major junior, and probably not until I was into professional hockey.

Do you make adjustments in motivating players who have an elite skill level?

Yeah, I think it is a little different. **In motivating highly skilled players, I try to get them to understand the level of competition that they have got to be at, and that there are different spectrums of competing.** Luckily I have been around some elite players and have been able to see the level of commitment that Joe Sakic has, the level of commitment that Patrick Roy has. Knowing that Markus Naslund has that level of talent, it's been nice to see him build that level of commitment; the same thing with Todd Bertuzzi. Todd has come leaps and bounds from where he was. He's gone from a guy who played well about 50 percent of the time, to now performing at that level well in excess of probably 80 percent of the time. If we can get it to over 90 percent, then you're starting to deal with what the Joe Sakics and the Ray Bourques have.

It takes a huge commitment to get to that level. **It's important for skilled players to understand that the commitment is huge, and that's one of the things that I can help motivate them to do. You've got to appeal to their sense of competitiveness and their desire to be the best.** If they have that as a core strength you can build on it. I suppose from a coaching standpoint if they don't have it as a core strength, then you have to try to develop it as much as you can, make them realize how important it is for the team that they get to that level. There's a team element in it, and I have found that if most players don't buy into the individual part of it, which you hope, they are certainly going to buy into the team part of it. They don't want to let their teammates down.

Star players are usually easy to deal with, from my experience. Again, that level of commitment has to be there. A star player is pretty rare. There has been a huge price to pay all the way up for them to attain that elite level. I can't think of anybody who's been a superstar player who hasn't had a pretty extraordinary level of commitment.

Do you communicate with star players differently to get them onside?

I don't think that I do anything differently. Usually those superstar players end up being the leaders on your team, and we tend to communicate with the leaders in the group a little bit more regularly than with the other players. From that standpoint, yeah, that's the difference, a little more regular interaction with those people, especially in terms of team things.

What type of player is most challenging to coach?

The deep thinkers, but they are sometimes the most fascinating.

Describe a deep thinker.

A deep thinker has to have most things mapped out for him and needs an understanding of why we do things. He's got to sort it through in his own mind, and it's got to make sense for him to do it. He has to have thought out every aspect of the game. Then you've got the player at the other end of the spectrum, the blood-and-guts-type player who has no thought, just knows he has to play hard. He's got to go. He's got to play with passion. It takes both kinds to be successful.

There are a lot of people who are the deep-thinking type who would be so much better if they just allowed themselves a little bit more reckless-ness in their game, and allowed themselves to be a little bit more emotion-al. For them it's a real stretch, just as it's a stretch for the passionate player to take time to think more, but it's easier to get a passionate player to slow down a little bit and learn to think things through. You may have to tell them four, five, six times why it's done, but with the thinkers it's a stretch to get them out of their comfort zone. Sometimes they get overwhelmed and won't push themselves with passion. Their strength is that they have the best overall vision. As a player I was more of the passionate person who didn't have a great scope, and now I've moved more toward the middle in my coaching. I've realized how important that is.

How would you challenge an athlete who is performing below potential?

Most players who play for me understand what's expected of them. A combination of people have a part in setting the standard for what is expected of them, including the coaching staff and the individual player themselves.

Do you set that up at the beginning of the year?

We have meetings to establish roles and to deal with expectations and with areas that we feel need to be strengthened, areas that are im-portant to us. I think just making a player who is underperforming un-derstand that there's more for him to give and showing him the benefits of working harder, works. There's a big payoff to pushing yourself a bit harder. The coach needs to make them understand what that is, and then acknowledge or reward them when they show progress. That really is the satisfaction that comes with performing at a higher level or pushing your-self higher than you thought you could go.

How did you help Todd Bertuzzi get to the next level?

I think a lot of it is the individual player. The light has to go on for the player, and then he realizes that if he wants to be successful at this high level there is a certain commitment that has to come. Commitment comes, in a large part, from the individual, so the individual has a major impact on whether or not they become a successful player. **As a coach you have to set and adhere to a minimum standard of commitment that you expect from the players in practice, games, and from off-ice conditioning. Your bar needs to be very high.** In Todd's case our bar was pretty high, and it helped him along the way, but his individual talent and his individual commitment to better his play were the most important factors in his improvement.

Napoleon said there are two great levers to move men: fear and interest. Is there a spectrum there?

You captivate them with interest much longer. Fear is only going to work for a certain amount of time, although there is a place for it. There's a time for that in the short term to make players aware that they've got to give more, but I believe if you use that tactic you certainly have to explain it to the player afterwards. Maybe you don't have to explain it right away, to get the benefit, but you better have a little talk with them later and then explain exactly what you were doing.

Where on the priority level is the locker-room soapbox speech for you?

It works differently for different players because you get so many different personalities in our sport. There are a lot of thinking players who probably need to think things through. They've really got to have their interest prodded, and they have to rationalize things and practically see why they have to do certain things. The soapbox won't have a big impact on them, but you've got a lot of players who are very motivated by the passion they have for the game, and those guys may need that little juice. **I don't think it ever hurts to show a little bit of passion for what you are doing, because it's going to have somewhat of a positive effect.** If you do it constantly game after game after game, though, it will fall on some deaf ears. I'm of the belief that you do what you feel is right and trust your instincts. It's more of a gut feel than anything, and sometimes it's dumb luck. I've had games where I just don't like the way things have gone, for some reason, and I've gotten in some players' faces and in some people's ears, and it's worked. I think I have a better sense the other way about when to back off, and that's really important.

Do you learn that? Is it an experience thing?

Yeah, it's an experience thing. We all have characteristics about us that allow us to read people, and you can tell pretty quickly just by how people are looking at you and from their body language, how they're receiving you. Am I reaching this person? Am I scaring this person? Am I pushing too hard on this person? You develop that read as you go along.

My personality, ever since I was a kid, and I think it's probably because I come from a big family, is to look for acceptance from people, whether it's been my teammates, the players who play for me, classmates, all those areas. When you understand that you've always been looking for that acceptance, you start to develop an instinct about whether or not people are accepting what you're saying. I think that is a big part of my instinctive strength, and that's kind of how I've developed over time.

Do you look for an angle every game, for something new that will spark or focus your team?

I try to. It depends on what is needed. Sometimes there is an emotional angle to your strategy to beat a team. You may attack a strength that they have or give your team a task that you know they have a good chance of successfully achieving, and try to bring some confidence to the group. For a lot of teams in hockey right now, it's a very tactical approach to a game because most coaching staffs are pretty tactically sound. You find very few teams that are ill prepared. Most teams execute at a pretty good level, at the very least, and therefore the emotional level of a game isn't as big a factor.

Having said that, I still think that every edge that you can get is important. If you get a little boost emotionally, if you can get a little boost tactically by coming up with a strategy that is going to serve you well, if you can get a little boost to the cohesiveness of your group, that's important. Conditioning is important, and so is staying with what you've got to do at the crucial times. If you look at all those elements, the great teams have balance in all those areas. They've got a very strong mental group, they've got a very strong tactical group, they've got a very strong execution group, they stay focussed at key times, their conditioning is at an elite level. Therefore, what they do might not be different from what we do, but it's just a little bit better in each of these key areas, and that's what makes the difference.

When somebody thinks of a Marc Crawford team in the NHL or at any level, what is the identity that they are seeing, and what do you want them to see?

The summer after I came to Vancouver our coaching staff spent about a month trying to identify what we wanted our team to look like three years down the road. We went over every aspect, from how we would play and practise to how we would interact in the community and with our alumni. This became our identity, our trademarks, and from that season we haven't wavered from that plan, even though at times there has been pressure to do so. Our management group has been excellent in supporting what we do.

I'd like people to notice our speed right away. I think speed is a big factor. Speed can come from different areas: from quick feet, player movement, puck movement, or a very active defence. I think the speed should also be evident in the work ethic that the club has. You may not be the quickest individual, but because you work hard you maximize whatever speed you have. We like to think our work ethic is at a high level. All the teams I have coached have always had a pretty strong, determined work ethic.

Does that come from the beginning of training camp?

It comes from day one. Three of my siblings are teachers, and I think I learned this from their influence. **The best teachers realize that they must establish the discipline and regimen that the class is going to have the first month or two of school, because they understand that once their class gets that, all the learning is going to be easy.** But if you fight to get that for the whole year, you're really minimizing what you're going to have a chance to do.

How important is practice?

Practice is really important, but quality practice is more important. You must get your team to understand that they have to come prepared to work for the time that you have with them. Your team is going to play at least 100 games in 200 days if you make the playoffs. Therefore, you don't have a lot of quality practice days. If you're looking for at least a one-to-one practice-to-game ratio, you'd better maximize what you can get. I believe it's ultra-important to get your team to understand first and foremost that practice is important; there is no bargain there. Much like in school: The kids come into class, and they understand right away this is the work-place and there are certain levels of expectancy from the teacher. That's where a good coach is like a good teacher. You may not teach a great many lessons to them, but you get them to understand that it's a workplace and it's organized, and that's how it's going to be.

How do you keep your players focussed on what's good for the team when there's so much attention on individual accomplishments?

It's complicated, and it becomes more and more complicated because those factors are there. It's work, but most players play because they love the game. If they make it to the National Hockey League, then they've had success at some other level, whether it's in minor hockey, junior, or the American Hockey League. They've had success someplace. Before they've come to us they've been exposed to winning, and everybody likes to win. Everybody has good memories of winning, so **you try to tap into those triggers of the enjoyment of the game and the great memories they have had of winning.** We understand there are individual needs or goals and there are individual demands that the players have, but as coach-es we have to make them understand that individual goals don't mean as much as team success. That's the challenge.

You have to sell it and you have to do a decent job of trying. Most of all, it's a pretty common-sense argument. You just have to look at the 40-goal scorers who have never won, and match them to the 40-goal scorers who have won, and then ask them who has more notoriety, who do people respect more, and definitely it's the guy who's won. Winning is a big fac-tor, whether it's the monetary enhancement they get, the respect that they get, or just the feeling of satisfaction they get. **Sure, there's satisfaction with scoring 40 goals, but the common-sense argument is there's more satisfaction with scoring 40 goals and helping your team win.**

Do you have any examples of tactics or strategies you use to enhance team cohesion?

Well, you know what? It happened a lot more readily when I played, and before I played, because teams were together all the time. Team build-ing is just trying to foster that bond that playing on the team has, and you see it at every level, even at the atom level in minor hockey. When my son played atom hockey a couple of years ago, their team was as close as any team that I've seen. They were a championship team that year at their level because they were a very close team that cared about one another and enjoyed being together. They knew a lot about each other. That's what team building is. It's trying to foster that in your team and get them to be a little bit more caring and a little bit more together as quickly as you can.

The difference now is teams don't stay together like they once did. The old Montreal Canadiens players all came through their system together. They either played on the Montreal Junior Canadiens, the Montreal Royals, or on one of the five or six other junior clubs that they had, and there was a certain closeness that came from being in that organization. When they finally made it to the big club, they had been together for a long period of time. There wasn't free agency or the ability to move, so teams were close because they were together.

The other reason that they were close is that they spent a lot of time together. There are positives and negatives to that. The guys would practise, and then after practice go out together, and a lot of times going out together started in the afternoon and went into the evening. The by-product of that time together was cohesiveness amongst the group, and there was a togetherness that forged naturally. There were some negatives that came with that, probably some weakened marriages because of the time away from the families and that sort of thing.

Now a lot of players have individual things going on, and they spend less and less time together, so I think you've got to work to develop that closeness within the group and get them to do some things together. We try to do some things not only with the team, but with the spouses too, and make it more of a family atmosphere. **If you look at one of the similarities of all winning teams, there was a family structure and closeness to the team that was pretty special. In most families you can't fool your brothers and your sisters, and I think with all the best teams you can't fool the guys on the team.** There's a degree of accountability within that group that comes from the closeness that you have. **As with all families, there's usually nothing that is left unsaid and no hidden agendas that aren't exposed.**

How do you establish tradition within an organization?

I think it evolves. I think you have to use what's there. If you don't have a strong tradition, you've got to look at what you want your team to be and find a way to implement those things and assess whether or not they're happening. If your team doesn't have a tradition as the hardest-working team ever or having the best special teams, you've got to find a way to assess its strength and be able to have that as something you can tap into. Teams that do have great traditions, for example the Montreal Canadiens, Toronto Maple Leafs, Philadelphia Flyers, the New York Islanders, are usually teams that have won. They can tap into what made those teams special and put them out front and say that's what we are.

The Edmonton Oilers do a great job of that, and they've got an air about them, an edge about their team that's very apparent. It means something to be an Oiler. You have to play hard to be an Oiler, and you can't fool anybody with how you play, other than to play that Oiler way. That's been something that's evolved over the years, and it certainly comes from Sather's influence, first of all. I think after that it comes from Gretzky's competitiveness, his desire to win all the time, and paying a price to win all the time. Other guys followed and developed the tradition: Messier, Lowe, Anderson, right down to the goaltending of Andy Moog and Grant Fuhr. They found something to tap into, and now you see it in their current players and the ones who are coming in.

How do you communicate that?

Most people have it in their memory banks. If they know anything about your organization they will have remembered the great teams and how they played. If you haven't got it established you've got to establish it, and if you have it established you have to continue to re-establish it and reward people who are promoting or fostering those types of traits among the group.

We talk about our identity all the time with the team. In Vancouver we have almost 100 people who work for the organization in various capacities, and after our first year we set up what is now called "coffee with the coaches" to try to tie everyone into what we are doing and how we are going to become an elite team. At the beginning of the season we invite everyone down to the dressing room and have a few team-building exercises to get to know the group and then talk to them about what we are trying to accomplish as a team and how they can assist us.

The first year was very interesting. We had everyone break down into small groups, and their task was to come back and report how they could impact our team's success. The groups were made up of the people in finance, ticket sellers, ice and maintenance staff, marketing, public relations, and when they left the room they all thought we were crazy because there was really no way they could impact the score of the game. When they reported back it was amazing. One woman in finance said when the players come up to her area, often they don't know where to go, so she helps them out by introducing them to the right people, and by doing so maybe they are less stressed and can perform better. The ice maintenance staff said if they improve the quality of the ice this would help our team play that up-tempo style. The ticket sellers would try to get more people into the building to create an exciting atmosphere, and it went on from department to department, and everyone had a way they could impact our success. It was great, it was motivational, and the best thing now is that everyone has an understanding of what we are trying to do with the team, and they feel a part of it, and the players recognize that. The little things make a big difference.

How do you build the right atmosphere?

It isn't easy to develop. You've got to work pretty hard at it. You've got to have everybody on board. It comes from everything you do, from the top down and from the bottom up. It can't just be the general manager, the coach, and the players; it's got to be the dressing room attendants, it's got to be the people who sell tickets for you, and it's got to be everybody buying into the excellence that you need to demonstrate.

Define success for Marc Crawford, for the Vancouver Canucks.

I think it can be defined in a number of different ways. We're a very result-driven business, so results do a lot of defining for us. You can't get away from it; the result is important. It determines whether or not you stay employed, first and foremost, and it determines whether or not you can stay together. Successful results allow you to continue to build the crowds, and provide the ability for ownership to invest more.

The other way that you define success is through the satisfaction that you get. It comes down to what we were talking about first: What motivates people. Motivated people, if you want to get down to the nitty-gritty of it, always perform at the absolute highest level they can or close to as high a level as they can. If you do that, then you're going to have success. **If you focus on being the best that you can be, the results will take care of themselves.**

You have won several championships. Is that success?

You have to be realistic. I think it's the ultimate goal in our business, because only one of 30 teams can do it every year. With the talent pool being so close now, there's a lot of parity. There are probably seven or eight teams who have a chance to win right now. Prior to the last 20 years there were probably only three or four elite teams. Still, there is the requirement that you've got to get to the elite level before you can win, you really do. You may knock off an elite team, but you won't get all the way. It's just so hard now. You've got to have the elite team mentality, the elite team habits, the elite team payroll, and the elite team conditioning, and getting there is a step-by-step process.

So can a coach then unequivocally say, "Success for me, if I'm a non-elite team, cannot be measured by a Stanley Cup"?

I think it's a yes and no answer. As I mentioned, we're a result-driven business, so at the end of the day you are going to be measured by the final result. To make the playoffs and vie for the championship is a pretty good accomplishment, and to win a round in the playoffs is a huge accomplishment. To win two rounds, there are only four teams that do it. To win three rounds, there are only two teams that do it. **The perception is that you haven't had a good season if you don't make the playoffs. I believe success is always improving. You've got to continue to strive to improve.** I'm a firm believer that the answer is always the same: If you have a poor result, you've got to try to improve. If you've had a good result, you've got to improve. The process is the same no matter what, so the way you approach it should be relatively the same. Now it gets complicated because the motivation that you have may change with the success or the lack of success that you have, but the process shouldn't change a great deal.

What is your most memorable coaching experience?

It changes from year to year. The obvious one was when I was part of winning the Stanley Cup in Colorado. That was just terrific. I've had a lot of great experiences. The improvement that we've seen in our club here in Vancouver has been terrific. Working with the Olympic team in Nagano was a great experience. Playing junior hockey and winning a Memorial

Cup was a great experience. Winning an American League Championship was a great experience. I've had a lot of really satisfying and fulfilling experiences in hockey, but I guess I'd have to say the Stanley Cup is the one. It's obvious. You say, "Hey, we won the big prize." It's so neat to win it because so many good things happen. You get to take the trophy home in the summer. It's really a lot of fun—you're the champion. It's interesting to see how it captivates everybody. It's pretty rewarding.

Do you win at all costs?

I don't think you ever win at all costs. You've got to try to do whatever you can to win, but "all costs" has a negative connotation to it. There are certain areas in life where you don't cross the line. I stretch the truth every now and then, but I don't cheat. I think it comes down to the individual conscience of each person, what they can live with. **I contend that what you have control over is how hard you work and your level of execution.** That's the price that you've got to pay, and it's a huge price, but also a very satisfying price when you know you've done that. **Each and every one of us has a conscience that tells us whether or not we're doing enough or whether we're crossing that line, and we have to listen to that.**

What are your most valuable skills as a coach?

I like to think I'm pretty diverse. People have told me that my communication skills are good. People have told me that my instincts are good, and I personally think technically and tactically I'm quite sound, although I don't get as much credit for that. If you get right down to it, you need a good balance, and that's important in every aspect of life. Everybody talks about everything in moderation, and it's important. You can't have so much strength in one area that it takes away from some of your strengths in other areas. I'd hope it's my balance, but I do believe that I'm probably strongest in the area of communication.

In what ways have you changed your coaching/leadership style over the years?

You learn more as you go along. A great deal of coaching is experience, so I've used the experiences that I've had as I continue to coach. It's very important to be open to new experiences and new lessons. If you do that you're going to first of all stay current, and you're going to be able to use them to your advantage. The systems in hockey have changed, but not a great deal. The game is still pretty basic, and I think everything goes in cycles. Different things are successful as time goes on, but the basics of the game are usually the same. Experience teaches us that when we change things in the game, whether it's the forecheck, backcheck, breakout, or power play, what we're doing is just throwing a wrinkle in that people may not have seen recently, and it will only be awhile until they figure it out. Then you've got to find a new wrinkle.

Do you trust your instincts and gut feeling to make major decisions?

I think you have to. If you don't feel good about something that you're deciding to pursue, then I don't think that's a great recipe for success. **What is a great recipe for success is feeling something strongly, believing in it, and then pursuing it. So really your instincts are your conscience. You should always let your conscience be your guide. Didn't Pinocchio say that?**

Then his nose grew. As a leader how do you shape the vision of your team and your organization?

You decide what's important to you and what you want as a head coach. What do you want your team to be? What do you want them to demonstrate? Then you come up with what your vision of your ideal team is. Now you have a responsibility to try to pursue what it will take to get that vision to come to fruition. Obviously organization becomes key to the execution of your plan. It is important to have some evaluation of what's going on so that you continue to revisit it and tweak the areas that need to be tweaked and refine the areas that need to be refined. **Most of all, with that vision there's got to be a really intense desire to accomplish, a passion, a love that will get you through a lot of highs and lows.**

If we were to interview some of your players, how would they describe you as a coach?

You know what? You'd probably get a whole different realm of answers. Most of them will talk about my competitiveness, my passion, and my intensity. Some of the smart ones would probably get the other areas. The other areas are harder to find with me.

How do you relax?

I lose myself in television a lot of times, watch movies. If I don't want to think about the team, then I'll get myself thinking about something else. A lot of times it's watching a sitcom. That's what I'll do on the road when I'm having trouble sleeping, or I'll get into a documentary about something else and try to focus on that. I'm not a bad reader, but I don't use it as a relaxant. I need to be relaxed to read.

How do you handle pressure?

I think you just need to understand what you're going to be faced with and try to deal with it accordingly. From a team standpoint you deal with pressure in a number of ways. You make sure that you push people to a level that you know they're going to be pushed to in games. You practise as hard as you can at the level that you're going to need to play at. If you can physically handle what's going to be required of you, then I think that mentally it becomes easier to execute at the level that you need.

Beyond the physical requirement, you also need to prepare mentally as well as you possibly can for what's ahead. Preparation is a big key, as well as being organized enough to understand what's ahead. It may be watching video to understand how the other people operate, how the other teams operate, how your competition is doing so you know what to expect. One thing that drives me is wanting to perform well at the crucial time and wanting to perform well when the eyes of the group are upon me.

How do you handle the low points in sport?

I think the support group that you've got around you is important for recovery. You need a strong family, strong people who care for you and make you understand that it's OK to have failed. I think that starts from a very early age when you realize how important it is to do your best. What's important is that there's always another day and the sun does come up the next day. That's how you recover: You pick yourself up, you dust yourself off, and you start all over again realizing that you can. The more you've both tried and succeeded, and tried and failed, the better you realize that. You try to take the lessons you've learned and put them in place for the next time that you're going to be faced with a challenge. Coaching is dealing with the series of challenges that you are faced with, just as life is.

Does a coach have to be resilient so that he can not only respond correctly, but also have his team learn to be resilient under pressure?

I think that's a part of it. **As a coach you've got to provide that fatherly advice, where you give people credit for what they've done both in success and in failure, but also make them realize that there is going to be another day and there is going to be another chance for success. We'll be all right in the last few days of our lives if we live right to the end believing there's always a chance to be better.**

Getting back to some of the worst moments I've had, I've gotten through them because of the support that people like my parents, my wife, my friends, and people whose opinions I respect have shown me. Don't ever lose sight of how important that is. I just wrote a testimonial for one of my old high school principals about one of the nicest things that ever happened to me. I don't know if you remember the Scotty Bowman incident after the series with Colorado when I literally made a fool of myself in front of a few million people. It's not one of my prouder moments. Well, this principal wrote me one of the nicest letters I have ever received. I was impressed that she would take the time to put into words exactly what we're talking about right here: being resilient. She said, "There are a lot of good things about you, and you can't let this get you down. You've got to find a way to forge ahead. There are always going to be ups and downs." Really, in some way, shape, or form Old Sister Mary Theresa was saying, "It's better to have loved and lost than never to have loved at all," and it's true.

How would you counsel an individual player who was really experiencing adversity?

Do whatever you can to be there for him as a friend. I think it's important to allow them a chance to express themselves. Just being around and available is key. The other thing you can do is offer advice and counsel, or, if you're not qualified, point them in the direction of someone who is qualified. Let them know you have confidence in them and support them when they are down. It will pay dividends down the road for you at some level, and really, if you get down to it, it's the right thing to do. **You should be guided by what's right; it doesn't get more complicated than that.** Do the right thing; it's usually the right thing to do.

How close do you like to get to your players?

It's an individual thing with each player. There are some players who probably need to be close with the coach or at least a member of the coaching staff. We have enough people around at the National Hockey League level that those players who need that closeness, even though they might not get it from the head coach, are certainly going to get it from one of the assistants.

It's important that you stay on top of what's going on in the individual players' lives. You don't need to know everything that's going on in their private life, but you should have an understanding of what makes them tick, of what's important to them. I like to know where my players are at, what motivates them, what's important to them. With a younger team like ours we've got to do a little bit more teaching and we've got to do a little bit more individually.

How do you handle all the responsibilities of a head coach?

I'm a delegator, there's no doubt about that. When Jacques Martin was my assistant in Colorado he told me that one of my best qualities was delegating really well. I have realized that it's important to have people around me who have very strong organizational skills, because I don't.

You also delegate because you want people to feel that their input is important. I know from my time as an assistant coach I found my greatest thrills came when the head coach took what I said and implemented it. That makes you feel like you have impact, and we all want to feel important. Delegating fosters that feeling of importance.

I delegate well because I hire good people, people that I usually know and have a feeling for and whose strengths I understand. Hopefully they feed off my strengths. Every staff that I've ever had has always been virtually the same. Anyone you employ should feel the freedom to express what he or she feels, and if they feel it strongly they should make you aware of it. One of my strengths as a coach is that I do look for the opinions of people, and I think I have a good ability to sort through the various opinions and take what I think is right. Sometimes it's going to be all of what people said, many times part of it, and then I'll add my own influence to it. Sometimes I'll dismiss what's there, but people should have the strength and conviction to express what they believe, and it's twofold that you should have the ability to listen to that input and take what's good.

Do you feel that the dressing room environment influences your team's success?

Yes, players and coaches socialize in the dressing room, and it has to be a comfortable place first and foremost. It's got to be a place they want to be, and they have to feel a certain level of comfort so that they do want to perform well. That goes for any workplace. If people are comfortable in your workplace, your productivity is going to be that much better, which in sports is very, very important.

What do you do to shape that environment?

I think my style is one of openness. Every place I've been I've always changed the coaches' room to be an open room instead of individual offices. I'm a person who wants everybody around and likes to hear various opinions. I like to have an open-door policy so the players have the ability to come in and speak to us, we have the ability to come in and speak to them, and they feel that they're not hindered by the fact that we go the other way.

We go into their room and talk to them a great deal. It's easier that way because that's usually the way players are brought up. The coach comes into the dressing room, into their environment, to speak to them. We'll sometimes have our meetings in the players' lounge, or we'll take them into different areas so that it's not always regimented the same way. You've got to have an ability throughout the year to make sure that that communication and interaction with your staff, trainers, management people, and coaches is constant and informal, although you do take certain times of the year to get more formal. It's the same thing with the players. Most of what you do is formal in the dressing room, but a lot of the communication that you have is informal. We take a few times during the season to have formal meetings with the players where they can plan on expressing their opinions, and they will be asked for their opinions.

Define your leadership style.

It's very important to be who you are. The players will certainly read if you're not comfortable doing something. I'm a passionate person. I'm passionate and excited about what I am; therefore I express it in the leadership that I demonstrate. If I were to be totally controlled I think the players would read that I was uncomfortable. It's not who I am. It is important to be yourself and to do what you think is right. If you feel something strongly enough, then go with it and trust those instincts that are so important.

It's important to foster leadership amongst the group and to get them to be accountable not only to you but also to each other. That's a way of expanding the leadership of the group. That applies to the staff as well.

How important is leadership in your room, and what qualities do you look for when you're selecting your captains?

Well, we went through the process a few years back, and truthfully we didn't have any players at that time who jumped out at us as candidates. There were a number of strong candidates but no one who was overwhelmingly special. First of all the presence that an individual has is very important. Honesty is a big part of what captivates that presence in the great leaders. People can sense realness, something true in that individual that doesn't need to be spoken. While what you do and how you perform is ultimately important, the ability to express yourself is key. Being able to express yourself is an added feature that great leaders have.

Does that presence also include confidence, which we hear about so often in hockey and in sport?

I don't think you can have presence if you aren't confident. You wouldn't have presence if you didn't command a certain amount of respect because of how you play or who you are.

Have you ever had a fourth-line leader?

Yes. There are a lot of good fourth-line leaders.

Would you put a "C" on him?

No, I don't think I've ever done that. Fourth-line leaders can be the leaders of fourth-line players, but it's pretty tough, in my opinion, for a fourth-line leader to lead the top end of the group. Hopefully you've got top-end people who have some fourth-line characteristics. People who play in those roles have to have so much character and they have to have a depth of leadership and a depth of passion, but I think it's a huge burden for them to be forced to motivate or help motivate the highly skilled people who are at the top end of the lineup. Hopefully as he develops, the guy with those fourth-line characteristics is good enough that he can be a top-line player, and then obviously you have ideal captain characteristics.

Do you try to teach your players life lessons along with hockey lessons?

Yeah, I'm still learning them myself, so it's a work in progress. It's important to point them out as you go along, to sit back and smell the roses every now and then, and help them to understand that these life lessons are happening right in front of us and that they are going to be things they carry with them throughout their lives.

Do you ever tell stories to the team?

Yup, I tell some stories.

Does that have a positive effect at the NHL level?

Yes. This is one of the fallacies I had when I started to coach professionally: I thought a lot of the motivational tactics were a little corny and wondered how they would be received by National Hockey League players. You know what? Players who play in the National Hockey League pursue excellence, and any little bit of an edge that they figure they can get, they'll take. Stories are good because they usually have a lesson and a reason behind them. The reason you're telling them is just to tweak some interest.

Do your success principles spill over into other areas of your life?

Yeah, I think what you're talking about are values. The values that I have are pretty constant in my life, and really they come down to common sense. I was taught at a very young age to always try to do my best. When you're coaching that's what you're trying to do. You've got a responsibility to do your very best, and you're trying to push people to do their best. **Your job is to try to squeeze as much as you possibly can from your players, so you're sometimes getting people out of their comfort zone.** They have to push themselves past their comfort zone to be successful in the highly competitive pro sports world that we're in. In life, probably the same is true, yet I think you can have a little bit more balance to coach in life. I don't think I ever want to mistake the level of competitiveness that I have in the arena for the level of competitiveness that's needed to live an everyday life.

I do push for excellence. I try to instill those same characteristics in my children. I think the values that you gain from sport are important. The values of hard work and friendship, and the values of doing what's right are all transferable from sport. The value of common sense, as well, is very transferable: If it makes sense, then you should be doing it.

Where do you go when you need advice? Who are your mentors?

I go to different spots. I talk with my father a lot. For most people our parents are pretty strong mentors. Family is important. My wife is pretty important for advice. She knows me better than anybody, so she'll know if I'm not feeling good about something or if I am feeling too good about something. She can keep me on an even keel. I don't think those types of people change a great deal. It's the people that you love and trust the most that you respect the most for advice. I have some very good friends that I talk to a lot. A couple of them have nothing to do with hockey, yet they understand sport and they understand psyche, so they're good people to talk to.

How about in hockey, other than your dad, or was it your dad?

My dad's probably the most important one. I trust the guys that I work with a lot. When I was coming up through the ranks, Joel Quenneville and I were very good friends. I trusted Joel a lot when he worked with me, but now that he is coaching against me, I don't trust him quite as much. I really trust Jacques Martin. Jacques is very honest. He will always give me the absolute right answer.

I really trust my assistants, Mike Johnston and Jack McIlhargey. Mike really thinks things through and has got a great demeanour and great presence, and I haven't seen many people with a better read of the game. Jack is black and white, so if you talk to Jack about anything he's going to give you exactly what he thinks. There's no grey area. Also within our organization I talk to Steve Tambellini a lot, and I've got to say that Brian Burke and Dave Nonis were excellent.

I do have a couple of older people in the sports world that I talk to, and I really just love their approach. When I worked in Toronto I got to know Dick Duff. I love talking to Dick, and I will often call him for advice or to get his reaction to certain things because he has such a great understanding of what it takes to win and what it takes to be successful. Look at where he's come from. He was in Toronto in their heyday in the early '60s, he was in Montreal in their heyday in the early '70s, Toe Blake and Punch Imlac coached him, and he's just been around so many great people that I like talking to him.

Who influenced your philosophy and development as a coach?

My parents, first and foremost, have shaped my coaching through the impact they've had on me growing up. I realize that's pretty fundamental in what you become as a person. After that, the coaches, players, and the teams I've played on have developed my persona and my tactics and my abilities as a coach. I've had some great coaches throughout the years. **Roger Neilson has been a big influence because he was the first great coach that I played for. He was so organized and prepared and thoughtful, and I like to think that I carry some of those qualities.** I like to observe other coaches and take some of what they do as my own. I'm glad to have been around Pat Burns when I was in Toronto and around Glen Sather when I was with the World Cup team, and to have been around Pat Quinn, just watching them operate and thinking that's pretty neat how they did this or how they did that. All those people help you develop. I am a work in progress. I hope I'll always continue to be a work in progress. I really mean that.

Brian Sutter

The Sutter family, from Viking, Alberta, has more than 100 years of cumulative experience in the NHL as both players and coaches. The Sutter name has always been synonymous with intensity, honesty, tenacity, and hard work, and Brian Sutter has brought these traits to the players he has coached over his career.

Following his junior playing career with Lethbridge of the Western Hockey League, Sutter was drafted 20th overall by the St. Louis Blues in the 1976 entry draft. A three-time NHL all-star, he played his entire 12-year NHL career with the Blues, nine of them wearing the "C" on his jersey.

Upon finishing his playing career in 1988 Sutter immediately joined the coaching ranks, taking over the reins of the Blues. He spent four seasons as head coach in St. Louis, posting a mark of 153–124–43, which exceeded even Scotty Bowman's record. He currently ranks second behind Joel Quenneville as the "winningest" coach in Blues history. Sutter received the Jack Adams Trophy as coach of the year the following season, when he led the Blues to a 47-22-11 record, second in the NHL.

Sutter became head coach of the Boston Bruins in the 1992–93 season and held the position for three years. In his first season the Bruins had the second-best overall record in the NHL, 51–26–7 for 109 points. It was the first season in 10 years in which the Bruins had won 50 games, earning Sutter runner-up honours in the Jack Adams Trophy ballot. Sutter had a coaching record of 120–73–23 in Boston, for a .609 winning percentage.

After leaving the coaching ranks for two years, Sutter returned to the bench in his native province of Alberta to be head coach of the Calgary Flames for three seasons. On May 3, 2001, Brian Sutter became the second member of the Sutter family to coach the Chicago Blackhawks (his brother Darryl coached the team from 1992 to '95) and the fifth of six hockey-playing Sutters to be associated with the Blackhawks.

In his inaugural season, Sutter guided the Blackhawks back into the playoffs with 96 points and a tie with the Detroit Red Wings for best home record. In recognition of this dramatic turnaround, Brian was selected in balloting by his peers as *The Sporting News* NHL Coach of the Year while concurrently earning runner-up honours for the Jack Adams Trophy in 2001–02. As a Blackhawk coach Sutter posted his 400th career victory on April 7, 2002, becoming only the 15th coach in history to achieve such a milestone. In the 2003–04 season Brian Sutter surpassed the 1,000-game mark as a coach.

A recipient of the Alberta Sports Hall of Fame Achievement Award in 2000, Brian Sutter continues to be a dedicated member of the Alberta community, on and off the ice. He coached the Bentley Generals to a Senior AAA Provincial Championship in 2007. On July 12, 2007, he became the head coach of the WHL Red Deer Rebels. He is also a founding member of the Sutter Foundation, which annually raises thousands of dollars for underprivileged children and local charities.

The Interview

Tell us how your playing career evolved into a coaching career.

I was drafted by St. Louis and played 12 years in the NHL. I turned pro in '76, and my wife knows exactly when I quit. It was just something out of the blue. Jacques Martin was coaching St. Louis at the time, and Jacques Demers had coached a couple of years before. I was 31 years old, and they asked if I was interested in coaching the team. Judy and I and the kids were going to drive down to Florida, and they wanted an answer right then. I said, "You're not getting it right now." I was 31, I'd just signed a new contract the year before, and coaching was the last thing on my mind. We spent a week in Florida and thought about it, and I ended up accepting the job.

It was an unusual year. I was obviously very aware that nobody had ever gone straight from playing to coaching, but I thought there were a lot of bonuses to it. I talked to guys like Al Arbour and Scotty Bowman, whose name I had heard every day from the time I got off the plane in St. Louis when I was 19. I had some good people like Emile Francis to lean on, and they thought that with the things I'd gone through and my knowledge of the situation in St. Louis, I would be fine. I knew we had a lot of work to do.

I ended up coaching four years there. In my second year we had only four original players left from one of the best teams. There were young guys who became really good players with us in St. Louis. We had a young Brett Hull and Adam Oates, and we signed Scott Stevens. We had a very good young team.

They thought they had a Stanley Cup contender, but the team was in the middle of what we went through in Calgary, ownership moving around and uncertain in the direction they were going and disagreement within the group. We had seven or eight owners in my 12 years of playing there. They had just changed general managers and, as a result, coaches. It was an interesting scenario because we had to learn the rules of general managers and waivers, so I hired the most experienced people I could find to help as assistant coaches. Bobby Berry and Wayne Thomas had both coached a long time. I named the two son of a guns Oscar and Felix, and that's exactly how they were. We were in a big room, and I put my desk right in front of them and pushed their desks against each other. Bobby's side was upside down with papers, and he was smoking all the time, with holes in his shirt. We coached there together four years.

When I was done in St. Louis I was offered coaching jobs with 12 teams. It was really interesting. There were a lot of new teams coming into the league. I always thought it would be neat to work for an Original Six team, so when Harry Sinden called, we went to Boston. It was a similar scenario to St. Louis. They had just finished two of their worst years in a row out of the last 25. In the three years after I arrived there were only two organizations that won more games than we did. Once again we rebuilt a team using eight or 10 rookies a year. We had a wonderful time. It was so different being with Harry. I absolutely loved those three years we had in Boston. If we could have stayed together and could have kept the kids together, we would have had a chance to win a Cup. We were among the three best teams in the league but the teams that beat us, like New Jersey and Detroit, were better. We spent three years there and then quit and came home for two years while I got the farm on its own two feet again.

When I was home for the two years I became a fan of the game again. I never realized how different I had been as a player until I was done playing. Everybody always said I was intense but I didn't know what intense was. I had fun. I wanted to win and I would do anything to help my teammates and everybody in the room get it. We did it because we wanted to do it for each other. We didn't want to let each other down. It was really neat when I came home because I could sit back and be a fan of the game again. **When I played I always wanted to see people do well. I was cheering for them to do well.** There are two different ways to watch a game: You watch it as a fan or you watch it like I do, as a coach. You never forget what a certain player did at the 12-minute mark, who was on the ice and who came off. You never forget those things, and then when you play them again, you're two changes ahead of those people all the time. But it was neat to be a fan again and watch the game and just let it happen.

The two years we were home in Alberta I coached AAA midget, and I remember saying to my brother Brent when he took over the Red Deer Rebels WHL team, **"Teaching kids in junior is no different from the best teams in the National Hockey League. It's fundamentals: Have fun coming to the rink, outwork the opposition, help the players to be as good as they can be."** I was talking to one of the best players in the National Hockey League this morning. He's a good friend and he's looking forward to getting going again. He told me, "I never, ever forget when I'm down, just to be myself, and be as good as I can be." It's neat, whether you are a kid or you're 14 or 16 you've got to enjoy what you're doing and live every day right to the fullest. The fundamentals don't change from peewee to bantam to junior to the National Hockey League. The team that executes the fundamentals and has the most fun doing them and understands that all your work is done in practice, **usually gets success**. Preparing to win and preparing to be good, playing hard and practising hard are the keys. **I always say good people make good players.** Everyone needs direction. I take mine by listening and watching, and certainly not just from hockey, but being out by myself at 5:00 a.m. someplace and thinking about things.

What motivates and drives you? Why are you at the top of the NHL game and coaching elite players?

I want to win the last game. It's like we always tell our players: "I want to win the last game of the year. I want to win the Stanley Cup." Why else would you do something except to help people along the way? All the young guys went through it in Calgary and Boston, and the bottom line is if we're going to lose a game they realize that all that has happened is the clock has run out on us. The other team's always going to know they're in a battle that night that they don't want to be in again. With regard to the Calgary situation, obviously winning the Cup wasn't the goal. The goal was to make them a better team and get them to the next level.

A coach is responsible for three things: preparation, conditioning, and discipline. Those three things could all come together, but before you win you've got to prepare to win, and to prepare to win you've got to motivate. **Motivation is making a bunch of people want to play for each other together and not let each other down. The key word to that is accountability.**

How do you motivate the people around you?

I always tell our teams it's being accountable to yourself. I found out when I arrived in Chicago and our coaches had 10 things to do, that it wasn't possible. **I never realized I did this at the time, but on the farm I picked two or three things that we were going to do well every day.** We were going to finish those before we went on to the next one, but you've always got to be prepared that some moose might run through the fence and break it down and you have to do something you didn't expect to. In a hockey game if you're always ready for the unexpected, you're ready for anything that confronts you. Motivation is preparing to win, and it's not a sometime thing; it's an all-the-time thing. Then the discipline falls into place. You don't walk in and click the light switch on. I found this out when you go on a losing streak. It just doesn't click on; it comes over a period of time. **You've got to reach people to motivate them. You've got to understand people. They've got to get to know you and you've got to get to know them.** Most important, you've got to understand it's not "I" and "me"; it's "we." I've told some very good general managers when they have asked my opinion of a player, that there is nothing that bothers me more than comments that people don't like this or that player. I can honestly say I have been in the league 25 years and there are maybe one or two players that I don't think are good for a team. I'd find it hard saying I don't like them because that's not right.

I can't put my finger on what motivation is, but before teaching comes motivation, and before motivation comes reaching people. You've got to make people understand why they're doing it. There have been times I've had to make even the best players in the game understand what leadership is. **Everybody craves respect and discipline, but sometimes you've got to teach people how to do that, and when you make them understand, you can really help people.** I guess you don't realize it, but in a sense you really protect them and you understand them, and then they become a little bit more motivated. You might take responsibility away from them in some areas without them knowing it, but really what you're doing is just making them relax and have fun.

How do you keep players at their peak level?

I always tell my players that it's my job to make them play to their abilities as individuals every day, and it's not measured in goals and assists.

How do you measure an individual player's performance? Do you have criteria or a gut feel?

I think I have a gut feel because I really care for the game. I learned over the years as a player that if I don't think a player is going to play well, he never does, so as a coach I tell my players, "I expect you to be the best you can be every night." I understand there's a lot of adversity coming into the picture—there's the other team, fatigue, the referees, there might be injuries, there are people who are tired—but the bottom line is you expect them to be able to play up to their capabilities every night. The toughest thing by far for a coach is to get teams to play hard. There's no other thing because most of the guys in the National Hockey League have skill. Some of their skill is to play hard, but nobody ever talks about that. They talk about skill as skate, pass, and shoot. Talking to the Al Arbours and the Bill Torreys over the years, I have often asked, "Is it God-given? Do we come out of the cradle that way?" I think that has a lot to do with it, but I know when people say it can't be taught, they're full of baloney. I've been around some people who have lost their way and didn't know how to get there, and I have helped them understand how to get there. Once you get them to understand that, they feel pretty good about themselves, and then the sky's the limit. It's really special and really neat when that happens. I've gone through it with some of the top guys that everybody said couldn't play. I've had two or three of them on every team, and even their organization said they couldn't play, but they do more than play. **I say we're not coming to play, we're playing to win, but then I simplify it. I pick out some things that make us successful so things aren't complicated.**

You can teach people to be mentally tough, and that's something you can lose just by the flick of a switch too. As a coach you have to make players understand that and want to be better, and then when you get them playing at their capability, be careful how you push them beyond it, but make them accountable. **I always tell them after the game, "Let's remember how hard it was, let's remember how good we feel, and let's remember how tired we are."**

I played 12 years and I never broke a curfew. Part of the reason was I thought everybody else kept the curfew, but as I got older, Jeez, there was hardly anybody that did it. Al Arbour told me, "Brian, people say you're stubborn. You're not stubborn. You just want to win." It never changes, the way you want to win. Some nights you've got an "A" plan that everybody knows about, but I've always got a "B" plan ready to go to if "A" isn't working, and I've always got a "C" plan, which I'm never afraid to go to. Al always said to be consistent, stick to your morals and values, and always care for your team.

Lots of times it's like raising kids. You've got seven people in your car, and you're not going to keep them all happy. I'm lucky to have been with a lot of great people: Scott Bowman, Sam Pollock, Lynn Patrick, Dickie Moore, and Glenn Hall. We're all good friends. Some of them aren't with us anymore. They all say, "Just be yourself and be as good as you can. **Don't try to be something you're not, but have fun doing it. Be honorable and don't let your teammates down."**

Is the fear of losing more motivating to you than the joy of winning?

This is really tough to explain. **There are two types of people in life: There are people who are afraid to fail, and there are some people who are afraid to succeed. I want to be around the people who are afraid to fail.** If there was a war tomorrow I know I could make a few phone calls and get about 50 guys that I've played with who would jump on a plane and I'd enjoy going there with them because they're afraid to fail. What that means is they are afraid to let other people down. They *won't* let other people down. There are 20 players in front of me every night who say they want to win. That's easy, but when you're afraid to lose there's something inside you. When Michael Jordan came back and played, his biggest motivating factor wasn't that his dad died. He was afraid people would say that he couldn't do today what he was doing yesterday. I can walk into a room with 20 guys, and I know who's listening.

What if they're not listening? What do you do?

There are a few players who go from team to team. People say they're lazy and that they don't care. There might be some who are like that, but most of them are just misunderstood and some of them have problems. To get to know people you've got to understand them. People don't realize the intensity and pressure the players are under because they all want to succeed. I know the limits of their attention span. When I am talking to them, I pick two or three important things that we have to look after for the game. It might be making sure we're paying attention to you or not letting Al McInnis shoot the puck, but it's not 10 things. That's their preparation. Most of their preparation started at the morning skate. Once the game starts it just happens.

How long is that speech?

I keep it short. I don't want to be in there any more than three or four minutes.

What happens when you turn your back on the dressing room and walk out?

Most of the time I know they're ready. If you walk out and you know you've missed your point, or you've touched on it but you know that there are two or three guys who didn't get it, then that's why you have two or three coaches. For me there's no such thing as an assistant coach or associate coach. They're all coaches. They're all important, and they can make sure the right message is getting through.

Is the pre-game speech important? Dave King said, "When I turn my back and leave, a healthy dressing room has more carriers than it has people that have to be carried." What is your take on this?

That hits the nail on the head. You've got to have leaders in the dressing room. You've got to win off the ice before you win on the ice. Your morning skate and your pre-game speech are the two big-time keys. **You can't win a game in your morning skate or in your pre-game speech, but you can sure lose a game in your morning skate and your pre-game speech.** Again, that's preparation, and that's motivation. You've got to back off when you know the guys are ready in the morning. After being a player you know when to back off and you know when to push. I know I can help teams win, help teams give themselves the chance to win. That's the key. You're an arrogant, ignorant coach if you say you're going to make teams win, and yet at the same time, I've played for coaches who walk into the dressing room and read the pre-game speech off a piece of paper. Players read through that. It can't be 10 minutes long.

My dream as a coach is to do two things. One of them I get across pretty well, and I don't think any coach is going to get the other one. The first one is where we are totally prepared and we're going to determine how it goes. It might not be being up 1–0 or 2–0, but hey, we're going to determine it. The second one for me, and I don't think it will ever happen, is where I could just stand behind the bench and not say a thing. I know I'm very organized. Every guy knows who's up and who's coming up, not just for us, but for them too, but to not have to say a thing, not one thing behind the bench, that's my dream. I'm kind of like a duck. There are times I don't think I'm moving, but I'm going like a son of a bitch underneath.

Is it different today to motivate players from the way it was in your day?

No matter what league, if you took your final two teams in the NHL, American League, the East Coast League, or at the Memorial Cup, essentially the morals, values, and principles that they work on every day as a group are all going to be the same. They haven't changed today from 1975 when I turned pro. We all have our own way of doing things, **but the bottom line is if money is a motivating factor for them, I don't want to be around those people.** It's one of the first things I say every year, and I said it as a player. I knew I was an older player and maybe making a little bit more, but I was no different from anybody else in that room. **One of the first things I say as a coach is, "Empty your pocket at the door and leave your egos there, because the only ego that matters from here on in is 'us' and 'we.'"** "Yours" has to be involved in that "us" and "we," but it's not "I" and "me." It's called self-respect, and it means giving yourself respect. **Respect and trust are the two most important words in life, really.** Being accountable requires trust and respect, and that's not just with your teammates. I always tell my kids, "Treat other people the way you want to be treated, and you're not going to be too far out of line in anything you do." That might be walking home after a game or driving down the highway and helping someone in need. Those aren't important things; they're just things that should get done.

From a motivational point of view, is the player the same because the standard is the same?

Really, the difference is the money. If only we could somehow take out of our mind that the average salary is $1.6 million. When I finished, it was $225,000. About 1985 salaries went from $125,000 to $225,000 to $875,000. The average of the top-end guys has come down a bit, but what I wanted in the years I played was the bottom-end guys to move up. I didn't care about the top-end guys because they're going to get it, whereas the guys at the bottom are the ones you're concerned about. We went through more adverse situations than anybody in hockey in the 12 years I played. I went through years that I never got paid most of my salary. For years I was the only guy in hockey who didn't have an agent. I did my own contracts in five minutes.

Why did you do your own contracts?

When I turned pro I signed for $30,000, $35,000, and $40,000 in '79. I led the league in goals for a left-winger, and the average salary then was $125,000. I thought if I got $75,000 on my next contract I would be happy. Bernie Federko thought he was going to get $150,000, and he and his agent, Norm Caplan, negotiated all summer. It was 2,000 miles from the farm to the rink in St. Louis, and I only left two days before camp because when you were combining you couldn't leave the farm earlier. I remember talking to Norm after the first night. He said, "You and Bernie aren't going to camp." I said, "Yeah, I'm halfway there."

I drove into St. Louis about 7:00 p.m. that night. I was so excited about being in St. Louis. I'd been gone for the summer and I was 21 years old. I went upstairs to see Mr. Francis. It was my first time in his office, and he's the president and general manager. He's one of the gods in hockey, and he says, "Sit down, son." I asked, "What's the problem, Mr. Francis? I'm excited about getting going. I made some great changes, and we're going to have a good team."

He said, "There aren't any problems. You just don't have your contract signed. Write down on a piece of paper what you think you're worth."

I said, "You write down on a piece of paper at the same time and put it on the coffee table, and the deal is I'm going to read yours first." I made $40,000 and I thought if I got $75,000 I'd be in heaven. The average was $125,000 in the league then. Bernie wanted $150,000. Mr. Francis writes on a piece of paper and opens the piece of paper up. Mr. Francis had written $75,000, $100,000, and $125,000. I thought, holy smokes, here I am at $40,000. I'd already written down $150,000 but I knew I wasn't going to get it. From negotiating on farm equipment you know there's some medium ground, so immediately I knew I'm going to get $100,000. He looked at my piece of paper, and I said, "Mr. Francis, I'm going to give you another piece of paper." I wrote $125,000 three years in a row and said, "I'll sign right now if you give me that." He asked, "What about bonuses?" I said, "No, to me that's real good. I don't need bonuses." It was that simple, and Bernie got his $150,000.

How important is finding an angle to get your players to the next level?

It's very important, and it's interesting because the angles don't really change. Your team's got strengths and weaknesses, and the other team does too. Now, I'm somebody who never dwells on weaknesses. I dwell on strengths. When you're talking about strengths you're really narrowing up the weaknesses. **When I'm talking to an individual I make sure that when that guy walks out of my office he is so high off the ground, all he's thinking about is how good he can be.**

If you have to be critical in a meeting, do you start with the critique and end by building the player up?

Absolutely. They know when they're not good. A lot of players don't understand that there's a fine line between good, being on top of their game, and not being on top of their game. If you're a good coach you see that coming a long time before it gets there. We went through a stretch one season, after starting on the road in Vancouver and Calgary, where we were 3–5–2 or something like that. I knew it was nowhere near what it could be, but I also knew going through those times that losing five out of 10 wasn't good enough for me. I knew that we could be better. When we lost in Edmonton the final shots were 28–11 for Edmonton, and in reality they were 29–9, after I went over scoring chances. They beat us 7–1. Our whole season changed around right there. **Before you truly win you have to get kicked on your ass. You can't just fall on your ass; you've got to fall on your shoulders and your head.**

You can really judge people by their reaction to adverse situations. Doug Risebrough said, and I've heard this from guys who have played with the Islanders and Dickie Moore, "Just because you won a Stanley Cup it doesn't make you a winner." The Montreal Canadiens are classic because young guys go from there to other teams and never do anything. They fall off the face of the map. The Islanders are also notorious for that. And yet on the other hand there were players that Montreal and other teams didn't want who came to us in St. Louis because we were always at the bottom of the pay scale, and they became damn good players. So you don't have to win the Stanley Cup to be a winner.

What is the identity of your team and each of the teams that you have coached?

That we'll never, ever quit. We're willing to do whatever it takes as individuals to help the group. The neat thing for a coach is it's a constant challenge for you. There are always new individuals coming in, and you need to make everybody feel important and help them to be as good as they can be. A team that sticks together and cares for each other and wants to be together is so important. I remember an eight-game road trip early in the year that ended up in Boston, and Boston road trips early in the year are notorious for being a total failure. There are generally eight or 10 games, and after the first game in San Jose we were going to a hotel. Three guys wanted to get off the bus here and two there, and I said, "No, boys, you stay here. You can call your wives from your cellphone, but you're all getting off together." You win together. You lose together. **Nobody is any more important than the team, myself included as a coach. Be accountable, and most important be proud of the sweater that you're wearing and what you're representing.**

How do you keep players focussed on what is good for the team when so much attention is placed on individuals and their accomplishments?

That's the neat thing about hockey: Like football and baseball, it is a team game. How do the Yankees win year after year? They're fascinating. They're proud of each other. The position players are proud of the pitchers, and the pitchers know they have to do their jobs. Hockey is a unique game because you have to go to individuals on a daily basis and make sure you're reminding them and patting them on the back. They need your approval. I have a tough time saying, "Yeah, you're good." Most of the time when you tell people they're doing a great job the human element makes them relax. **There's a word inside success that nobody talks about: complacency. As a coach you've got to see, and maybe I learned this from being a farmer, that before the smell gets there, you know it's coming and it ain't good.** If you stay on things and have a close pulse on your team all the time, sometimes you can be losing, but you recognize you have to lose before you truly win. **You have to learn to find the buttons to push in every individual to make them make a difference on the team.** Even though you say it is a team, you have to make people want to be a difference. You can't just play to win; you've got to be a difference. Everybody finds that in a different way. They might find it in five minutes of ice time, or they might find it in 10.

I believe as a coach I can make everybody feel important and wanted. When I hear somebody upset at the coach I kind of grin and keep walking. I can take it because they want more. It's fine for them to say they want more; it's like saying I want to win, but what do you want to do to make a difference? That's where you've got to get to know the individuals and when to back off. Everybody cares differently. **That's what coaching is. It's not manipulating; it's motivating, it's managing people, and to do that you've got to be extremely disciplined in your approach and extremely consistent.** You can't be way up here and then down here. In other words, you can't be totally off the wall when you lose or get too high when you win. You've got to make the guys understand they've got to feel good when they win and it's got to hurt when they lose.

What types of things have you done to enhance team cohesion?

Going on the road is very important.

Do you find your team's play fluctuates a great deal with the length of the NHL schedule?

The tough times of the year are Christmas and that little time in January around the All-Star break. Why don't players play the whole game like they play the last five minutes of the game, ahead or behind, with that sense of desperation and that sense of urgency? I've got to do the little things. If you do the little things right, their skill will take over. **I always say the game is like a horse race. If you train and prepare properly and discipline yourself, you start well and you finish well; then everything in between always looks after itself.** You might lose some at the end but that's because the finish line just came too quickly. You need that mentality that tomorrow is a new day.

How do you establish a tradition within an organization? Or does it evolve?

First of all, you've got to set your standards, and you don't set mediocre ones. I tell the players I'm never going to compare them to something that's average. "We're all paid very well and we're paid to be good, not average, so set high standards for yourself. Don't be afraid to dream, but compare yourself to the best." It's something that evolves, and the coach has something to do with it. You can't be so set in your ways. You've got to be prepared to change. You can't be afraid to play players against people that they didn't think they could play against. It's your job as a coach, whether you're coaching kids or in the NHL, to put players in the position to succeed. That's the key; you want them to want more.

How do you communicate a tradition of excellence, and why do so few organizations reach that level of excellence?

I don't think there's any doubt why they don't reach it. It's because coaches and management don't stay together. The thing that was consistent about Edmonton and the Islanders and Montreal was who ran the show. **I always say success is like a manure pile. It starts at the top and runs down. If it's not very good on top, it's going to run to the bottom, and there's going to be a big pile of smelly stuff with a bunch of people in it.** You've got to be consistent. You can't go through four coaches in five years. You've got to be consistent in your approach. People read that and people see that.

Also, there are few players who are loyal to teams anymore because there's so much money out there. They're loyal during the year, but once the season ends, it's different. People think that as they get older they should be making more money, but it doesn't work that way. There are not many 38- or 39-year-old players who are still playing.

Define success. Is it goal driven? If this was the end of the year right now, what was a successful year for you?

It's staying on course. Making the playoffs has to be the benchmark because otherwise franchises go under and coaches are replaced. Success is what's staring you in the face. In reality, it's how good your people have become. The press and fans are going to judge you that way, but as a coach you never forget the people who would do anything for you, and you know that if you went out and played hard and they looked up to you, that's what success truly is. **Hockey is just a small part of our life, that's all, but it's also a reflection of our soul. It's not always winning and losing. It's being respectful to everybody and everything around you and treating people the way you would want to be treated. If you don't do those things you have no chance of winning.**

Success isn't how much money you make. The grass isn't greener on the other side of the fence. Sometimes it looks like it is, but there are a lot of other more important factors. Success is how people look at you. It's not just what you did for me yesterday, but what can you do for me today? Unfortunately that's the way it is in sports and in every business. Just winning a Stanley Cup doesn't make you a winner. There are a lot of winners who didn't win a Stanley Cup.

What was your most memorable coaching experience?

I've had some really good ones. Taking a team in St. Louis and making them one of the top teams, and the same thing in Boston and Calgary, and Chicago in 2002–03 was memorable. I've always said putting a uniform on every game for 12 years was really neat and very satisfying. Every day it was special to come to the rink and practise. I know I had more fun than most people who play the game, but as I look back I should have raised a little bit more hell and had a little bit more fun. I always feel I never quite get enough. The most gratifying things to accomplish in life, the things that mean the most to you down the road, are always the ones everybody says you can't do, the ones you can't accomplish. Certainly a special moment was when we won the Canada Cup in '91. That year we ended up having 60-some guys in camp, and it was so hard because you knew a bunch of guys weren't going to make the team that should have made the team. The Swedes had just come up with the trap and the Finns were getting better and the Russians had a really good team.

What did all your successful teams have in common? Was there a common thread?

You never meet two players the same. If they came and played hard every night for each other and they had more respect at the end of the year and were more accountable to their teammates than they were at the beginning of the year, that's what makes a success.

Is there a business process to get success?

There absolutely has to be because to be successful you have to plan to do it. There are three things you need to do to be successful in life and to reach your goals: (1) You've got to decide what your goals are; (2) you've got to plan how you're going to achieve those goals; (3) you can never forget your goal and how to get it. Obviously you have to have strong people at the top. There's definitely got to be a plan. You ask about winning a Stanley Cup and building a tradition, a so-called dynasty, which is what it is. You're setting goals. You've got to be honest in your approach. You've got to be firm but never afraid, flexible and prepared to change. **You've got to be selfish and do anything to win, but you've got to be prepared to be totally unselfish in giving yourself up for what's good for the team.**

How do you measure success at any given time in the season? How do you keep track of your team's success, and how do you keep your team's success on track?

Just looking at the black and white can allow a player to stay focussed. Players have to stay focussed for the short term. **In any business and as a coach you have to have a long-term goal in mind, but that long-term goal will be lost in a hurry if you lose sight of the fact that we've got to win tonight and look after the job tonight, and then tomorrow**

will look after itself. You've got to get players thinking that way. All you have to do is look at baseball players. A baseball player on a streak is in there before anybody else and taking his batting practices. He prepares to win and to be better every night.

Do you win at all costs?

During the game you do anything. Every coach tries to do it differently. I look back and wish I'd done things differently. Things seemed way tougher to me at times than they actually were. You play to win. That's the way you play. It started when we were little kids. You weren't afraid to kick the line of scrimmage back two or three feet at a time until your team gained 20 feet. Everybody talks about changing the rules because of obstruction and stuff. There's less obstruction in the game now than there has been in 10 years. The guys who are talking about it don't know anything about hockey. The game's great now. I always say the best team cheats the best within the rules and does anything to win. It starts from the time the puck drops by treating the officials with respect so they give you that extra couple of inches when you are offside, or when you might have interfered with the goalie. Hey, treat the officials the right way and they'll give you that inch.

Do you ask your players to treat officials well?

Either you're disciplined or you're not. Either you're a good teammate or you're not. **I always tell our players you treat officials like you treat your parents. If they tell you something, do it.** You might not agree with it, but do it.

I was a captain in the league when I was 21, and it was "Yes, sir" and "No, sir." Nobody likes to be embarrassed in front of 20,000 people, so don't do it to the officials. If there's a trademark to being on one of my teams, you've got to be very, very disciplined, and it's a tough thing to teach. To get your team to play hard with discipline is a very difficult thing.

Do the principles of success that you have in hockey spill over into other areas of your life?

As you get older you realize they are very similar. As you get older you may actually be embarrassed by how you went about things when you were younger, kind of ashamed of yourself. The guys who weren't involved with the players don't understand the pressures and adversity from day to day, separating your job from your family, but that's what life's about: learning. After you learn, admit it and change. Be flexible.

How do you handle pressure?

It's very important to prepare for the toughest possible challenge every night so that in every situation you're mentally prepared and motivated to play. **When you play with that sense of urgency to make a difference all the time, then those adverse situations get easier.** Life and death is adversity, not winning and losing.

I react a lot differently now from when I was younger, both in terms of at the rink and away from the rink, and it's helped me in tough situations. Not playing was tough for me. Getting hurt and having my little boy say how I looked when I came home bothered me. Wondering what my teammates thought about me was adversity. Not scoring with 10 seconds left in the game that would have allowed St. Louis to go to the finals instead of Calgary is adversity. The adversity to me was getting hurt and not having the ability to help our team win, not winning and losing.

What was your worst moment, and how did you recover from it?

My worst moment was probably just an injury in hockey. I had never been hurt in 10 years, and then I fell into the boards. The doctor said I broke my back. A player had never broken his scapula like that before in the National Hockey League.

What was your toughest time as a coach?

The toughest by far was when they released me in St. Louis. We had built a good team, but there was squabbling. Any time management listens to the press there will be problems. There is always one guy who is negative, irresponsible, disrespectful, and not a good human being. One guy got on a kick there, and it was kind of the same thing in Calgary. There was a guy always against you. It was interesting that after I had to go someplace else those guys were out of the business. They had to find another job, and they couldn't. They were pretty good profile people in the media, but they were disrespectful people.

How did you respond to your tough times?

The first time I was relatively young, 34 years old, and it was hard on my family. We had spent 16 years in St. Louis. Only two players in hockey have spent as much time in one place as we did.

What did you do the day after you were fired?

I am disappointed now by the way I felt then, how I thought I wasn't a good coach, I didn't do a good job, and I let my family down because I had to move them. It was totally devastating for my son and was really hard on my wife. She left home when she was 19, we were married, we were drafted at 19, and we were in St. Louis for 16 years where we raised the kids. It was probably hard because I was so loyal to St. Louis.

How did you get yourself out of the hole?

The best thing that ever happened to me was learning that if you get bucked off a horse, you get right back on. Don't be afraid, and make sure you learn from it. Just don't get back on and fall off again. There were calls within about one day. I look back at every one of those great opportunities and realize they were all special.

How do you help individual players who are experiencing adversity?

First you have to make people honest with themselves and help them to understand that nothing is as complicated or as deep or as difficult as it seems. You've got to get people to understand that. You've got to have the ability to make them understand that this is how you can make them better. It is important not to put them in a situation they are not capable of accepting and responding to. You've got to put people in a position to succeed. **I will never, ever embarrass a player. I will never, ever take away his dignity, and yet I will never, ever let a player bullshit me or his teammates, and a lot of them try that, a lot of them.** I know when a player is playing his heart out; nobody else has to tell me. Lots of times after a game you go into the press room saying, "Boy, he scored a goal but he was one of the worst players on the ice."

Do you deal with each personality type differently?

You absolutely have to. God didn't make any two of us the same way. I think you learn that from being in a big family. In this business you don't have a chance to spend Christmas together. We're all a close-knit family, yet we'd run over each other to get something done because it's competition. You want to do better than the next guy, that's all. I tell my kids that they're not always going to like everything that goes on. If I liked everything that went on for me all day ... nothing's going to go exactly the way you want it to. **You're going to get dirty and cut. I tell my players, "If you don't have those problems, if somebody isn't hacking you and calling you names, then you ain't doing your job."**

What types of players are the most challenging to coach?

I don't know if I could put my finger on any one, but the challenge that I enjoy the most is getting players to find out how good they can be. The agent always says, "This is a good player, and he can do this and that for you." Harry Sinden once told one, "You're not the expert. We are."

How do you challenge an athlete who's performing below potential? What do you do with the lazy player, and how do you challenge your star players?

The third one is a little bit different from the first two. Obviously the star doesn't always play well. The one area that a coach has control over is ice time. I **don't care whether he's a star or not, if he's not performing and he's letting his teammates down, I've never had a problem with taking away his ice time.** I always felt when I played that I was the one that everybody counted on to make a difference, to score the goal, but that still didn't mean as much to me as playing in the other areas of the game. You can take away somebody's ice time, but there's a major difference between a player underachieving and a player not playing well. I always tell guys, "If you keep down this [underachieving] road, your next step with me is the press box or to the minors because kids aren't sitting in the press box."

I don't believe in cutting a player's ice time when he is not playing well. **I'll play him through it and help him play through it. It might hurt us a game or two but it's going to make the player better, which is going to make the team better down the road.**

I am not afraid to play a player that other people won't, and I make sure the team knows that. I'm going to stick with the player in different situations when other guys wouldn't, but I'm not stupid either.

I tell the players, "In my mind every one of us starts at 100 percent every night. Every one of us is different. We might get 10 minutes of ice time or it might be 20, but that's 100 percent, even to the five-minute guy. If you drop off during the game and go to 95 percent, somebody else might go up to 110, and then we're going to win." That's why we're playing that guy at 110, but the next day they are all the same again. If somebody is not playing well, coaches don't button their lips, and yet they don't spout off to the press. What goes on in the dressing room stays in the dressing room.

How close do you allow yourself to get to the players?

I want the players to feel good about themselves all the time. To do that they've got to be able to look in the mirror every day when they leave the rink and be totally respectful to themselves and not let anybody down. You're with your players all the time. **When I arrived in Chicago the players had no idea how to prepare to win. They were prepared to play, but they never prepared to win.** People don't realize that players need more support than they ever have because there are more pressures. There is more adversity. They need somebody to talk to.

Everybody coaches differently. I know Scotty Bowman inside and out, and I've got more respect for him than any other coach. I know him and I know what he's going to do, and he does it. He coaches differently now. You can call it hands-on. What you see in coaches behind the bench is not necessarily what they're made of. You have to lower the boom on people, and you can't be afraid. The toughest thing is to teach players to play hard and to teach them team defence.

Can you read a player's ability or willingness to perform by looking him in the eye or at his body language?

I know when people are ready to play 100 percent of the time. I know if somebody's going to be sharp or not. I wasn't very impressed early in the season. Our preparation was awful. How would you know how to prepare to win if you haven't won? It's like tying your shoelaces: They're either tied or they're not. I know before a game. Sometimes you're close to the player without even talking to him. You can't be in there talking to him all the time and getting on him. I know when somebody is totally sharp.

I tell the guys to never miss the net in warm-up, never, ever. Don't ever because, guaranteed, then you're going to miss it in the game. That's a habit. **There are only two types of habits in life: the good ones and the bad ones. There's nothing else. There's not an OK habit or a so-so habit or a sometime habit. It's either good or bad.**

I'll call time outs two or three minutes into the game and say, "One more shift because we can't wait. There are too many guys on this bench who are relying on you." That's the ability to see things before other people see it. I know before they go on the ice. It's a gut feeling. I know it sometimes in the morning skate. As I said before, the toughest thing is to prepare your players to win and to play hard.

Define your leadership style. Eisenhower said, "Leadership is the art of getting someone to do something you want done because they want to do it." What do you think?

You can't say it any better than that. That is leadership in a nutshell. It's the ability to have other people follow you, to be sincere in your thoughts, to always be totally honest, and to never, ever do something because you want to do it. You do what is best for the team. It's not something you can just put your finger on. I was given the advice that the key to being a successful coach is to always repeat yourself. **When you think the players are tired of hearing something, make sure you repeat it again, and then when the players are tired of hearing it and you think they're tired of hearing it, make sure you do it again, always.** When you hear a coach say, "We have to go back to fundamentals," you know they're in trouble because why should you get away from fundamentals if that's what makes you win? But what are fundamentals? You have two or three two-on-one drills every day. You have some three-on-two drills every day. You might pick two or three out that work for your team, or it might be a breakout and you stop at the net, but you hit the net every day. No matter where you are, you hit the net. No matter where you are at, you stop at the net. You've got to repeat that.

Are you a philosopher coach? Do you try to teach your players life lessons?

Absolutely. Every day. **The game is just a small part of our life. I always say the game is just a reflection of our soul.**

Have you changed your coaching style over the years?

I think I have. I'm always going to be myself but the thing I learned the most after what happened to me in St. Louis is that although at one time I honestly believed I could make a difference in every situation, I now know I can't control it. I think it's age. **I laugh a lot more now, but there's nothing I despise more than losing.** I tell players we don't get paid to lose. Coaches who don't win don't address problems. You have to make the players compete hard every day.

Clare Drake

Clare Drake stands alone as the "dean" of Canadian intercollegiate hockey coaches. The Canadian Interuniversity Rookie of the Year Award bears his name and Hockey Canada's first National Coaching Certification Program, based extensively on his written coaching philosophy, bears his imprint.

Drake took over the University of Alberta Golden Bears hockey program in 1956, six years before Canada established its first true university championship. He coached the Bears for 28 seasons, taking time off to focus on coaching various national teams and the Edmonton Oilers of the World Hockey Association for the 1975–76 season.

Drake transformed the University of Alberta Golden Bears into the best collegiate men's hockey program in Canada. Under his tenure the team's record was 697 wins, 296 losses, and 37 ties, a .695 winning percentage. His commitment to winning led the Golden Bears to six University Cup titles and 17 Canada West Conference championships.

On October 8, 1985, the Golden Bears beat the Red Deer College Kings for Drake's 556th victory, making him the most winning intercollegiate hockey coach in North America. Only Ron Mason, the legendary coach of the Michigan State University Spartans, has subsequently surpassed his record.

As an innovator in university hockey, Drake has no peer. In 1975 Drake was named the Edmonton Sports Man of the Year, and the CIAU

Hockey Coach of the Year in 1975 and 1988. He also received the Canada West Hockey Coach of the Year Award in 1985, 1987, 1988, and the year he retired, 1989. He has been granted a University of Alberta Distinguished Alumni Award and an honorary Doctor of Laws degree, and was the first coach to be inducted into the Alberta Hockey Hall of Fame. In 1981 he was inducted into the Alberta Sports Hall of Fame, and in 1989, into the Canadian Sports Hall of Fame. In 2006, the Coaching Association of Canada honoured Drake with the Geoff Gowan Award for a lifelong contribution to coaching, based on his "We, Not Me!" philosophy.

In international hockey, Drake led the Canadian team to gold at the 1981 Student Games in Jaca, Spain. He also led Canada to two other podium finishes at the World Student Games: silver in 1972 at Lake Placid, New York, and bronze in 1987 in Poprad, Czechoslovakia. He was a co-coach of the Canadian men's team in the Lake Placid 1980 Olympics and went on to coach Team Canada to victory at the Spengler Cup tournament. Throughout the 1990s, Drake served as a "mentor coach" for the Canadian women's hockey program.

Hockey is not Drake's sole passion; he also coached the Golden Bears' varsity football squad. In 1968 not only did the hockey team win the University Cup, but the football squad, also under Drake, beat McMaster 10–9 to win the Vanier Cup. With these two victories Clare Drake reached a unique milestone in North American sports, leading two different sports teams to national titles, a feat that may never be equalled.

Drake continues to live in Edmonton, Alberta, where he is a consultant to NHL teams (the Edmonton Oilers, Winnipeg Jets, Dallas Stars, Vancouver Canucks and Calgary Flames have all been clients), a presenter at coaching clinics (he has taught in North America, Europe, Asia and Australia over the past 30 years) and continues to watch hockey at the Clare Drake Arena on the campus of the University of Alberta.

The Interview

What motivated you to get into coaching and then remain as long as you did?

I was fortunate to be in a sporting environment as a youngster growing up and always enjoyed playing sports. My dad was a teacher and coach. I probably felt that I was going to reach a particular plateau in terms of performing myself, so my main motivation to consider coaching was that I thought I wasn't going to play very long. I played to the university level and then I played some senior amateur hockey, and for a year in Europe. Everybody recognizes there is a limit, but I really enjoyed the atmosphere of athletics, and had some really good experiences. I felt the best way to stay in that atmosphere was to get involved in coaching.

Do you feel that coaches have a responsibility to motivate players, or do you let them take ownership at certain times?

Sometimes I think back in a fuzzy way because I can't remember things as well as I would like, but I know I started out as a fairly autocratic coach. I was young, coaching players that were almost the same age as I was. I took the initiative in terms of trying to motivate the players to begin with, and then eventually, as I got a little smarter and learned a little more through going to clinics or reading things on motivation, I recognized that you've got to sell your players on the importance of internalized self-motivation. You try to give them some ways in which to do it and then let them start to take ownership. To the best of my recollection that's the way I would say that it happened.

When would you or your assistants go into the room with the purpose of motivating the team to try to get a win, and when would you let them deal with it themselves?

Quite often we'd go in and make an emotional plea to bring the game up to a particular level, but I think we did it the right way. I couldn't put a number or percentage on the times that we did that. Sometimes we just left them alone. We were fortunate, and I've mentioned this in several clinics, to be in an environment with a lot of skilled, intelligent athletes who bought into the character things that we talked about, the guidelines we were developing, and as a result became self-motivated. We looked to the veteran players to provide leadership and motivation. Our veteran players, with very few exceptions, developed into great role models for the rookies.

Were those players leaders before they came in, or did they learn those skills?

I would think it's a combination of the two. They were probably leaders to a degree in the environment that they came from. **They had what you might call a propensity to be a leader or certain qualities that would let them move into a leadership role, such as their attitude, intelligence, and their ability to recognize what is important.** We tried to encourage and develop leadership by often rotating the captain's role early in the season, having different players lead the warm-up or drills. Often we would have a player who was very skilled in a particular area work individually with two or three teammates. We also tried to identify and praise leadership actions when they happened.

How does a coach instill confidence in his players? Can you instill confidence in your players?

I believe you can. When I think back to myself as an early coach, I recognize how I've changed, how I've matured, improved, and gotten smarter about different things like assisting a player in developing confidence. You can structure the environment and bring certain things to the attention of players, things that they have done successfully. You can structure practice to allow your athletes to experience some success on their part and become more successful, say, this week than they were last week. Then you need to make sure you really give them extra praise in that regard, like, "John, you're doing the one-on-one coverage so much better this week than you were last week. Nobody seems to beat you out of the corner anymore, and that's great. You're really moving up." Confidence can be a very fragile characteristic in athletes because they are getting instant feedback on their physical performance. Our "self-talk" sessions were done in part to help build self-confidence. We tried to have players build a positive, yet realistic, perception of themselves.

If a player comes to the bench and breaks his stick or gets upset, and you see that his self-talk is too negative, what do you do?

This is something that came into my coaching repertoire as I progressed as a coach. I believe self-talk is very important. I actually designed a little handout for the players on self-talk that defined it and explained its importance. **You talk to yourself 1,785 times a day. We tried to get the players to make as much of it as possible, positive, focussing on the good things they do.** We talked to them individually about not getting down on themselves too much, telling them, "We think you're being a little too negative. You're taking away some of your energy and enthusiasm by being too tough on yourself." We stressed positive reinforcement. I can't remember how many years ago we introduced it, but we tried to have a teaching session on that subject each year. We usually did it with the whole team, but eventually we started to do this with new players to talk to them about the importance of self-talk.

Is body language, the way they carry themselves as an athlete, the same type of thing?

We didn't want anybody skating over to the bench with his head down after a goal was scored against him. The goal is scored and that becomes history, and you skate over and get ready to go again. We had to address several times, over the course of the years, players not being upbeat, not being positive, kind of sitting there with their heads down in the dressing room. You notice those things when you come in. Once in awhile if you come in right after the period and you want to mention something while it's fresh in your mind, and you see guys shaking their heads and muttering or whatever, that's the time to talk about the kind of atmosphere you want to have in the dressing room and make it as positive as you can. If guys want to sit together, if you have the defence pairs sitting together in partners in the dressing room or a line sitting together, we always want them to feel free not to criticize each other but to bring up some things that they thought the other guy maybe wasn't doing or maybe could do a bit differently. **We want to have a little bit of interplay and communication between them. If you had something you wanted to say to your linemate, you should be able to say it to him, and the linemate should be able to accept it as long as it's given in a positive way or in a way that will make things a little better.**

People often ask what the coach said in between periods to get the team go-
ing. How often did the "soapbox speech" occur in your locker rooms, and
was it a major factor in the game?

Not very often. I like to tell a story sometimes in clinics or sports
banquets about when we played Loyola University in the national finals
in 1967. Some of the older guys hadn't been playing well early in the season, and some of them had lost enthusiasm for the game, and we talked to
them and said maybe it would be best for them to leave at the end of the
first semester, and they were OK with that. A couple of them left, a couple
of them stayed, and there was a general malaise with the team and very little enthusiasm. We brought this rookie line up about halfway through the
season, and they sparked things in the second half and played really well.
We got into the National Championship final game against Loyola at the
Forum with 12,000 fans, as far as I know the largest crowd to have ever
seen a Canadian college game. We're down 4–2 at the end of the second
period, but eventually come back in the third period, and this rookie line
once again sparked things. They got two of the goals to bring us back to
4–4 at about the 15-minute mark, and then we scored the winning goal
with about 17 seconds to go in the game to win the National Championship. I was asked this question a lot: "What did you say? I mean, it's got
to be magic. What did you say?" I didn't really say anything at the time.
The things that made the difference for us were the things I said to them
on September 10th and October 15th and November 1st and January
20th or whatever. I just reminded them of the things we had worked on
all year to try to get better in certain areas, and those things fell into place.
You know there's no magic. I can't think back to exactly what I said, but I
didn't jump up on a table or kick the garbage can or anything. We knew
we were playing with them; we knew we were close.

Have you ever come in and made the difference in the game with some-
thing you said?

Yes, I've done it the other way too the odd time. I've gotten a little
excited when I thought we were really a long ways away from the way we
should have been playing as a team, for our capabilities. I may say, "You
guys are shortchanging yourselves. You're shortchanging each other," and
get a little excited, a little upset, a little mad, but I never have been a grab-
the-stick-off-the-rack-and-crack-it kind of guy, although I have kicked a
couple of garbage cans. I guess you've got to get the right mix, as most

coaches know, but sometimes it takes coaches a long time to figure it out. The yelling becomes pretty ineffective fairly quickly with an above-average team. I think you can scare some kids, and I've heard this said about some coaches. The intimidation factor is probably a little higher for the younger players, and there is maybe a little more yelling, but in my experience with the older players, you don't need it that much.

Do you try on game days to look for some sort of angle that makes this game different from last week's game or last night's game?

I believe you're always looking for an angle or a little bit of an edge. How are we going to react to the challenge of what they did to us in that last game if they did some things particularly well and took away our ability to do some things? I would imagine you'd have to look for that angle a little more in professional hockey. One of the nice things about coaching at the university is that there is kind of a built-in motivation because of the shortness of the schedule. There is extra importance to every game, but that said, I still look for that something to draw on.

It's very difficult for organizations to build a dynasty. How did your teams' identity evolve?

I think the university itself, or the organization itself in this case, has a recognizable tradition connected with it, if it has been fairly successful. When I joined the University of Alberta, their basketball and hockey programs were really strong. **One of our major focusses was the work ethic. We really tried to use that as the cornerstone.** You want to build the feeling in the players that they do not want to have the coaches or fans say they really got outworked over the course of the game, that the reason they weren't successful or didn't play well, or it wasn't a very good game to watch, is that the U of A Bears were just not working. We wanted to be an upbeat, hard-working, enthusiastic team, and supportive of each other.

And then we've always talked about sharing the puck. We've been using that expression for a long time, the co-operative support concept. We wanted our players to recognize that's the way we wanted them to be, the team identity that we wanted them to buy into. We also tried to focus on self-discipline and prided ourselves on quite often being the least penalized team in our league. These identity characteristics became the key components of our "team guidelines."

Along with outworking the opponent and the self-discipline, we tried to be as proactive as possible. **We talked about trying to set the tempo in games and not sitting back to see what the other team is going to do.** I've never been a big proponent of matching lines; I think personally there are more problems with it than advantages. Sometimes it's a lot easier not to worry too much about matching lines if you feel that your talent level is at least equal to theirs and maybe a touch better. We always tried to sell our players on the fact that we were going to try to be good in all aspects of the game and that if anyone wanted to worry about matching, we'd let them worry about matching us. That would be an indication to us that we were setting the tempo, we were dictating the course of the game.

I don't mean that we've never matched; on occasion we've decided that it was going to be to our team's advantage to match. I can remember one time that Bill and I should have matched because we had a scouting report on a player by the name of Don McLaren, who played for York University. We were going down to play them in the playoffs, and our scout said that McLaren was their best player by far. We talked about it and decided not to do any matching, not to start with anyway, and just see how the game goes. Well, he scored three goals in the first period. We outshot them 52 to 16 and lost 3–2.

How did you create and maintain that identity?

A lot of it comes from within. One of the reasons for our success was having a core of really good players. You'd like to think eventually that guys who play here for two or three years are all going to buy into the things that you're trying to sell. Initially we used to have 180 people out for tryouts. The rookies would try out separately, and then we would gradually phase them in with the returning players. We used to meet with the returning players just before this happened and tell them to show the guys who are trying to make the team what it takes to play on this team. I can remember when Ace Brimacombe, who was trying out and later became a very good player for us, said to me, "I couldn't believe it. I saw these veterans smashing into each other and winning all the races." He said it really opened his eyes. It's kind of a role-model thing on the part of the veteran players.

I guess we initiated it in terms of building an identity, but the veteran players did most of the internal leading just by role-modelling what was necessary to play. To maintain it we always tried to bring in some new players every year. We occasionally cut returning players, but it didn't happen that often. The graduation cycles, where four or five players are leaving every season, gave us a chance to bring four or five new players in. That was the big reason for maintaining our identity; we never had to completely reload.

You say a lot of the communication of your tradition and your identity came from the players. Would you do anything special to subtly communicate key messages to your players and the new guys coming in?

We definitely made a conscious effort over the years, to develop a set of what we called "team guidelines." They were a set of beliefs or values or behaviours that we as a coaching staff believed would help us be successful as a team. We introduced them early in the season and referred to them often. They're intended to guide behaviour, and I know from experience that they help encourage the development of mature behaviour and self-discipline. When you start the season with new players, often coming from a wide variety of backgrounds, it is important to let them know what is expected of them and what they in return can expect of their coaches. The guidelines apply to everyone connected to the team. We felt it was important to get player feedback in order to build their ownership stake in the guidelines.

Some of the guidelines stressed the importance of being personally responsible for your actions and maintaining a positive, enthusiastic attitude. Showing respect to all those involved in the game, developing consistency, and strong habits of discipline. These characteristics were part of what we felt would become our "championship habits." We talked about being accountable to one another. Co-operation and unselfishness were a key for us. The catch phrase we had displayed prominently on our dressing room wall was John Wooden's "It's amazing what can be accomplished when no one cares who gets the credit." Of course we were always reminding players that hard work would be the cornerstone to our success.

The bottom line on guidelines was we wanted things spelled out clearly, discussed, and understood, and we wanted everyone on the same page and committed to the guidelines. They became a very important factor in our success.

Why do you think so few organizations can hold their teams at the top for long periods of time, the way you were able to do it?

Maybe it's just getting the right combination of people to start with.

I'm really big on the role-model concept. If you want to improve yourself, have a mentor who is very positive and who's achieved something, and try to hang around with successful people. Some teams are successful for a period of time, and I don't know if complacency is the word, but sometimes they kind of lose track of the fact that there's something that has to happen for it to continue.

Do you think it had to do with you and your assistant coach Bill Moores being there for a long time? Some organizations change their leaders and key people. You talk about your players being role models, but it's also the people at the top.

Absolutely. I'm glad you mentioned that. It hits the nail right on the head, really. The continuity factor and stability factors are so important. I hadn't thought of it in those terms exactly. Players appreciate that too, especially if the core people, say a coaching staff that they have some respect for and faith in, stay there. That's a big, big factor, absolutely.

What made you want to remain coaching at the University of Alberta?

Just my enjoyment of it, I guess. There's kind of an internal feeling of satisfaction in knowing that you really enjoy your job. I enjoyed going to work every day, having been a Phys. Ed. graduate and kind of a jock. The other part of it was that we started to enjoy some success, and I think that helps motivate you. **If you experience success, it makes you feel a little more confident and a little more self-assured. That's a motivating factor in itself, and you want to continue in that environment.**

Coaching at the university level is the best environment for coaching in terms of the athletes. They are not as talented and as skilled as athletes at the professional level, for example, but I think there's more opportunity to sell concepts to university players and more opportunity to influence them. It's a little more satisfying. I don't know what professional hockey is like now, but my experience in 1975 with the Oilers was that there was a core group of players who were great, and you could do a lot with them, but at that particular time there was also a smaller group that was somewhat noncommittal. My experience with the Winnipeg Jets from 1989 to '93 was different; there the players were committed to try new things and open to new concepts. I never had a problem going back to the university level. I was kind of happy to go back, in some ways, because I was in a good situation and always enjoyed it there.

How have you defined success through your career?

I think success is obviously a winning record. As I look back I see that we've had a tremendous number of our players who have come through the program and have gone back into the community and done a really good job. We have about eight or nine players that I can think of just offhand who are coaching Tier II junior hockey. We've never had a lot of people go on to play in the National Hockey League. We've had a number, but **I think the better measure of success is what the people do as they graduate and go into the community and really contribute back.** Almost all of our players have gone on to do extremely well in their chosen professions and have become very productive members of society.

What were your most memorable coaching experiences?

I guess you always remember the National Championship games that you win. One of my most memorable experiences relates to a good friend of mine, Wayne Fleming, who was coaching Manitoba when we played them in the finals of our conference to go to the Nationals. It was a three-game series in Manitoba, and we split the first two games. They were leading 4–2 in the third game going into the final few minutes. We scored a goal to make it 4–3 with about 1:23 to go, and then we scored another one to tie it with about 30 seconds to go. We went into a straight 10 minutes of overtime. They went ahead 5–4, we tied it up 5–5 and then I remember Dennis Cranston scored on a faceoff with about 15 seconds to go in overtime. It was a devastating game for them to lose, but it was a game that really sticks out in your memory. Wayne and I talk about it once in awhile.

The other memorable experience that stands out is the year I was asked to also be the head coach of the football team in '67. We played in one of the early College Bowls against McMaster. It was a really tight game back and forth, and we were ahead by two points, 11–9, going into the final minute. They were pushing us back, and they were in a pretty good position to kick a winning field goal. It was a rainy day. They had tried a field goal a little earlier, but because the weather was bad they decided to try and push it down and get a little closer. One of our linebackers, John Wilson, who later went on to play for the BC Lions, intercepted the pass, and we won that game in the dying seconds. That was in November, and the following March we were playing in Montreal in the hockey Nationals. This was the year, as I mentioned earlier, that we played against Loyola University in the final. The memory of that year really sticks with me.

I coached with Dave Chambers and Andy Murray at the Spengler Cup in Switzerland, and we won in a nail-biter, in the last minute of play. A player by the name of Rob Plumb scored for us. The fans in Davos and the atmosphere in the rink were great. It was 1985 and Canada's first gold medal at the Spengler.

Another game I remember well was one we lost. We played Toronto in the National finals in our rink. There was a big crowd, it was packed, and at that time we had an organist playing and it created a great atmosphere. They got up on us 3–1 in the first period, and from then on we really dominated the game. Tom Watt was coaching, and when I kid him about it he says, "We just threw the puck off the glass and sent you back down to your end." I can't remember what the final shots were, but even though we were quite dominant, we couldn't come back to win. I told the team afterwards that was as good as we'd played all year because Toronto had a great team. We really controlled and dominated them, but we couldn't score. We hit sticks and legs on shots, and they just dumped it out. I told our team we were proud of them because we had played our best game of the year. You remember games like that too.

Was there anything that your championship teams had in common?

We won three championships in a row, two when I was there in '78 and '79, and when I was away with the Olympic team in '80. Bill Moores took over the team that year and they won. They got in as the wild card and ended up winning in Regina. One thing we did a pretty good job of, maybe kind of happenstance, but it seemed like four or five players would graduate and we would replace them with four or five players in their first year. When we had the run of '78, '79, '80, '81, we had really good players who were quite young, like Don Spring. I don't know if you remember that name; he played with the Winnipeg Jets in the NHL for five or six years after he graduated and came from Edson, Alberta, as a 17 year old. John Devaney, who ended up playing on our Olympic team also, came out of juvenile along with Randy Gregg and Kevin Primeau. Dave Hindmarch came from B.C.; he was 18 out of Tier II junior. All these kids came into our program at 18 and grew up in the program. All five players made the 1980 Olympic team, and four of them went on to play in the NHL.

The common thread for our team has always been the work ethic. We were fortunate that way, and I've said quite often that I attribute a major part of our success to the fact that the players bought into, and demonstrated a lot more consistently than some other teams, the work ethic. We hustled and checked well, so that would kind of be the cornerstone, but obviously you have to be fortunate enough to get some talented players. **Another key to our success has been that the guys who were graduating were always great role models for the younger players.**

What do you consider to be skills that have made you successful?

I know I've been a pretty detailed person. Some of the players have said to me that I try to reach for perfection. **We did believe in the "agony of repetition."** We had good variety in our practice drills because I think we introduced new things when they came along, but we spent a lot of time on the basics and we strove for quality of execution. That's one of the things we talked about with the players, that we didn't want to try 101 different things, but the ones we wanted to do we wanted to do well, so I guess that is attention to detail.

When you think back on your career, you really recognize how you've changed. I coached by myself to begin with, and believe when I was quite young I was a little more authoritarian than I'd like to be now. I look back and say to myself I would have been a better coach at the time if I had done some other things that I know about now.

So your skills have changed over time?

I don't know if dramatically, but I know they have. I know you get a little smarter. Towards the end of my career I was a much better people person and communicator than I was to begin with. Initially you're a little more authoritarian and a little more distant from your players, and I felt I had to be that way because the age gap was narrow. When I first started coaching I wasn't very much older than some of the players. I've seen some coaches fall into the trap of being buddies or friends to the players, and I think teams take advantage of coaches like that. I felt I had to keep myself a little more distant, and as a result I wasn't as close socially or as good interpersonally with players at that time. That was a deliberate thing on my part but I gradually got away from that to a degree where I felt comfortable. It would be foolish for anybody to say they didn't evolve in coaching techniques and approaches.

Does the way you coach and the way you are around the team spill over into your family life, or do you find you're totally different away from the rink?

In those earlier days there was a difference, but now I'm pretty much the same away from the rink, although a little more outgoing and social. **I don't want this to sound the wrong way, but I think there's a little bit of an acting component in coaching. You take a persona onto the ice that you think enhances your ability to get things across to the players.**

What do you do to relax and unwind?

I don't get too uptight. I used to go out after a game and have a smoke, before I quit. Quite often we'd go into the coaches' room and go through an evaluation of things that went well and things that went badly, a summary of the game. Then we'd open the filing cabinet and pour a drink and sit there and chat socially, and quite often our wives would come in and join us after our evaluation of the game.

Is there anything else? When you're at home do you read or work out?

I am a pretty faithful workout guy, and I like to read and listen to music. I've got quite a few Sinatra and Tony Bennett tapes, the old guys. I guess you could say music and family; I do quite a few things with the family, and I think it's great for relaxing. My wife, Dolly, is really great for bringing me back to normal. She gets pretty involved. I think she went to every home game and she travelled a fair amount with us when we went on trips overseas. She got to know the players really well, and they liked her a lot more than they usually liked me during the season because she was always good with them. I think they appreciated the support Dolly gave me; they could sense how important the support was at home. I'm really lucky in that both our daughters, Debbie and Jami, and their families live nearby so we have weekly get-togethers, barbecues, and socializing. In the off-season I get to do a lot of golfing and socializing with old friends.

Has it ever been difficult to find a balance between your family life and your coaching obligations?

When I first went to the university I was an assistant with the football team and Don Smith was still coaching the hockey team. I was going to help Don too, but then he quit coaching quite soon after, so I was coaching both football and hockey. Football practice was from 5:15 to about 6:30, and then I went in and had a sandwich and took my cleats off and put my skates on, and we had hockey practice at 7:00 until 8:15. At that time we didn't start hockey until about October 6th or 10th, so there was about a month of an overlap that I didn't get home until about 8:30 p.m., just in time to put the kids into bed. Summers were more of a family time for us.

Do you win at all costs?

I can answer that quite readily. We've always tried to put a value component into our coaching, and the key is working with players and making them better people. We've talked at different times about things that are important in terms of ethics and the ethical component, so I would say no as an answer to the question. Do you want to win at all costs? No, and we've talked to the players about making sure that they retain their respect for the integrity of the game.

Everybody has adversity and failure in their career. How did you handle it?

I guess over the years I've probably gotten better at being able to handle that. We've tried to sell that very point, that we're always going to face some adversity, and personally I believe it's great to have some. We talk about it so it doesn't jump up on people. There's going to be an opportunity for us to face adversity and see how well we've come along as a team and as individuals. We've talked about the pressure and the fact that it's going to be there and it's an opportunity for us to gain something from it and learn a lesson and go on. **Adversity can be a healthy thing for you because it often exposes your current shortcomings. It can act as a wake-up call to things you have to improve on, either individually or as a team.**

How do you help individuals who are facing adversity, whether it's a scoring slump or a personal issue they're dealing with?

We help by attacking adversity in general and by talking about it, by meeting with the player individually and trying to build him up and recall for him the good things that he's done to this particular point. We try to help identify things like he's been a good player in a lot of areas for the team but now he's struggling a little bit and this happens to just about everybody. **There's a point in your year or your season where it's going to be a down time, and you just have to try and think back and remind them of what they do well. There's an old saying: "This too shall pass."**

What types of players are the most challenging to coach?

I would say one of the most challenging types to coach are the players who have the attitude that there's not an awful lot that they're not familiar with, there are not a lot of things that they haven't heard before, and they're reluctant to change. They may have been in an environment in which they were familiar with only one type of play. Fortunately we haven't had too many of those, and once again you've got to go back to the role-model concept. If you can point to the success that people are having doing certain things you know are important, you can then ask the individual to try them.

We've had a couple of players over the years who had anger management problems, and they've been difficult. One who comes to mind was a problem. We worked with him and I suspended him from the team for a week. I wanted him to sit back and think about whether he wanted to make a good effort to change his ways. Finally we did work through it, but it was difficult. I found out later that most of it resulted from his home upbringing.

Are some players tougher to deal with than others?

I keep going back to the role-model theory. **When you're surrounded with positive, enthusiastic, upbeat people, it's hard not to be that way too.** It's hard for them to stay pessimistic if there are a lot of optimistic people around, so I think that the environment is key. The idea is to build championship habits. It's a championship habit to think optimistically, to believe that things are going to turn out.

If we were talking to some of your players, how would they describe you as a coach?

I think that some of the players I coached earlier in my career would probably describe me as being a little bit distant, maybe a little aloof. Gradually that would change. You always hope that they don't think too badly of you. The majority of my players would think that I have had quirks and foibles. Some of them might say I was kind of a perfectionist who harped on little things. We used to bug guys all the time about stopping in front of the net after drives and shots and trying not to turn away from plays. I think they'd describe me as a bit of a taskmaster in terms of trying to force them, not force, but encourage them to execute really well.

I hope they would say that I helped teach them about a few other things, a few of life's values. It's hard to pinpoint exactly what they would say. I guess it's better to ask some of the players. I'd have to give you a list of the players I got along well with! I hope they would say I'm a friendly person, fairly approachable.

How close did you get to your players, and how did you interact with them?

When I got a little bit smarter, I didn't do it deliberately, but I tried to talk to a couple of players personally at practice every day. I don't know how successful I was at it. I tried to interact on a personal basis as often as I could, by just chatting with them about things, sitting with them on the bus once in awhile, sitting with a couple of players talking about their courses and general things, once in awhile leading a singsong. We always had a couple of guys who had guitars, so I made up a songbook. I've still got 20 copies of it in the basement. We used to do a lot of singing, and I loved to jump in and sing. I never got into the card games they were playing, penny ante, at the back of the bus. I believe that the guys at the back of the bus are your informal leaders.

How do you get the most out of your players?

I think maybe in a general sense **I try to appeal to the tradition and pride that the program has generated in the past, not letting the history of the program down, trying to do their best, trying to maintain the integrity that the program has built up.** Those are the kinds of things you appeal to when talking to the team. Appeal to their pride and the fact that they belong to a group that's got a good tradition of winning and they've done an exceptional job to put themselves into that group. They should want to try to maintain it. I appeal to them to maintain a sense of accountability to the rest of the guys on the team, to try to do their particular job so everybody is accountable to each other. I continually remind them of our team guidelines and the team identity we want to maintain.

You originally handled all of a head coach's responsibilities on your own because you had to. How do you delegate, or do you prefer to be hands-on?

Well, going back to the early days, when you are doing it by yourself obviously there is not much delegation. When I think back, I couldn't have done a very good job, really, in terms of what you could do, but I guess I did a good job for what I was able to do, because most teams were coached by only one person.

Later on I was really fortunate in the assistants that I had. I almost always got players who had played a few years before and were out teaching or had graduated but had a coaching mentality. They usually didn't stay all that long, but then Bill Moores came on staff. I really liked the qualities he brought as a player; he was fantastic. I guess I was a mentor for him when we started out, and then we ended up as co-coaches.

Did you share responsibilities?

Towards the end he was in complete charge of the power play. I did the penalty killing. We talked about the two things at different times when we were on the bus or at our coaches' meetings, but it was complete delegation. He would tell me the guys he wanted to go out. We usually had two assistants, so I was very fortunate. I had some other really good people with me too. Dick Wintermute played football and hockey and was a great assistant. **I always feel one of my strengths was delegating, or what they call now empowering people.** We didn't have that term then; it's a good term. I was fortunate to be able to work with a lot of great assistants.

How would you interact with your trainers, equipment personnel, or other staff who worked directly with your team?

We used to meet with the trainers, and when I say we, Bill and I did most of these things together. We called the trainers in fairly regularly to keep us on top of any problems in the dressing room. We wanted them to help us if they spotted anything like a lack of harmony and the same thing with the equipment managers. We always got along quite well with our staff. As a coach you have to recognize early in your career how very important your support staff are to the success of your program.

How important is the dressing room environment to the team's success? Did you do anything to try to control it?

First of all we talked about it after we had the team selected. We explained to the players how important we felt the dressing room environment was. We gave them an outline of some things that we thought were important. In the last 10 or 12 years that I was there we posted a list of reminders of things that we wanted to see happen. We told them that the trainers and equipment managers were an integral part of the team, and they had authority in the dressing room area in terms of talking to the players about medical or equipment needs. I believe it's important that coaches remind players, early and often, of the important contributions made by various support personnel.

What reminders would be on the list?

Making sure that your stall is neat; making sure that any towels you use don't go down on the floor. We had the manager go through how we wanted the stalls to look at the beginning of the year. We talked to them about the importance of the social environment of the dressing room. We wanted guys to be positive and upbeat, and we didn't want guys coming in hanging their heads and complaining and throwing sticks. One of our values was to try to be enthusiastic, to be upbeat and positive whenever possible, so they're not affecting somebody else. I think the dressing room environment is very important.

The whole practice environment is key because you're there to try to accomplish something; you want to try and get a little bit better than you were the day before. Sometimes I tell a story about Randy Gregg, who was in medicine, and medicine is a tough, tough program. He had 45 minutes for lunch and courses went from 8:00 until 4:50. We practised at 5:15, and there were only a couple of times during the four years that he came to me and said, "Coach, I've got this lab," and couldn't make it on time. He was on the ice at 5:10 every day for five years with the odd exception. I sometimes use that as an example if I'm talking to coaches about the sacrifices people have to make if they want to accomplish something. We had a number of players, in very demanding courses, who made the same type of commitment.

How important is leadership in your room, and what are the qualities that you would look for when identifying your core people, your leaders?

Leadership is tremendously important. I don't think anyone would question that, and I really believe that if you don't have a real good core of people in your dressing room or connected with your team, you can get into a lot of trouble. I have to keep bringing up the role model, but in a sense we were always fortunate in having quality people. You want to try to select talent and quality of character. We've always had guys like Randy Gregg, Kevin Primeau, and John Devaney over the years who have been really good leaders. They were players who seemed to have a little more maturity. I believe there are some inborn character qualities in people that make them leaders. We have been fortunate to have a lot of quality players as team leaders.

I think they are players who have a good sense of themselves and feel confident. Part of it has been from success, but I think a big part of it is that they've had a good family upbringing where their family has made them feel that they do things well. It's kind of an inbred sense of confidence in themselves partly from what they've done, from their athletic accomplishments and maybe from their school accomplishments, but a key ingredient is also their family environment. They reach maturity a little earlier, and they make great leaders. **When they come into a group, other players start to recognize their leadership qualities and gravitate towards them. It's a confidence those players exude, but a confidence that's got a little humility attached to it.** They're not bragging about things, but they just kind of exude the fact that, yeah, we've done that or I'm able to do that, I can take charge of the situation. This is quite often the distinction between them and the rest of the group.

What other specific qualities would you look for when you pick your captains?

We never selected our captains right off the bat. Some schools select their captain a year ahead. We never did that. We had a checklist with about four or five points. I can't recall them exactly now, but key ingredients were maturity and good emotional control. We want the captain to be able to speak for the team and speak rationally to the team, and to be a leader in his actions on the ice. Sometimes as a coach you develop a bit of a sixth sense looking at people and being around them about who would make a good leader. Often we would allow the players to vote on the captain.

So they picked the captain?

No. We told the players when we allowed them to vote on the captain that we as coaches have a vote as well. "We want and value your opinion and are going to give it strong consideration, but we will have input in this process." I can only remember one time in all the years I coached when the players didn't select the same people as the coaching staff. That's the ideal scenario, when you can go back into the room and announce your captains, and say, "These are the guys that you, as players, want to lead us this year." Now the guys feel good about having a say in the process.

What is your leadership style?

It has gradually changed from being autocratic to more democratic. I like to exert a degree of control at the outset, but then I like to gradually let the control slip into the hands of others. I like to delegate a lot, so I guess **I'm a meritocratic leader as opposed to democratic. When I see somebody who is doing something really well and they've earned the right to be in charge, I like to let them have control. They have earned it through merit.**

When you were coaching at different levels, did you try to teach players lessons you thought were valuable?

I made a real conscious effort, once again, later in my career. We coaches always used to say that if we have to stop the practice or point something out at the end of the game or in between periods, if there is a teachable moment, try to grab it. Sometimes the lessons were related to hockey and sometimes they were life value skills.

Would you talk to them after the game, or would it be the next morning?

It could be at any time. I can remember a lot of times talking about respect for people. We'd be in a hotel and see a player doing something that we didn't think was particularly respectful or treating a waitress in a cavalier manner; you don't jump up from the table and address it then, but as soon as possible after. Sometimes it related to the whole team, not just the particular player, so after a pre-game meal on the way to the rink I would say something like, "I noticed a behaviour today I don't think is a great character trait for our team … We didn't respect this particular person as well as we should have." We would try to point out those things whenever we could.

Do you feel it's the responsibility of youth coaches to take these moments and try to have an impact on some of their kids?

Absolutely. I've said this in many presentations. **We have to be a combination of a skills teacher and a values teacher as much as we can, particularly with young players.** It's a little harder in the professional ranks; you don't always get a chance to talk to players in that sort of vein, but I think it's vital. You shortchange the kids if you have an opportunity to teach something related to values and you don't.

When you coach do you trust your instincts, your gut feeling, or how do you react?

I'm a firm believer that if you feel this is the right thing to do, then go ahead with your instincts. There might be some pressures from somewhere else. We didn't have any external parental pressure in university hockey, but you know that there are people who think, hey, that's kind of a goofy thing to do, but I think you have to do it. You're trying to do the right thing at the right time, and sometimes it's not necessarily the conventional thing, but you think it's right and you do it.

If you go into the game with a plan, how do you react according to your instincts and your feel?

To me one of the most important characteristics of a good coach is that ability to see something and be able to recognize it and adjust and adapt. If the things we thought were going to happen aren't happening, we have to change it, and I think I'm fairly good at that. I do believe it's important to be adaptable and flexible without being wishy-washy and changing with the breeze every five or 10 minutes.

How do you deal with confrontation?

With difficulty! I've had to deal with it a couple of times, like the player with the anger problem I told you about. He was a problem over a period of time and he was such a talented player that you hated to let him go. The reason I don't like to let a talented player go is not because of his talent but because I want to try to help him. I've heard some coaches say, "He's good but he is causing a lot of trouble. We'll get rid of him." To me that's kind of the easy solution: Get rid of him and he goes somewhere else and maybe gives somebody else a problem or maybe doesn't get help. If I think I can help him, I'd rather have him stay and try to put up with the problems and see if I can change them.

To answer the question about confrontation, I think you have to try to be as calm as you can and try to go opposite to what he's upset about. Sometimes it's about not playing, and he thinks you're not judging him fairly. You've got to just step back from it, maybe change the scene and just say, "Let's you and I get together out in the stands or over in the office and we'll talk about it. I'll let you know in more detail." I've found over the years that you always have some players who are not as perceptive about their own ability as the coaches are. They have a different perception of how well they have played, so you've got to talk to them about that and let them know in the most positive way you can.

How do you develop that sense of accountability?

I think it's something that takes time. You have to point out a player's deficiencies as positively as you can. We quite often didn't have that many players, so if I sat a player out we were able to tell him he would likely play the next night, and then we'd switch guys.

For some people, changing their perceptions can be quite hard. It may help to have another coach talk to him about some of the same kinds of things and maybe have one of the captains, if he's really pushing, just give him a pat on the back and say, "You're coming along. You're still not quite there but keep working." After awhile most players improve their perception of their abilities. Once they're in the environment and playing, practising, and competing in practice drills against other players, the realization of which areas they need to improve in starts to become more evident to them.

We had players do some personal evaluation at different times of the season —maybe watching a game tape by themselves or with a team-mate. We had them rate themselves in areas like competitive toughness, emotional control, and work ethic. **We wanted to have players develop a realistic perception of their current abilities. It helped them set im-provement goals and to take personal responsibility for their own per-formance and how it related to the goals of the team.**

I know you began as a young coach and you jumped right into it, but did you have some mentors over the years?

Yes. To me a mentor is a little like that role-model thing; it's a per-son you look at and you admire for some particular qualities and then build your philosophy or value system from there. You admire a person for something, and you try to adopt part of that quality for yourself and try to make it into something that fits your personality.

My father was a mentor for me. I watched some of the things that he did and some of the qualities he had, and I tried to adopt them. I was pretty fortunate in the coaches I had along the way. I had a really good coach in junior, Murray Armstrong. When I look back, I think some of his other players would agree he had a tremendous program. I'm talking 1948, '49. He was way ahead of the curve then, in my opinion. When I went to UBC our coach there for two of the years was Frank Fredrickson, an NHL Hall of Famer who was a perfect philosopher coach. He must have been 65 when he was coaching us, which I don't think is old now, but he was great. He was sharp about the game. He had thought about the game, and he was the first coach to give us a sheet with some diagrams and explanations on it.

Beyond that, I think about university people I taught with that I really developed a respect for: Murray Smith. He and I bounced thoughts off each other so often and still do, and there have been so many things that he has said and thought that I think are wise and that I've adopted. I could name eight or 10 coaching colleagues as mentors, and you, Mike, would be one of them. People that I've listened to, respected, and watched doing wise things, either confirm what I've been doing or provide me with new ideas. I think of Dave King and George Kingston, Father Bauer, Andy Murray, Tom Watt, and Ken Hitchcock as mentors. They are not older mentors—in fact most of them are younger than I am—but I don't think of mentoring quite in that way. I try to look for good qualities that I think are rational and that I can accept and make part of my beliefs.

I think I've done that for other people as well. I would classify Bill Moores as an equal mentor because I know that I helped him a lot and as he grew more experienced he helped me a lot. He brought things to the table that helped me in my coaching that I didn't necessarily have. He had a better sense of toughness than I did and a different approach. I was never a tough player myself, but he had a little extra edge that I knew was a positive thing for our team. We recommended to our players at the beginning of the year, coming into a new university environment, that they try to associate with people that they looked up to and that had qualities that they would like to emulate. **Associate with positive, enthusiastic, and optimistic people if you can and eventually these will become your qualities. That's the mentorship role to me.**

Do you have any advice for young coaches?

If you want to get better at something, you decide what level you want to get to, and it becomes what you'd call a dream goal. A minor hockey coach's dream goal might be to coach a midget AAA or bantam AAA team. He'd really like to go that far and maybe no further. Then it's important to focus on a game plan or series of skills that you want to give your team to be able to compete. Decide how far you want to go, and then try to gather as much information and knowledge as you can to get you there.

I can remember when I was younger and just started teaching, going to as many clinics as I could. Murray Smith and I took our wives down to Reno, Nevada, in my station wagon, to one of the best clinics I've ever gone to. It featured Bud Wilkinson, who was coaching Oklahoma football at that time and had 50 straight wins. Adolph Rupp, the legendary basketball coach from Kentucky, was also there, and it was fabulous. I was coaching high school football at the time. There are so many little things that are cross-related in sports, not necessarily tactics or techniques, but just different little things. You have to work at getting better as a coach. Just as work ethic is probably the base for improving your skill, I think work ethic is also the base for improving your knowledge. **Youth coaches need to focus on how to help the 14 kids they're working with become better players and better people. Give them the techniques and values to do that, but don't get too complicated, and make sure they're having fun.**

Jacques Demers

J acques Demers found success the same way he taught his players to win: through hard work and determination. Born in Montreal, Quebec, on August 25, 1944, Demers lost both of his parents at a young age and immediately took over the responsibility of caring for his younger brother, Michel. Realizing he was unlikely to achieve his dream of joining the Montreal Canadiens as a player, he discovered the coaching path instead and set out to make his dream a reality.

Demers started coaching juvenile hockey in the 1960s, then coached Junior B in St. Leonard, Chateauguay, and Montreal, all the way to the Provincial Championships. He got his professional start in the World Hockey Association, first for the Indianapolis Racers from 1975 to 1977, and then as head coach in Cincinnati in 1977–78. Maurice Filion hired Demers to coach the Quebec Nordiques for the 1978–79 season, which was the WHA's final year of existence. He remained as head coach the following season, after the WHA merged with the NHL.

Demers spent the next two years in the American Hockey League as head coach of the Fredericton Express, where he was honoured as the Coach of the Year in his second season. The St. Louis Blues brought Demers back to the NHL to be their head coach for three years, from 1983 to 1986. In the 1985–86 season, Demers was runner-up for Coach of the Year and led his Blues to the Conference final.

He then moved directly to the Detroit Red Wings for four seasons, from 1986 to 1990. The team's profound 53-point improvement over his first two seasons as head coach earned Demers the Jack Adams Trophy for Coach of the Year in both 1987 and 1988. The Red Wings advanced to the Conference final both years.

After a stint as a French-language television analyst for the Quebec Nordiques, Demers realized his boyhood dream of joining the Montreal Canadiens. He returned to his hometown to become the Habs' head coach from 1991 to 1995. On June 9, 1993, Demers led Montreal to their 24th Stanley Cup victory.

Jacques Demers coached the Tampa Bay Lightning for two seasons, from 1997 to 1999, before moving back to broadcasting with the RDS television network. He was one of five head coaches to have coached more than 1,000 consecutive NHL games, with a playoff winning percentage of .561, so no one was surprised when *The Hockey News* named Demers the 100th most influential personality in hockey in 2007. The world was astounded, however, when Jacques revealed in his biography *En toutes lettres (All Spelled Out)*, by Mario Leclerc, that he is functionally illiterate. While many were shocked by this revelation, they were not surprised that Jacques had never let this handicap stop him. His drive to succeed has been an inspiration to the players he has coached and to his wife, Debbie, in her battle with cancer. He will continue to inspire students, teachers, parents, and fans everywhere.

The Interview

How did you start coaching?

I had to leave school at a very young age to work on a Coca Cola truck. My mom passed away when I was 16 and my dad a few years later. I wasn't a very good hockey player. I played a little bit of Junior B, but I was very, very average. There was no possibility of a career in the game. My objective when I was young had been to play in the NHL with the Montreal Canadiens, but it wasn't to be. That's when I started coaching a juvenile team in St. Leonard, Quebec, in the '60s.

My brother-in-law at the time, who was president of hockey, talked to me about coaching. We had some quick success, and I started to enjoy it. When I played Junior B I was always competitive, but not being a good hockey player I became more of the grinder. I always seemed to be in the front row in terms of intensity. When I coached, it was like what I wanted to be as a hockey player. I always brought the intensity behind the bench. I was a lively guy. I was emotional. With time I've changed, although I can't say I control my emotions all the time. I went to Junior B coaching in St. Leonard and Chateauguay and then in Montreal.

I started to get recognized and was offered a job in the Quebec major junior league, but I had to ask for a leave of absence at Coca Cola. They didn't want to do it because there was no leave-of-absence policy, so they said I couldn't coach major junior. That was basically my only goal. Our Junior B team went to a provincial championship, and it was then that I realized that maybe I had some kind of talent here. **I have always had the opinion that you're born an athlete, and I also think you're born a coach.** You have that in you. I don't think just anybody can coach.

How did you get to the NHL from junior?

Marcel Pronovost noticed me and brought me to the WHA from Junior B. I spent seven years there as an assistant coach. I moved a lot, but both athletes and coaches have to sacrifice to be successful. I always believed there's a price to pay. There's no such thing as a free pass to success. The WHA brought me recognition, if you want. General manager Maurice Filion hired me to coach the Nordiques in Quebec City in the last year of the WHA, which was '78–'79. The WHA, as much as it got a lot of people in the NHL upset, was my springboard to go to the NHL. There was no way a little guy coaching Junior B in Montreal would ever have been looked at to coach in the NHL.

Walk us through your NHL career.

My NHL career was full of ups and downs. The ups were many but there were also some downs. During my first of two years with the Quebec Nordiques, one in the WHA and one year in the NHL, I gave an off-the-record comment to a reporter who proceeded to put it on the record. I learned a lot from that and then went to the minors to coach. I went to Fredericton in the American Hockey League and worked my way back. I became the American Hockey League Coach of the Year in my second year.

When there was an opening in St. Louis, I was hired by Ron Caron in 1983 to be their head coach. There we had the likes of Bernie Federko, Doug Gilmour, Mike Liut, and Brian Sutter, all character players. I've always loved character players. I've had a hard time dealing with soft players. **I don't judge an athlete on their talent as much as their desire to compete and their desire to want to play at whatever talent level God has given them.** You've got to use that talent. If you're soft I'm very, very uncomfortable with you.

For three years the owner in St. Louis, Harry Ornest, promised a contract but never delivered. I was nominated for Coach of the Year my third year in St. Louis. I lost to Glen Sather, but went to the final four. In 1986 I signed a five-year contract with the Detroit Red Wings to become their coach. I took over the worst team in hockey. They had 40 points and were called the "dead wings," but I had a young kid, a very determined young man that I named captain, Steve Yzerman. I recognized instantly during my first conversation with him that he was dedicated to his profession, and we had an instant good marriage with others added to it. Gerard Gallant, Harold Snepts, Tim Higgins, and Glen Hanlon were solid guys. Together we took the Red Wings into the playoffs and the conference finals in my first year there. We improved by 53 points in two years from 40 to 78, and then 78 to 93 and went to the conference finals again, this time against Glen Sather and the Edmonton Oilers. They won the Cup both years, in '86 and '87.

It seems that a coach's welcome wears out after four years, especially if you have the same players and they tune you out. It does happen. They all say that you can fire one coach or trade 25 players, so instead of firing

25 players, Detroit got rid of one. From Detroit I went to do radio in Quebec City and went back to working for the Quebec Nordiques, where I started. After two years of radio, Pat Burns was moved to Toronto and Serge Savard gave me the opportunity to coach his team, the Montreal Canadiens, which for me was a dream come true. A French Canadian kid back in Montreal with all my family and friends, that was instant success. We won the Cup my first year, and after my third year, which was the year of the strike, I think, Mr. Corey decided that he was going to clean house, and everybody left. They kept me in the organization, but Rejean Houle, who became the general manager, decided he was going to hire Mario Tremblay to coach. I stayed on as a pro scout so I could get paid and be seen around the NHL and maybe have a shot at coaching another team.

It ended up that way. I coached Tampa Bay Lightning and wasn't very successful. The team made the playoffs once in 10 years. They still missed the playoffs the three years after I left. Artur Williams, the owner, had given me a four-year deal, and about a year later decided to sell the team. The new owners came in from Detroit and decided to hire Rick Dudley, so I was out of a job. Timing is important, and I've been fortunate to be in the right place at the right time for the most part, but maybe in this case I was in the right place at the wrong time. I had worked very hard to establish myself around the .500-mark in this league, but in Tampa I really slipped lower than that. Those things happen. It was a gamble on my part, but it paid off financially, and the money is important because I have four children.

What motivates you as a coach?

I really believe that the motivation came from my youth. We were brought up in a very difficult situation, and when I was working for Coca Cola at 17, although I don't knock that, I thought I could do better. I had difficulty in school, and I thought there was a way to prove to everybody that even though I went through a hard time, I could still do something and be successful at it. I love hockey and I was dreaming, but dreams don't come true. You wake up and they just go away. **I keep motivated by always wanting to prove something.** I think a lot has to do with having been ridiculed, but I'm always out to prove that I can do it. I'm motivated by getting up in the morning and putting in a day's work. **I'm motivated by success because success is healthy. Success is joy. When you're successful in life, everyone else around you benefits.**

If you want to be successful at something, however, you have to pay a big price. There's the moving. I am, unfortunately, a divorced father, as well as a grandfather. I am still very, very close with my children and will continue to be, but it also motivated me to keep working for them. They needed me. I was the provider in the family. I was the one who continued to give them a good education. My son is at university right now. If I'm not there physically, I'm there with my heart. I call them a lot. I didn't see them as much as I wanted to just because of the job I had, so in return I wanted to give them a good life. That motivated me.

Does the fear of losing motivate more than the joy of winning?

The joy of winning is so short and small. The fear of losing stays with you. Without it you could continue losing. If you have the fear, you're going to do something about it. **I think losing becomes a habit, and I think winning becomes a habit.** When the Red Wings had 40 points, there was a habit of losing there, and Stevie Yzerman wasn't comfortable when that happened. He enjoys winning.

The lows in professional hockey are much greater than the highs. You play 82 games. If you have a .500 season it still means you may have lost 41 games. If you have 90 points you have lost 35 times.

So what really motivates me? I would like to think I'm a perfectionist, but if the table is crooked by one-tenth of an inch I'm not going to bother fixing it. I'm not a perfectionist to the point that it bothers people around me. I want excellence, but to a point where there is also a margin of error. If I wasn't going to be able to give my players that margin of error, they couldn't function as human beings in the fastest game in the world. There is that margin of error, but there is also that push for excellence.

Did you, as a coach, believe that you had the responsibility to motivate players?

I think that is the coach's responsibility in many ways. People talk about motivation as yelling, throwing tantrums, kicking Kool-Aid buckets, and breaking sticks. That's all part of coaching, and we've all done it. We've all said things that we've regretted, but I think personally it's the coach's responsibility to motivate. Bringing a team together motivates players. Having a system motivates players. Having a good and organized practice motivates players. Having discipline and being on time, at the bus on time, at the airplane on time, and having a curfew motivates players because this says to a player that if he is well organized he will be a better hockey player. He's going to win because I am well structured. **If I'm not well structured and not well organized I will pull my players down.** They won't go to practice if it's not a good practice. It's not going to work if we have a meeting at 8:00 a.m. and one player doesn't show up until 8:05. If I kick the late one out it's going to motivate the other 20 players because they will realize with this kind of attitude we will progress.

Were there any techniques that you used to keep players at their peak level?

I'm very strong on compliments. I will compliment you, I will compliment success, and I compliment effort. If you do not buy into the team concept I won't drag you down, but I'll put you in your place. I don't believe in dragging people down to the point of taking their self-esteem away, which you can do. Coaches who have done that have really destroyed a human being. I've blasted some players at times, but I always thought I chose the right timing. **The strength of a coach is to be able to understand each individual**. There are players that you could put in their place in front of a group of 24 or 25 and it won't affect them, but if you do that to other players, then you just took them out.

Are different players motivated in different ways?

Absolutely. If any coach said that he treated all his players the same way, he'd be lying. **I'm telling you honestly that I didn't treat all my players the same way. That's impossible. I show respect for the fourth-line player. I show respect for the sixth and seventh defencemen, but I don't treat him the same way as my first defenceman or my first centre or my number one goaltender.** I respect them. If a coach does not show respect for his players and only looks at one or two or three guys on the team, he is going to eventually eliminate the other players.

I had to recognize that if I was going to win in Detroit I had to start somewhere. My number one guy was Stevie Y, but I knew if I put him out there against four guys, no matter how good he was, he wasn't going to win. So I had to give each of those players who were going to be with Stevie Y a role. You determine the role of each player and make sure every player understands. Every player wants to play 25 minutes, but everybody can't play 25 minutes. Those who are persistent and don't understand that they can't play 25 minutes, are going to eventually have to be parted with, because everybody can't play 25 minutes. Every player has a specific role.

A coach is a salesman. He has to sell his system and his way of dealing with people. He has to be honest. I've learned very quickly that there are things you can't say. Give each player an opportunity to manifest or express himself in his role. After you've given the player a role make sure as a coach, and I repeat myself, that you don't change that role. Be consistent in what you do. You can't put in a system on Tuesday and say, "Boys, we're going to be a defensive-minded team," and a week later say, "Boys, by the way, we're going to be an offensive-minded team." You think about a decision, because if you're changing your mind all the time you're not motivating your players; you're putting them down. They'll say, "This guy's not organized. This guy doesn't know what he's doing or where he's going."

How do you get that little extra out of your players?

They say I wasn't a great technician, but I've always said that I understood the game. I've coached five teams in the NHL, and never once did I come up to my players during the first training camp or when we picked the team and say, "Boys, I'm your coach. You have to respect me." **Respect comes from your actions. Respect comes from your decisions.** When you're dealing with men, treat them like men. Now, if that man you're treating with respect goes overboard, there's going to be a fine line. I learned in my 14 years in the NHL that you can't have players dictate to you, but I think the most important thing is to show respect for your players.

Successful coaches communicate with their players so that each player understands exactly why he's benched, why he's put in the press box, why he was scolded in front of teammates, and why he wasn't put in the situation with five minutes left and you're leading 2–1. **It is so important never to embarrass your players. If you treat them like men, then everybody lives by the team concept.** The players start saying what they like about the coach: He's organized; he's fair; he's honest. When the time comes to win that game on Tuesday night, the player understands that you might have to shorten your bench. If he respects your decision and you're consistent, he will accept that.

How does a coach instill confidence in his athletes?

You put players in situations where they can excel. I'm one who likes to set goals. You set team goals that are attainable. For example, team goals for and against, or points by segment. I can't say in October, "Guys, we're going to get 100 points by the end of the season," because maybe in December five of my best players will be out. Monthly goals are more realistic. If I tell a player who has scored an average of 20 goals a year for five or six years, "This year if you're going to help the team I want you to score 40 goals," I just cut his legs out from under him. I'm taking away any drive that this guy had. I just cut it. It's not attainable. I took away his desire, his spirit, and his enthusiasm because I'm asking him to do something that he can't achieve. If I come to him and say, "Listen, by the way, Ryan, you scored 20 goals last season. You've had a little more experience in the league now, and I saw at the end of last year that you're getting better. I'd like to see you score between 25 and 30." You could score 27, but it's seven more than last year. Don't ask for unrealistic goals. Instead, put your player in a situation that he wants to be a part of. He's a gamer. He's a competitor. He's a character player, so put him in a situation where he can achieve.

Could you read a player's ability or willingness to perform? For example, before a game if you looked into a player's eyes or at his body language, could you feel whether he was going to have a good night?

I always loved to go into the dressing room before the game. There's a time to go into the dressing room where you don't speak. There's a time to go into the dressing room, and there's a time not to. My timing was good, and I always looked my players in the eyes. I was intense. I looked my players in the eyes and didn't say a word just to get the feel of the room. Too noisy a room is not a good room. There's a time to listen to the music, but there's also a time to get prepared. There's a time to get focussed. There's a time to get ready to compete. I could tell if my team was ready, and I could also tell if my team wasn't. You have to get the feel of the pulse of your team.

Do you concern yourself with a player's self-talk or body language?

Yes. I will accept poor body language in a player who competes every night and for whatever reason is not going that night. If he's having a bad week or a bad game and I don't play him on the power play where he's used to playing and I can see poor body language, I can live with that. **I can't accept a player with poor body language who fails to do the job that I ask him to do and then reacts when I don't put him back after**

giving him numerous chances. If you're going to give a guy a chance, don't do it once. If he fails once, what kind of chance was that? You put him in a situation five times, and if he fails five times, at least you gave him a chance. If that guy is going to show me some kind of sign of negative body language, it means he's putting his own personal stats or his own personal ice time ahead of the team concept. So I accept negative body language from a warrior who plays hard every night, gives me everything, competes, and has won me games. **Every team has soft players. It's up to the coach to determine who that soft player is. You hope you don't have more than two or three, because then you're not going to win.**

Describe a soft player to me.

A soft player is the type of guy who will pick which team he wants to compete against. He's not a guy who competes every night. He could be very talented, but he will pick his team. We could be playing a more physical team, and you don't see him all night, even at home. The soft players generally have a tendency not to show up on the road, but there will be times when you don't even see him at home. These players are judged more severely at home because of the fans. **A soft player is not willing to pay the price to make the play.** He will put his teammates in a difficult position on the ice. He will say, "I want to win," if you ask him the question, but you can see just by the way he competes on the ice that he doesn't really actually mean it.

Have you ever taken a soft player and turned the corner with him?

No. I've coached some soft players, and I knew eventually we'd have to part with them. When you're the coach you're not the GM, but if you have a strong rapport with the GM, it might be possible for changes to be made. When I arrived in Detroit and they had 40 points, they obviously had a lot of soft players. One of the great motivators of any character player and self-motivated player is seeing that the coach identifies those players who don't compete every night and doesn't use them in key situations. That will motivate a team. If you're competing every night and you see the coach keeps putting that guy back on the ice in positions where you had given it your all and you're a character player and you're competing, you're going to think, "What the hell is the coach doing? Why does he keep coming back with a soft player?" **I've never turned a guy without character around, and I've never been able to turn a soft player around.**

Is there credibility to the locker room speech, the soapbox speech, the big speech before games? Was it important for you with your teams?

If you had the right players you didn't need a speech. If you had the wrong players you had to have a speech. If you have too many speeches the players tune you out. If you have the right players there is a time for speeches. There is a time to put people and everything into perspective. Throughout my career, 80 percent of the time I had the right players. That's why I was able to last 14 years and coach 1,000 games. If I hadn't had them, I would have been gone. It's not the coach; it's the players. **A lot of people think it's the coach, but if you don't have the right players you are not going to be successful.**

Describe to me what a "right" player is.

The right player is not perfect. The right player is a little difficult at times. The right player will miss a curfew at times, but he will play guilty. He will feel responsible. The right player is not afraid to express his feelings if he's not in agreement with the coach, but he'll do it in a very respectful way. I never had a problem when a player said, "Coach, can I talk to you tomorrow morning?" and then sat in my office and said, "Coach, I don't agree with you." "Well, fine, let's talk about it. What don't you agree with?"

If you don't agree with me, come into my office. I know there are five or six of your friends, maybe seven others in the room who don't agree with me. That means maybe one-third of the team doesn't agree with me, so let's talk about it. There have been players who have brought up great suggestions. I would always leave the door open. That's the best suggestion.

I will give you an example. Guy Carbonneau played for us in Montreal against the Los Angeles Kings in the finals. He came into the office and said, "I want to play against Gretzky." He had a bad knee and was starting to get a little older, so I said, "Guy, let me think about it." Well, as soon as he left the office I knew he was going to play against Gretzky. Guy came in a respectful manner and he knew when he left the office the coach was going to think about it. So leave the door open. There is an opportunity for communication, and as soon as you shut your door, there's no communication, there is no more team, and there is no more going through the wall for the coach.

Give us some examples of finding an angle to get players to another level that you used for your teams.

That comes from the coach being organized. **Players love a coach who prepares them well. A player loves a coach who moves his team to a higher level of competing.** You have to bring them into a level where the whole team can compete without being too high or too low. A coach or coaches who are organized is key.

I have always given my assistant coaches a role. Give your assistant coaches an opportunity. One has the power play, the other has the penalty kill, and another could take care of the defencemen. I know that players like a team to be well organized.

I've never prepared my team the same way for every opponent. It doesn't work that way. So that's my edge. You've got to set goals for the players, but you have to set up things so the players are able to identify what is going to happen in the game. You know you have to be aware when you are going to play Ray Bourque on the power play, so you show a little video: five minutes of power play and five minutes of penalty killing. Don't over-video. Don't show a half-hour every day, or you will tune the players out.

Players like to be matched against a key player on the other team. I might put in a challenge, for example, to have Guy Carbonneau check Bryan Trottier, or two defencemen, Eric Desjardins and Lyle Odelien, play against Gretzky every time he's on the ice. You are not telling the other four defencemen they're not good, but you assign two players specifically because sometimes it's tough to have five players on the ice match up. I always try to give everybody an opportunity to get involved. You may only play five minutes, but make sure you're involved. I didn't believe in sitting a player on the bench all night. If I have you dressed, it's because I believe you can be on this team and help out. I had units on the penalty killing, and those players, in my opinion, knew each other and enjoyed the role and the challenge. I used to always like to have Guy Carbonneau and Mike Keane together, as well as Kirk Muller and Vincent Damphousse. **Players like to be given assignments, and everybody has their specific assignment.**

Players go through life guided by everybody else. The bus is at 5:00, the plane at 7:00, lunch is at 12:30, curfew at 11:00, and practice in the morning is at 11:00. I believe players are motivated by assignments and by things to do. Just don't always be into a routine. You may be on a bit of a roll, but don't make it boring. Hockey is exciting. It's interesting. **It's a fast game, so set things up to keep the players tuned, not tuned out, but tuned in.**

Did you talk to every player every day?

No, I didn't do that. It's not possible. I would talk if I ran into a player in the hotel hallway, or on the ice. I would talk to the fourth-line players as much as I'd talk to the first-line players, but my captains are very important to me. I had a little committee with the captains to get their opinion. If you have the wrong players as captains, then they'll start telling you what to do. If you have the right players, you have tremendous success.

How close did you like to get with your players? Give us some examples of how you interacted with them.

The only player I really got close to was Doug Gilmour. Because he was young he had come to my house a little. You are never too close to your players. There is that balance of a coach and player, and you really don't want the player to get to know you well. We all have weaknesses, so it's not good if he gets to know you too well and learns some of your weaknesses.

At times I was very complimentary to my players. I love excellence. I love players who perform and succeed. I love players who are going through a stretch of glory, if you want, like Stevie Y two years in a row. I love to see great athletes perform to their ability, but I never got too close. I played golf with my players a couple of times. Maybe we needed to go play golf, talk, have something going, but there's a fine line between a buddy and a coach. You can talk, you can communicate, you can laugh, but it stops there. You never want to cross that line.

What is the identity of a Jacques Demers coached team?

The identity I wanted was to be a hard-working team. You would have to pay a price to beat us. That was the identity I wanted my team to have. I didn't want my team to be too defensive-minded. I wanted to let the offensive player express himself. If you played our team you would always be on the edge. We would play a good defensive game but also be able to provide good offence because I gave the offensive players the opportunity to excel. If you played against my team you knew one thing coming in: that I would play my best players at a high level of ice time. My best players would be put in every situation, and I would continually give them ice time. Whether I was down or up, my best players played a lot. I like a hard-nosed team. I like a team that will not allow the opposition to manhandle our smallish or, certainly more important, our best players.

How do you start and maintain that identity?

You have to establish the way you're going to play in training camp. You have to establish the kind of team you will have in your own head as a coach. If you have a team that has very little goal scoring, then you have to play the game differently. If you have an offensive-minded team and you have a lot of offensive-minded players, don't give these guys a defensive role. I think that's very important: to get to know your team and to prepare yourself well coming into training camp. You have 60 or 70 players your first few weeks, but as soon as those players are cut and you're pretty close to the team you're going to have in October, **be consistent with what you do in practice. Repetition is key, but not boring repetition. Don't be boring. Have fun doing it.** I really didn't believe in one-and-a-half-hour practices. I believe in a fast-paced 45 minutes to an hour. To the point, do it, do it well, go out, see you later. I love tempo. I love a transition tempo team. **If you get a team to practise with tempo, you're going to form good habits.** I dislike bad habits. Put good habits into your team and the players will get into good habits, not bad. I believe in repetition of the good things.

How did you keep your players focussed on what was good for the team when there was so much attention placed on individual accomplishments?

You cannot ever eliminate the individual skills, especially if you have big-name players, but the team concept is very important. You have to focus on keeping your team sharp by winning. **All players say they want to win, but not every one of them is willing to pay the price. The team wins. Individuals with high talent will win you games, but it all boils down to team wins.** I can really believe that the great players I've coached, Yzerman, Gilmour, Michel Goulet, certainly Denis Savard, are part of the team concept. They don't want to be higher than the team. I think Gretzky was the same. Superstars are thoroughbreds, and you have to handle them right, but it's important to keep the players thinking "team." You have to keep the players focussed through constant repetition on the ice to do the right thing, but there's no question off the ice you need to change the atmosphere and change the routine because you get into such a routine. It's such a long season.

I strongly believe in the team concept. At the beginning of the season I budget with my general manager to be able to take the team out a lot for dinner. It wasn't because I knew they couldn't pay; it was because I knew I'd have them together. I always said, "I don't want the same guys sitting at the same table. Just change. Get to know each other. Spend time with each other." Today you have the Russians, the Swedes, the Finns. It's very difficult, but I'm still a bit of the old school. Let them be together. Let them spend time together. Let them share things together.

Were there any other things you did to enhance your team play?

One of the things I did as a coach on Monday morning, if the players were thinking, "Boy, he's really going to give us a hard practice after we'd lost three in a row," was to say, "OK, boys, I'll give $1,000 to the winner of an east-west fun game." Now, they were expecting a hard practice. When you expect something, you prepare yourself for it. You may not be looking for it when that person who is going to dictate what you're going to do that day has a reversed psychological way of doing things. I like to always whet their appetite.

On a Tuesday morning after losing four in a row and all the players in the room are wondering, "Holy shit, what's going to happen?" I want to know from every player what we could do to be a better team. Every player on the team has a right to express himself, because it's not the coach's team. It's the players' team. If you don't have them in front of you, you're done, and that is one thing I always had as a coach. There are times when the coach thinks he makes a difference, and I think a good coach can make a difference, but the real difference comes from the quality of players you have in front of you. You may not have the greatest team, but if you have a bunch of competitors who play hard every night, you may have some decent success. So give every player an opportunity to express himself.

I was often tougher when we won than when we lost. When we lost I was very concerned about affecting their mental state and their confidence. When we won I didn't want them to get too excited and carried away. I would have the toughest practices the very next day after we won three in a row. You have to keep the players guessing to be a good coach. If you give them too much of the same, you've got them in a routine and they don't function right.

How do you communicate the tradition of excellence? You've set the bar, but how did you initiate it?

In Detroit our goal was to make the playoffs. We never talked about points. Our goal was to make the playoffs because making the playoffs is an accomplishment. If I come to my team and say, "We've got to get 90 points," and you get 90 points and don't make the playoffs, you didn't accomplish anything. You have to set your goals a little higher. **Get to know your players quickly. If you have a tremendous amount of talent, they'll win for you anyhow and a lot of times won't need that much coaching. Get to know them to the point that you know what makes them tick, what makes them click, what gets this guy pissed off, and what makes this guy happy.** The only way you can get to know them is with a lot of one-on-one, and a lot of team. Then when you talk to a player you can look him in the eye and say, "Don't bullshit me because I won't bullshit you."

Why do so few organizations reach that level of excellence?

I think it's bad management, bad trades, bad drafting, and continually panicking and making changes when you don't have success that keeps organizations from reaching that level. Everyone wants instant success, but 16 teams make the playoffs and 14 don't. **Everyone wants instant mashed potatoes because there's a tremendous amount of money involved, but it doesn't happen that way.** Patience is a tremendous virtue in hockey, as it is in life. When I won in Detroit it was chaotic, but they had a good owner who had just purchased the team. Before they had run out of money. If you have a well-structured organization the players will identify with that quickly. It starts from the top, not necessarily with the coach. **A coach will follow the pattern already established. So it starts from the top and filters down from the president to the general manager, with good drafting, patience with players, hiring the right people to do the right job, and once they are hired, letting them do their job.**

Success is often defined as winning championships. How do you define success?

There's no question, in hockey success is making the playoffs and doing well in the playoffs because only one team will win the Stanley Cup. You start the season with 30 teams, but realistically there are five that have a chance to win. **My definition of success is being consistently in the playoffs and consistently improving each year.** Failing to win the Stanley Cup doesn't mean you are a failure as an organization. Be consistent and competitive and gradually improve each year into the playoffs. Today you are in a different world because you are in a world of money. The one who has the most money could possibly buy the Stanley Cup. Success is what the franchise has as a tradition. **Tradition comes from winning. Tradition comes from the great players you have had who have worn the sweater with class and respect, and most important, every night that they put that sweater on they competed to the best of their ability.**

What would be your most memorable coaching experience and your greatest accomplishment?

There is no question, even though I won a Stanley Cup, that I will probably be defined as the guy who took the Detroit Red Wings from nowhere and brought them back to respectability, because I was part of that. I wasn't the only one, but to take a team that had 40 points and was called the "dead wings," that nobody saw any kind of future success in, and turn that team into a respectable franchise the first year that I got there, was the biggest accomplishment for me.

What did all your successful teams have in common?

They had the right players who competed every night. If they didn't compete, they had something wrong with them, because they had big hearts.

Is a lot of that attitude?

Absolutely. You have to have the right players with the right attitude, the right frame of mind, and, more important, who compete every night. If you have too many players who take the night off, you are not going to have a competitive team. My success was the Mike Keane of this world, the Kirk Muller of this world, the Lyle Odelien, but my bigger success was the Stevie Yzerman of this world, the Vincent Damphousse, the Guy Carbonneau, the Michel Goulet, the Denis Savard, the Bernie Federko, and the Brian Sutter.

When you were coaching, did you win at all costs?

We never cheated. I don't believe in cheating. I believe in following the rules. I was called everything in the book for calling an illegal stick on Marty McSorley in the Stanley Cup playoffs. I was called gutless, classless, everything, but I just followed the rules. Other coaches disliked that I did that. They said, "I wouldn't do that." Well, too bad. I did it. I didn't cheat. Marty McSorley was cheating. I talked to Marty, and he said, "Coach, you made the right call." I admire him for that.

How did you know his stick was illegal?

We lost Game 1, 4–1. I found out, after talking with some of my players in the third period, that his stick was illegal, but the timing was not right to call it. It was very visible after it was pointed out to me, so I waited for the right time.

There was a game where I was caught throwing five or six pennies on the ice in St. Louis. For those who don't know what really happened, we were playing Minnesota, and we were called for penalty after penalty. We heard that Lou Nanne, the Minnesota GM, went to talk to the referees between periods, which is a no-no. So at a stoppage in play during the fifth game in a best three out of five, when we were overwhelmed with penalty after penalty and knew what was going on, I took a bunch of pennies and threw them right in front of the bench. I would never do it during the play; I have too much respect for players on both sides. I then called the linesman, and he and the referee came over. If they want to call that cheating, they can. I wasn't cheating.

What happened in that incident?

Well, they took the pennies. Brian Sutter and Doug Gilmour were killing the penalties along with Rob Ramage, and it gave them an opportunity to get a 30- to 45-second break. Apparently a policeman was somewhere near the bench and told the referee what I had done. The referee said to me, "I don't know if it was you, but I've been told it was you. If that ever happens again you'll get two minutes." So no, I don't want to cheat. If I'm going to win I'm going to beat you fair. I'm going to get into the boxing ring to fight you, but I'm going to fight you fair. I may lose, but if I win and kick the shit out of you, take it.

How do you handle pressure as a coach?

I hope I handled it well, but I really don't know. That's for other people to tell you. When I was a youngster I had all kinds of problems. It wasn't easy growing up. I thought I handled it by working harder and being even more determined. Adversity in hockey comes from losing, and sometimes from having problem players. I tried to handle it as best I could by communicating and showing the right way to do things. I hope I was able to handle it, when things weren't going well, by being positive instead of negative. Dwelling on the negative is too easy. My strength was dwelling on the positive. They call me Mr. Positive in Montreal. I think it bothers people if someone is too positive because many people are negative by nature. Being positive is in my nature. I can't come into the room saying, "You can't skate. You can't shoot. You can't stop a puck. We're no good defensively. We're not good offensively." If I did that, I'd be just killing my team. Find the positive and build on it. "OK, we've lost four in a row, guys. Let's go out tonight and play the first period like we've never played before. Let's win the first period." Don't worry about winning the game. Worry about the first period. If you win the first period, then you come into the room with a short speech and say, "Boys, a couple of adjustments. Now, let's go into the second period," and then you're back on a winning streak. **Find a positive. Too many coaches are negative. Coaches who are negative are hurting kids.**

What was your worst moment, and how did you recover from it?

My worst moment was when I found out my wife, Debbie, had cancer. I think I did a bad job of coaching as well. I was coaching the Tampa Bay Lightning, and the woman I loved the most was battling cancer. We had been together 20 years. I was trying to coach, and we had no family and very few friends in Tampa. I was not a coach; I was trying to be a husband. I missed a couple of games to take care of the woman who turned my life around. That was the most difficult time.

How do you deal with team adversity?

I dealt with team adversity by being a Joe Field guy, as difficult as the losing can be and as difficult as it is to sleep at night. I used to always show up early at work and leave late. When I got on the ice I was like a Jekyll and Hyde. My personality was "OK, boys, what do we do about this?" I always believe "Let's find a way." We have to find a way, find solutions, and present different types of practices. I'd say, "We've had difficulty in this area. We are having difficulty in our zone. Let's work on this today. Let's work on it 15 or 20 minutes, but as we work on it, let's put all our attention and all our focus on what we're doing." As we work on these things we're having difficulty with, we're having fun doing it.

If you show on the ice as a coach that you've lost, don't ever forget the players have lost too. If you have the right players, they're hurting just as much as you are. The only difference between a player and a coach is two or three guys could go out to dinner after a game with their wives, while the coach goes home by himself or with family or a friend. Players can talk about it more, but the coach basically ends up by himself. The responsibility of losing really falls on the coach more than anyone else.

So find solutions. Run practice differently. Don't panic and change the system. Don't panic and start thinking you don't have the right players. When they were winning in November you certainly had the right players, but if they're losing in December you start thinking you have the wrong players. They may have lost a bit of their confidence, so you have to build their confidence up: "We know we can do it. We've done it before." Take out a couple of videos: a nice goal, a nice defensive play, a big stop by the goaltender. "Look at that great save there." It's just building on the positive. Find energy, because when you lose, the energy goes down because of sleepless nights. You're tired when you lose. If you win you're never tired, even if you play 10 in a row. **I think it's the coach's responsibility to find the energy and not ever touch on the negative. Find a positive way, because if you touch on negative, you're really going to go on a losing streak.**

What would you do with an individual player who is experiencing adversity?

I need to know that I have a good rapport with my player if he has a personal problem. If he tells me he has a personal problem at home, I'll deal with it, and I guarantee no one else will know about it, not an assistant coach, at times not even my wife. You're dealing with a player one-on-one if he is capable of sitting down with you and expressing himself in an honest manner that he's suffocating in some area: divorce, girlfriend pregnant, father asking for money, maybe a drinking problem, anything that could pull a player down. There are all kinds of things an athlete can go through. At times you have to take that player and say, "We're going to start slowly. I may not be able to deal with your problems at home, but now that you've told me, I'm going to be a little more patient with you. Still, you're going to have to come out of it by yourself. You have to understand one thing: If things are going badly at home and you let your job go down, then you lose everything. Don't fail at the one thing that's keeping you alive, or certainly don't be negative about it. If you do your job well, everything else around you is going to be taken care of."

What would you do to me as your player when I'm going through a goal-scoring slump?

I will have a talk with you. I want to know if something is going on, but I don't want you to tell me about the stick and skates stuff, because that's just an excuse. Don't give me that or "I've hit the goalpost five in a row." If you hit the goalpost five in a row, I'll know that. Are you playing hurt? Is something going on? I want to know. Tell me, because if you tell me the truth I'll help you, but don't lie to me, because I can't help you if you lie to me.

I will often try to put the player in a different position. Instead of giving him the second half of the power play, I'll give him the first half. If he's a first-guy power play and the power play is not running, maybe I'll put him in the second half. He'll get his 45 seconds, but with different players. He may be thinking he would like to be with different guys, but I hope he won't tell me. As a player don't ever come and complain to me about your teammate. Don't tell me that Joe is not passing you the puck. I can't accept that. On my own, I may give you an opportunity to play with someone else, and you may find a little more chemistry.

What types of players are the most challenging to coach?

The toughest player and biggest challenge for me to coach is the player who has a tremendous amount of talent but is not using it to the best of his ability. I have a hard time dealing with that. For whatever reason we've all experienced that as a player with a teammate, and now I've had it as a coach. You know that down the road this guy is going to be on three or four teams, and then he's going to eliminate himself. Still, you make it a challenge, and you really work with him. Maybe he has very little self-esteem. Maybe he was and still is being kicked in the ass by his father, who expected him to be Gretzky. You've got to be able to identify that. I also have a really hard time with a guy who is nonchalant about the game. You can sense those guys.

How would you challenge an athlete who was performing below his potential and get the most out of a lazy player?

You won't win with the lazy player. You won't be able to get them in the team concept, and you won't be able to have them compete every night. **I do not know if I was ever able to take a lazy player and make him what I thought he should be.** A coach's definition of a player is different from the players' definition of themselves. You look at a player and say, "This is what he could do for my team. This is what he could do for our franchise. This is what he could do for himself." A lazy player is soft. If you're lazy you don't enjoy the game, you don't like to work, and you don't like to compete. If you're lazy I have to motivate you and threaten you with the press box or single you out in front of your teammates, because as a coach if I don't get down on you, then the other 17 or 18 players are going to lose respect for the coach.

Let the best player play; he wants to play. A very high percentage of the great players want to be put in every tough situation. If you put them in a situation you know other players can't handle, they'll usually come forward. Great players do things from instinct. God gave them a huge talent. They are instinctive and they are usually hard workers. They may seem lazy, but like Mario Lemieux, who may seem lazy because he's floating in the neutral zone, they get the job done. You have to let him be Mario Lemieux. I've never tried to change any of my players. Let the players express themselves.

How did you deal with confrontation?

I dealt with it in an honest manner. I dealt with it frankly. I let them know that, no matter what, I was the coach and their boss, so if the player was a repeat offender at one point — I'm not saying 10 times — there was no giving. I could give. I am able to do that. I'm not stubborn enough not to change my mind. You have to be able to change your mind. It's very important to be straightforward, look the guy in the eye, and say, "This is the way it is, man." The character players and the competitors will accept it.

Do you feel that the dressing room environment influences team success,
and what did you do to influence a positive environment?

I believe that the players control the dressing room, and when you
have the right players in the dressing room, you are going to win. First of
all, if you want to win in this game, you surround yourself with winners.
Know that every night these guys are going to play hard, no matter who
the competition is. **Surround yourself with players who are willing to**
sacrifice and play hurt. I'm not saying a dislocated shoulder, but if you
are hurt, play hurt. That's part of this game. You have to play hurt.

You may not go out with your teammates and be best buddies,
but respect your teammates when you put that uniform on and when
you're in that dressing room. Respect them, because even though you
might not like that guy beside you, he may be part of winning a game for
you. He may be part of your living. **The guy beside you is the most im-**
portant person on the team, not the coach. If you don't have him, you
have nothing. Even if you don't like him, make sure that when the game
is on or when you're in the dressing room, you respect him. It's tough to
respect every player. If there are players who are not following the team
concept and are breaking curfew and all that, then the coach has to immediately put his foot down and start identifying those players. You may not
have the same thinking and you may not have the same focus, but once
this guy becomes your teammate, he is your teammate for years. You have
to respect that this is the guy who is going to bring you success.

How do you view leadership?

Leadership in coaching comes from showing your players you
really care. Showing your players that you respect them is part of leadership. Showing your players that you will not accept other players not
being part of the team concept and stepping in right away if you see the
team slipping. I identify the winners the first day, at the first meeting of
the first practice, by what they say to me, the way they perform in practice, the way they want to be put in every tough situation, and how they
will handle it with their talent as best they can.

I dislike players who are finding whatever excuse can be found. There
are so many excuses when you're with a hockey family. I call my team a
family, and it really boils down to knowing your players and putting your
players in specific roles. The players also really consistently need to know

how much losing affects you, that it's not just a slap of the hand. **If you show them you care, they'll care, and really, winners do care.**

What qualities did you look for when selecting your captains?

A captain is a player who will perform. The best player on your team may not be your captain. **A captain's leadership is demonstrated by the way he plays the game. He doesn't have to voice his opinion every day in the room, but if he competes hard in practice every day, follows the team rules, competes to a standard of excellence every night, and is willing to pay a price to win, you'll have identified your captain.** I also want a captain who's going to come to me honestly if I'm getting out of line or if I've just slipped away from doing what is good for the concept of the team. We're human; it happens to coaches. I want that captain to say, "Jacques, you're not being fair with John. You're not treating John right." Maybe I'm not treating John right, and I did not see it that way. I want a captain who will not be a sucky kind of guy to the coach. I want someone who comes in, tells me how it is, walks out, meant what he said, steps on the ice, and performs hard at practice. He should be disciplined all around, and once the game is on, he brings the game to a higher level.

How important is the quality of communication? The captain doesn't have to talk a lot, but is it important that he communicate with his team?

The captain in hockey is more important than in any other sport. He has to, at times, let his teammates know that he's not happy with the way they performed. **A captain at times has to speak on behalf of the coach, because if the coach has to come in all the time, he will eventually lose the attention of the players.** A captain has to be able to tell 19 other players every night that, "Hey, we've got to get it going here." A captain's got to be able to say, "Listen, the coach has been down on us, but he wants to win just as much as we do, believe it or not. I talked to Coach, and he's going to relax a little bit. Let's make sure we all get back on track." That is why a captain has a major role in a hockey club. **A captain has to be able to tell a teammate, "Move your ass because I don't like the way things are going right now," and also bring the guys together off the ice as much as possible.**

Define your leadership style.

I really believe that leadership comes from not accepting anything less than a high standard of performance. My leadership comes from being prepared every game. If I'm not prepared, then I'm not preparing my team. I think it comes from always being organized or trying to be well organized. A coach's leadership comes from the way he conducts himself behind the bench, and there have been a couple of times where I slipped, and I was very upset with myself and made sure I didn't do it again. A coach has to come ready to have his players come to play. He has to be alert behind the bench, make the right decision, make the right changes, and say the right things to the players. I don't believe that a coach should be swearing up and down the bench at his players. I don't believe in that philosophy. I believe in the importance of communicating with the players. If the players screw up, there will be a time when you have to tell them but not this swearing stuff like some coaches do.

What were the incidents that upset you?

There are specific things. When the puck comes around the boards you've got to be 100 percent sure to go up the middle. I gave my players an opportunity to be creative, but if you're winning 2–1 and there are a few minutes left in the game, don't come up the middle. If the puck comes around the boards, you have to win the battle and pay the price for that battle. If you don't have the play and there's no play, just put it off the glass. Flip it out. If you're going to go in the corner and there's an opportunity for an icing and you hear footsteps, pay the price and go get that puck.

Play the game the way it's supposed to be played. If you're coming down three on three and there's no room on the blue line, you want to be persistent, but if you want to be cute and deke the guy and you lose the puck and it's three on two the other way, that would bother me. If you stay too long on the ice because I didn't give you the amount of ice time that you thought you deserved, and then I've got another line going with only two fresh players, you just deprived another player of ice time. If you make an honest mistake, if you compete and make a mistake, you have no problems with me. That happens. But don't give me a soft play. Don't take a bad penalty because the guy gave you a little shot and you wanted to retaliate.

In what ways have you changed your coaching and leadership style over the years?

Every decade from the '70s to the '80s to the '90s was totally different. In the '70s we were a lot more demanding from players, and in the '80s we were more demanding vocally. The players in those days accepted it. The athletes were still the same guys in the '70s, '80s, and '90s. The character guys had character, the competitors were competitors, and the cheaters were cheaters, but their way of thinking and living was totally different. The players and athletes today are more independent in their ways because they are more financially secure. If you are financially secure, your whole life is pretty good. They used to play to secure their finances. Now when they are playing you only have to touch their pride a little and their ego a little. Over the decades I have had to adjust to the times.

What kind of adjustments did you make?

You couldn't push the players as much in the '90s as you could in the '80s or the '70s. I think the players' time around the rink was different then. They want in and out as quickly as possible now. They want to spend less time around the rink than they used to, so structure and organization in your practice is important. Don't ask them to play ping-pong in the dressing room after, because they're in and out. It's all about accepting how times are. In the '80s you didn't see the agents, but now the agents are there waiting for the players. You have to adjust and accept that they seem to be playing younger than ever. Athletes think differently and are more independent and less team-oriented today than they used to be in the '70s and '80s.

If we were to interview some of your players that you have coached, how would they describe you?

I think they would say they could talk to Jacques at any given time. "When things were tough, Jacques was a very positive coach. When I was in a slump, Jacques stuck with me as long as he could, maybe too long at times, but he stuck with me. Maybe at times Jacques was too emotional, but maybe the emotion he brought made us a better team."

How did you handle all the responsibilities of a head coach? Were you hands-on, or did you delegate to assistants?

I liked to delegate to my assistants because I always believed that if the players hear you every day they are going to get damn fed up with

you. I would tell one of my assistants, "You'd better talk to Paul today because I'm really starting to have enough of this stuff, and if he doesn't get back on track or do what he has to do, he's going to have to deal with me." I thought that I'd let the players know when I was happy with them, and when the coach wasn't happy with their performance. Sometimes players think everything is going well. They are not even competing or playing well, but they think it's OK because the team is winning, so you have to be careful with winning. I think it's very important to delegate, but I also wanted the players to know that if there was that meeting in the office it wasn't because they screwed up. It was because they had been screwing up for quite awhile.

How did you manage your time?

Just to give you an example, if the practice was at 11:00, I'd show up at the Forum at 7:00. I just wanted to be there, preparing. Never in my career have I been late. The players respect a coach who's there. They don't respect a coach who walks in after they are already there or has left from his parking spot when they're still working out in the gym. You don't have to tell the players what you're doing off the ice, but the bottom line is my time to my team was spent trying to make the best team possible for that one game that one night. If you don't prepare your team, you are taking away their opportunity to win. If you prepare them well and they know what to do and then you give them an opportunity to be creative, no matter what, you will be successful. They are not robots. Give them an opportunity to be creative.

How did you relax as a coach, and what did you do to get away from the game?

Actually, I never relaxed. I never took the game home because I think your family will suffer from that, but I took it personally. If we lost I questioned myself. Did I prepare my team well enough? Did I put my players in the right situations? Did I say too much? Did I not say enough? Did I show enough video? Did I show too much video? Did I use the proper strategy? There is a strategy in this game that you have to use against different teams, and I always questioned myself, but I kept it more inside, always thinking about what I could have done better.

I was able to admit when I screwed up. I have told my players in meetings, "Look, I screwed up last night." It may not be the way to coach for some. Everybody has his own style. If I put the wrong players on the ice at the wrong time, then it's not the players' fault. It's my fault. That's what I'm paid for. That's my responsibility as a coach. I did do that at times, and when I did it, I knew right away. There was nothing you could do about it, and if I was lucky the other team didn't score. I was always trying to do better the next day.

Was your down time in the summer, or when did you take a break?

I think that in the summer you basically have a month. I spent quality time with my kids. The hockey season is a lot longer than we think. It is 11 months instead of 12, because you have the month of July off, if you want, after the draft. There is very little time. Maybe your general manager has signed a free agent or made a trade at the draft. Even in July I would be sitting down with my wife, Debbie, and be making lines of who I'm going to play with whom, and this was about three months away from training camp. I think hockey stays with you 12 months of the year, and maybe that's a fault. Maybe I handled it wrong, but I was never able to put the game aside. It was always within me.

Jacques, are you a philosopher coach? Do you try to teach your players life lessons?

I try to teach my players non-hockey life lessons: the importance of family, the importance of being a good citizen. I've had some players who have disappointed me because they went astray, but I try to conduct my life the way I feel is appropriate. I never want a player to see me drunk. I never want a player to see me in a position with other women. I want to live my life as straight as possible. I never want my players to judge me, or to see me in a position where they could judge me or a position where I would be embarrassed. **I may have embarrassed myself with some of my speeches, and I may have embarrassed myself with some of the things I have said to players, but I don't think any of my players would say they saw their coach get out of line. Rather, when he was off the ice he conducted his life with respect and manners.**

Who was your mentor growing up?

Glen Sather. I liked Glen Sather's ability to coach a bunch of superstars and make them all perform at a high level every single night. I liked Glen Sather's approach to the game and the creativity he allowed for all those players, but also the way he coached them, because to tell you the truth it was very seldom that any of those superstars complained. I thought that Glen Sather changed our game in a positive way in the '80s. He made our game more interesting, and he gave every one of those great players the opportunity to express themselves every night, no matter where the game was played. I liked his cockiness behind the bench. That little smirk that he knew he was going to beat you. I hated it, but I liked that. He was the coach that I wanted to be like.

Who shaped you as a leader and as a person?

My mother. My mother died of cancer at 41. She gave me everything I have. She was and still is the most important person in my life. She gave me the desire to compete, the desire to better myself, and the desire not to accept mediocrity. She loved me. She cared for me. She pushed me to be better, she encouraged me, and she never let me down.

Where do you go today when you need advice?

I have some good friends, but I really turn to my brother, Michel. If I need a straight answer and no b.s., my brother Michel will tell me exactly how he feels right to my face. I respect him for that, even though I may not agree with him. At home, Debbie is my life. She is the one who gives me the motivation to excel and to continue to give her a good life.

George Kingston

Hockey has been a long and satisfying run for ultra-marathoner George Kingston from Biggar, Saskatchewan. The Detroit Red Wings snagged him as a "C" form player when he was 14 years old, in the NHL's pre-entry draft days. He played hockey at the University of Alberta while garnering Bachelor of Arts and Master of Arts degrees in education and physical education. Later in his career he received a Doctorate in philosophy. After playing senior hockey and enduring two shoulder injuries, Kingston decided to forego the NHL and took a job as an assistant coach at the University of Calgary in 1967. He took over as head coach in the final two games of the season and continued for 15 seasons over 22 years with a record of 245 wins in 373 games, reaching the playoffs 14 times and winning five conference titles. He was named Canada West Coach of the Year in 1980–81 and 1980–86, as well as CIAU Coach of the Year in 1974 and again in 1981.

From 1980 to 1982 George worked as an assistant with the Calgary Flames and was an assistant coach in the 1988-89 season for the Minnesota North Stars, where he helped the team post a 19-point improvement over the previous season. He was hired as head coach of the San Jose Sharks in their very first year of existence in 1991 because of his proven ability with young players and great technical knowledge of the game. He was hired as an assistant coach for the Atlanta Thrashers in their inaugural season of 1999–2000. After coaching in Atlanta for two years, he joined the Florida Panthers as an assistant coach in 2001.

George Kingston's track record in international hockey truly sets him apart. He was an assistant coach for Canada's Olympic hockey team in 1984. He won a bronze medal with Team Canada at the 1983 World Championships, coached Team Canada to the gold medal at the 1987 Spengler Cup, was a guest coach of the Canadian Olympic team in 1988, and was director of the hockey tournament at the 1988 Winter Olympics in Calgary.

George then spent two years as head coach of the Norwegian national team, as well as sports director of the Norwegian Ice Hockey Federation and a consultant to the organizing committee of the 1994 Winter Olympics held in Lillehammer, Norway. During this time Kingston led the Norwegian junior national team to a best-ever sixth place finish at the 1990 World Junior Championships. Under Kingston the Norwegian national team achieved a best-ever "A" pool finish in the 1990 World Championships and were relegated to the 1991 "B" pool by just one goal. The following season they won the silver medal in the "B" pool, yet another best-ever achievement.

In 1994 George Kingston became director of hockey operations for Hockey Canada. He was the general manager for Team Canada when they won a silver medal at the 1994 Winter Olympics in Lillehammer, losing only on the famous Forsberg goal. Later that year, as head coach he led Team Canada to a gold medal at the World Championships for the first time since 1961.

George Kingston is a natural teacher, a natural learner, and a natural achiever who "likes to take on challenges." He took up running at age 42 and has since competed not just in marathons (even in 95-degree heat at the "Original Marathon" in Greece), but also in ultra-marathons, 50- to 100-mile races over rugged terrain that can take up to 24 or 25 hours to complete. He has done everything in hockey from teaching sledge hockey to athletes with lower body handicaps to authoring more than 100 presentations, journals, and videos, to leading Canada's national team to world supremacy. He is the "Ultra Hockey Man."

The Interview

Tell us where you grew up and how you got started in coaching.

My grandparents, mother, and her six brothers were farm pioneers near Biggar, Saskatchewan. Biggar is noteworthy for its sign: "New York is Big, but this is Biggar!" The farm was a great learning environment, with most of my values derived from a pioneer family persevering in the face of the uncertainties and challenges of nature. My father emigrated from Ireland when he was seventeen years old, but was killed in a farm accident when I was three, so I grew up in a hurry.

Despite my grandparents insisting that all my uncles and mother get an education and leave the farm, I was not a good student. Many other things, including sports, were far more interesting than sitting in school. One thing was very clear, however: My grandfather would not allow any of us to be "baseball bums, rodeo bums, or hockey bums!" I reckoned there was nothing worse than being in one of those bum categories, so getting an education seemed a necessary salvation.

I was a "C" form player belonging to the Detroit Red Wings, so in order to advance in hockey I had to play junior for the Edmonton Oil Kings. At the tryout the general manager of the Oil Kings told me that "if you want to be a hockey player, forget about school." The line was very clearly drawn, but my mother and grandparents were adamant about getting an education. I went to school. Fortunately I was taught and coached by N.A. McNair Knowles, who, along with my stepfather Jim Murland, helped straighten me out. I played new sports, dropped down a level in hockey, and they pointed me towards studying to be a design architect.

In high school in Edmonton I had the good fortune of having Clare Drake and Murray Smith as teachers and coaches. Through having so much contact with Clare and Murray, I decided that I really liked what they did. They had a zest for life and were doing something important that I thought I wanted to do: They worked with people in sport. These men became my lifelong mentors. I had hockey scholarship offers to go to Denver University and the University of North Dakota, but neither school had a good Physical Education degree program. And neither school had Clare and Murray, as they had joined the Faculty of Physical Education at the University of Alberta. In order to pursue coaching,

I took what was then a very fledgling Physical Education program at the University of Alberta.

I became the first of my family to achieve a degree and teacher qualifications, but hockey was still the sport I loved the most. Although I received a contract offer for $3,800 to play for Detroit's farm team, I also had the opportunity to teach for $5,000 and make additional money playing senior hockey. When I examined the Detroit lineup, with Bill Gadsby and Marcel Pronovost on defence playing virtually 60 minutes except for penalties, and especially when I considered the circumstances in minor professional hockey, I decided that I had a really good alternative to teach, coach, and play senior hockey. Underpinning this decision was the fact that at the U of Alberta I had played with terrific hockey players such as Vern Pachal and Vic Dzurko. They, and others, told horror stories of their playing and life conditions in minor pro hockey under coaches such as Eddie Shore. By contrast, they loved to play for Clare and never regretted how hard we trained to play amateur hockey.

Prior to 1967 there were just six teams in the National Hockey League, so the owners had all the power. Players had no power and in most cases had no alternatives but to endure what amounted to sport slavery.

How did you eventually move from playing and teaching into full-time coaching?

I taught high school for six years and coached all sports, including football, basketball, track, wrestling, gymnastics, and soccer—about eight or nine different sports in all. I also coached community-based hockey, and we tried to start up high school hockey with the leadership of Clare Drake and a number of the high school coaches who were in Edmonton at the time.

In 1967, after playing a strong tournament at the first Canadian Winter Games, I was invited to attend the expansion St. Louis Blues camp. However, Dennis Kadatz, a former U of A classmate of mine and at the time the athletic director at the University of Calgary, offered me a job as a Physical Education instructor and assistant coach with Al Rollins, who was then the U of C varsity hockey coach. The team had gone 0–46 over the first three years of its existence. At the end of my first year Al had other commitments, so he could not lead the team in the final two games of the season in Winnipeg. We beat both the U of Winnipeg and Manitoba in one-goal games. Al left to coach Spokane; fortunately, I was given the opportunity to build the U of C Dinosaurs program. I coached many, many outstanding young men in my 16 years at the U of Calgary. Actually I was there 22 years, but because I went back to complete further degrees, to work as dean, and to take study leaves, I ended up with fewer actual coaching years. Included was a sabbatical leave to join Dave King and coach the 1984 Olympic team in the Sarajevo Olympics.

How did you develop into what many would describe as "a great teacher of the game"?

Although I had played junior, college, and senior hockey, when I stepped on the ice in 1967 to start teaching people how to skate, I suddenly realized that I didn't know how. **I began to analyze the mechanics of what we did naturally as players. I questioned everything and tried to understand all that I had taken for granted as a player. As a player, you just did it**. It was an exciting time.

If memory serves, the first coaching clinic in Canada was in 1965. Part of my responsibility at the University of Calgary was to undertake professional and community leadership, so I channelled effort into coaching clinics. In 1969 Hockey Canada was created to improve Canada's performance in international hockey. Both Hockey Canada and the CAHA sponsored clinics and coaching certification initiatives.

I had one very telling experience when I was playing with some very good players put together as an all-star team to play against a Soviet touring team. In the morning I watched the Soviet team practice. The team held a two-hour practice that was harder than I had ever experienced with Clare, and I'll tell you with Clare we worked hard. That night the score ended up 5–3 for the Soviet team, but it should have been 15–3. At that time, when the Soviet teams came over, they played a gentleman's game. They kept the interest high and made the extra, extra, extra passes to entertain and ensure another invitation so they could eat well and drink gallons of orange juice … and beer! On ice their fitness, balance, and dynamic strength was as impressive as their skill execution at top-end speed. As a player and physical educator, I appreciated that there was an awful lot going on in Soviet hockey that we didn't know about. Sweden, Czechoslovakia, and Finland also held curiosity for me, so it became a priority for me to find out how they were developing top-level hockey players.

You were one of the first Canadians to travel to Europe and the Eastern bloc countries to study hockey. What did you learn?

My first foray internationally was in 1971. I went over with my family and toured in a Volkswagen van for five months. I spent three and a half weeks inside the Soviet Union watching their '72 team. I made a comment, which was picked up and reported, that I thought the "Russians" would win the '72 series by one game. I saw first-hand how hard they were working that summer and how focussed their daily dryland and on-ice training was. My fear was that we would be caught with our pants down in the September series, as I knew our Canadian hockey mentality about players playing their way into shape in the NHL season. I already knew from being on the ice with them that these guys were for real. These were very, very good hockey players. They were totally focussed. They were preparing to go to war because sport in Communist countries then was "war without weapons." Their foreign relations and diplomacy were all built around exporting representative sport, the Red Army Chorus, the Moscow Circus, or the Bolshoi Ballet, where they were exporting the absolute best of their society. In fact, only athletes capable of winning gold were allowed out of the Soviet Union.

Because I'd called the series to be a one-game advantage for the Soviets, I was regarded as somewhat of a traitor in Canada. This was a viewpoint differing from the NHL people, who came back and said, "They don't have a goaltender, and they can't shoot the puck." In fact, their game style dictated that they only went for high-percentage shots, and when they shot, it usually became a tap-in by a player on the wide post. Having watched them for three weeks in dryland training and on-ice training, I knew they could shoot the lights out when the opportunity arose. They had shooting accuracy and velocity from wrist, snap, and slap shots, and they had the legendary goaltender Vladislav Tretiak!

My travel in 1971 only whetted my appetite for further international study. Every year thereafter I travelled to learn more about our hockey rivals, and eventually I completed a doctoral degree based on comparisons among the top five hockey-playing nations. In 1971, however, I never really knew the full significance of all that I learned through bribing (by using Canada pins) my way into all the closed practices which were the Soviet preparations for the '72 Series. **Overall, I learned that all hockey players and coaches the world over were more alike than different, and that every player and nation shared the same deep passion for the greatest game man has invented.**

Don't you find that players today are much more aware of the off-ice training commitment and preparation necessary to play at an elite level?

Canadian hockey players are world renowned for their will to win. Our younger generation now understand the absolute necessity of paying the price in all-round fitness training with a will to prepare to win. **Competition forces you to always improve what you do and makes you more effective, more flexible, more prepared to meet the challenge of change.**

The top levels of NHL and international hockey demand virtuosity, creativity, improvisation. It is vital that young players have experience in a wide range of sports and physical challenges, rather than only narrowly focussed, repetitive hockey training. Only through experience in gymnastics, martial arts, wrestling, ballet, skateboarding can individual qualities such as body control, balance, leverage, spatial awareness, and so on be developed. The current game demands high-speed, split-second solutions which go far beyond the weight room, repetitive hockey training, and more scheduled hockey games. Open-ended solutions are needed both physically and mentally. Nurturing the spirit of play is critical for players of all ages, including NHL players. Far too much of sport has become a business. At the same time, business leaders are desperately seeking ways to play. That should tell us coaches something.

Give us one or two or your most memorable coaching experiences.

After I got fired in San Jose I was offered the opportunity to be director of hockey operations for Hockey Canada. Ron Robison recruited me to accomplish two things: to build the '94 Olympic program in co-operation with Paul Henry while serving as a mentor coach for Tom Renney and Danny Dube; and to be the head coach of the '94 World Championship team. The latter was a dream come true because, other than the U of Calgary job, it was the only job I really wanted. It was going back to hockey that I respected.

I thoroughly enjoyed working in the National Hockey League, but I left San Jose knowing that I had unfulfilled business in the NHL. I was really hopeful that I would get another opportunity to have a shot at the Stanley Cup. Every day was exciting and fulfilling as you're working with the best players in the world.

The Hockey Canada experience was a marvellous year. I loved working with Tom Renney and Danny Dube in international hockey. I blended in and tried to uplift a couple of very, very good young coaches. We ultimately won the Silver Medal in the Lillehammer Olympics, losing on the famous Peter Forsberg shootout goal. We had some really bad luck. Manny

Legace was primarily our backup goaltender, but he was unbelievable in the shootouts, so we had decided we would put him in for any shootout. In the morning practice he took a shot in the kneecap, his knee swelled up, and he hobbled to the gold-medal game on crutches, and therefore we had no option of using him in the shootout.

Later that year I had the good fortune of working with Glen Sather when we built the World Championship team. Glen gave me a lot of leeway. We were very fortunate to have a number of very good players who came available, either directly by not being in the playoffs or by being eliminated in the first round. Our mission was to win the World Championship. Canada had not won since the 1961 Trail Smoke Eaters. Bob Murdoch was added to join Tom, Danny, and me as the coaching group. We had a day and a half of practice before departing from Toronto. We were the first Canadian team who had ever practised in Canada before going to the World Championships.

We planned to play a very aggressive offensive style with four men on attack. We felt that we had the right team to go for it and force other teams to handle our attack. To do this we needed special defensive players to handle the potential outnumberings which might occur. Our special defensive players were Luke Richardson, Bobby Dollas, and Marc Bergevin. We were criticized before we left Canada because these guys were not your typical international players, but they were all first-round draft picks who went through living-and-dying hell to establish a career in the NHL. Their character, personality, and their defensive responsibility was great, so they allowed us to attack with confidence. Bob Murdoch and Tom Renney ensured that they were clear in handling any two-on-ones and the three-on-ones with Billy Ranford and Stephane Fiset.

There were excellent teams opposing us, but the fact is we had the great good fortune to have very good players who bought into the roles our team needed. Joe Sakic led the way in saying, "I am here to win. If you need a penalty killer, I'll be a penalty killer. I don't have to be on the power play." To a man they parked their egos at the door and led our mission. We won the gold medal in a shootout with Bill Ranford in goal, and it was Canada's first championship since 1961, and full credit belongs to an outstanding group of players, aided by a great group of coaches and team support personnel. We were able to do something that 33 previous Canadian entries, many of which had better individual talent, couldn't accomplish. We were a team! It was not all roses; we had one blowout meeting in the middle of the tournament to refocus on our mission, but the bottom line was that we went undefeated in eight games. From an outsider's view that was probably the greatest accomplishment I have been associated with. The 1994 team provided me with a pinnacle memory.

What do you consider your strengths as a coach?

I think one of my main strengths is that **I have learned to be a listener, communicator, and problem solver who might be termed a "player's coach." I can go into any high stakes or highly emotional situation and find a win-win solution.** Normally the solution will be based on fully using the player's strengths and special abilities so as not to diminish his ability to take initiative and perform. **I am a great believer in giving full respect to a player, of expecting and demanding great performance, while never giving him any excuse not to perform or be less than he should be.**

Another key strength is my positive, optimistic, enthusiastic attitude. **I firmly believe that more will be accomplished in sport when a coach helps put the athlete in the zone to perform.** Most of the coaches I played for in hockey, with the exception of Clare Drake, motivated by negative means through use of fear, threat, guilt, belittlement, ignoring to unsettle, or other public means of stripping a player of his self-worth. **In my view if you give respect, you will get respect; if you do not, then you risk violating trust as well as losing a player's respect.** I maintain that "there are no problems, only situations to solve; there are no problems, only issues to resolve." Improving an individual's performance, attitudes, relationships, and communication and so on should be solved through one-on-one meetings rather than burdening the team. If it is a team issue, then it is dealt with and resolved on a team basis. Coaching at times involves handling egos, bumping heads, getting down and dirty, being frank, dealing with difficult situations and personalities, but we have to come out with a win-win solution. **In my experience, too many coaches have never learned to park their ego at the door, so too many situations become a one-way, public, "my way or the highway" stand-off.** Even though sport is a "now" business, it is important to take time to achieve solutions which give the players long-term ownership, accountability, and responsibility.

I am regarded as a very patient coach. Certainly I am more patient with players than I am with myself. Success in sport usually is based upon being more active, taking initiative, calculated risk-taking, going for it, and making mistakes. **Mistakes are an integral part of hockey. I always expect impassioned play, not perfection.** Players play; coaches pursue

SIMPLY THE *BEST*

perfection! While I demand improvement in performance, I also expect that if I do my job, players will reduce poor choices and mistakes. In a high-speed game like hockey, where a choice or decision is made in 0.4 seconds, there will be poor choices and mistakes. Our job as coaches is to help players choose higher-percentage solutions to game situations and related issues.

How do you keep your players at a peak performance level?

Absolutely the most important thing that you need to have as a player is confidence. It is the expectation in yourself that you are able to perform, that you are able to do all the things that you have special gifts or special capacity for. Hockey is so competitive and it is so tough to be successful that it is hard for a player to maintain rock-solid self-belief, rock-solid confidence, and to avoid self-doubt. Confidence is an ethereal, time-to-time quality that usually accompanies winning and personal performance success. When you are not winning or enjoying personal success, then it's an issue of confidence. **No issue is more important than ensuring player and team confidence.**

Related to this is the challenge of putting a player into the performance zone. In the zone you feel confident, you feel in control, you feel relaxed, and you feel like time is suspended. You see things clearly and in slow motion, you seem able to anticipate and see things unfold as you visualized them, you are focussed and enjoying performing, and you are experiencing the joy of effort and the spirit of play. There are golden moments and seemingly magical times when everything falls into place and you can go with the flow of being in the zone. The reality is that more often players need strategies for handling adversity and frustration and persevering through the tough times.

Most players try to ensure their own game performance by counting down to game time with a mix of routines and rituals and some superstitions which the players believe will help them prepare for a good game. The top players in hockey produce a consistent game-in, game-out performance. To accomplish this, they exert mind control during the game and from shift to shift to block out negatives and refocus their efforts towards their desired performance level. Recently I have directed a lot of effort towards helping players control and bring consistency to their own game performance.

How do you go about doing that?

It is all about finding a solution that works for each individual player. It is a process of guided discovery which starts with a one-on-one meeting and progresses by monitoring and fleshing out what works for the player. Initially the open-ended questions work backwards from when he had a good game. We flesh out routines, likes, distractors, annoyances, and so forth that were present before and during that game. Armed with this, the player builds a countdown for his pre-game routine and builds focal points for the game. Thereafter the player and coach monitor and modify as the player establishes his game control routines.

Specific strategies for handling adversity and coping with frustration must be part of a player's game preparation. This is doubly so for role players and players receiving limited ice time. They have the need to be always ready despite arbitrary and sporadic actual involvement in the game.

Most players seem to do a reasonable job in pre-game preparation. I find that players need more help in maintaining focus and readiness during the game. The more the coach juggles the lineup, then the more the player has to park negatives, reload, and refocus to be ready. When working a bench I endeavour to make comments to players to ensure their readiness.

More of my bench comments are targeted on finding players doing things right. **What gets rewarded, gets done. I am always looking to give feedback that closes the loop between a video session or practice session and use of an idea in the game.** That's probably where I'm most positive, most focussed, most enthusiastic in trying to find players doing things right.

What is your definition of success in any given situation, in any given season?

The normal way you measure that is by a team winning a Stanley Cup, a World Championship, an Olympic gold medal, or an important tournament. Unfortunately, only one team and one group of players can be successful in that definition. Coaches need additional measures which are attainable for more players and teams. The first measure of success is being the best you can be. This is attainable both individually and collectively by a team. Performance is measured both quantitatively using, for example, statistics and results, and qualitatively by subjectively answering the question: "Were you the best you can be?" A second measure is charting improvement and progress in performance. Again this can be measured both quantitatively and qualitatively for both the player and team.

One of my most important measures is whether the players play with passion. Passion should be obvious. Enthusiasm, enjoyment, fun, effort, energy, intensity, excitement, and a "can't wait to get back on the ice" spark should be on the faces of my players. If it is not, then I have not done my job of energizing the players.

Another related measure I use is the post-mortem of a loss. If you lose, it is never acceptable that you lose by being outworked, out-hustled, through lack of will or discipline, lose on less than 60 minutes of absolute perseverance, lose by leaving any of your potential untapped or by a faulty game plan or strategy. It is grudgingly acceptable to be defeated by a more talented or experienced team. Losses are going to happen, so lessons for avoiding the next loss should come from a loss.

How players handle the critical moments of a game is another measure. **In life and especially in a game, everything comes down to how players handle the few decisive seconds when they are central to a critical situation in a game.** Most often games are won or lost in a few seconds rather than 60 minutes. For example, so many times your team goes down and misses a golden opportunity to score, and then your opponent counters and scores. The critical moments involved in the power play, penalty kill, and especially the final moments of the third period where the goaltender is pulled are defining moments for measuring performance. Obviously you work to improve your player's ability to handle these critical moments. **Success is best measured as a journey in performance improvement. My bottom line definition of success is very simply "playing with passion to be the best you can be."**

Define the steps that allow your team to be in a position to win.

Winning starts with your selection of players. If you select players with character, then you have the foundation for success. **Talent will win games, but character will win championships.** Winning is an attitude; expecting to win is an attitude; not accepting a loss is an attitude. Attitude is an expression of character. Players such as Joe Sakic and Peter Forsberg always put Colorado in a position to win. Both are relentless when the game is on the line. Scott Stevens embodies the core values of New Jersey's Stanley Cup success. **Defining core values and developing core leaders who embody your core values is central to team success.**

When we started the franchise in San Jose, we identified Doug Wilson, Kelly Kisio, and Dean Evason as our core leaders. With their input, we defined our core values of what we expected a "Shark" to be. Later, other players were added to the core group to help cultivate the core values we wished to define as our team character. As an expansion team we did not have a full deck to play out, so we chose to emphasize selected core values to position ourselves for winning. Our core group was delegated the responsibility to implement and maintain who we were and how we played. Players brought into the team later were led by the core group. Doug, Kelly, and Dean did a great job in leading the Sharks, and it is heartwarming to see them all continuing to be leaders in the game.

I think that we all have visions of the style of play and type of team we would like to coach, but the reality of coaching is that you have a hand of cards dealt to you. **My job is to identify each player's strengths and special gifts, and devise a game plan to make each player successful and to ultimately make the team successful.**

To win, players need to know where they fit in, what is expected of them, and how they can contribute. Giving players roles and responsibilities addresses these player needs. Players should know that expanded roles and responsibilities can be earned through good performance. **Roles are not designed to be a straitjacket or coffin.** Labeling must not be disabling. The key is to recognize and reward your background role players as your unsung heroes. **My job is like that of an orchestra conductor: to make the sum greater than the total of the individual parts. I have to get things done through others by energizing, focussing, harmonizing, leading them towards a symphony of success.**

I've learned that at the pro level the responsibility for performing should always rest with the player. The players know how to play better than I. As a coach I don't want to be smarter than a player, ever. I prefer to keep the pressure to perform on the player. My job is to help or push to ensure that the player plays better. I want to make sure the player understands that I'm not a limiting factor or excuse for him not playing well.

Even in a short-term situation, for example the 1987 Spengler Cup, we took over a team to Davos, Switzerland, that in Dave King's view was not strong enough to win. We started by asking the players, "What must we do to win? What do you do best? How can we use you best? How can you contribute?" We ended up winning the Spengler Cup in 1987 on the strength of the players taking ownership of that team. The players were a great credit to Canada as they stepped up and played excellently.

Why do players step up? They feel important, respected, and are given the full opportunity and responsibility to contribute. Every book in business will point to these factors being the foundation for employee satisfaction. **Getting a team into a position to win games has everything**

to do with players feeling good about their play and being recognized for performing their roles. What gets rewarded, gets done.

Do you believe coaches have a responsibility to motivate?

No and yes! Genuine, gut-level, intrinsic, long-term, effective, passion-driven motivation comes from within the successful player. Wayne Gretzky's motivation was to be the greatest player in the game. **Athletes who craft successful careers set their own internal standard of performance and they hold themselves accountable to meet and exceed their standard.**

If there is need to motivate a player to play the game, then in my view something is very wrong and a coach has a serious issue to resolve. Hockey without passion is nothing. Actually, it is necessary to energize some players, but rarely the best players. In my experience it is an issue of character at the deepest level and of focus on the shallower level. You will never have to motivate the player who loves the game. They are passionately committed to playing and will pay the price to play. The second return of Steve Yzerman from a serious knee injury is a testimony to his passion and commitment to the game.

On the other hand, there are players who are in the game for reasons other than the love of the game: business, talent, social, recognition, pressure, expectation, to name a few. These are the players who want the game to come to them on their terms, as their focus, commitment, and willingness to pay the price is clouded over with other issues. They are the players who need help and extrinsic motivation from others, including the coach, in finding a more successful reason to play the game. **By observation a coach can readily spot the level of energy and commitment a player brings to the practice in dryland and on-ice settings, in the dressing room and in games.** Having said all this, we have an important role in short-term player motivation and, where necessary, in career counseling.

There is no stronger motivation than you find in the military: my responsibility to you when we are in the trench together. I will not let you get shot at, I will not let you get killed, I will not let you get injured, I am going to get you out of here alive. There is nothing more powerful than that responsibility for and accountability to another person. That is one very powerful motivational situation that we can use in hockey. My responsibility as a player is to my linemate, defensive partner, or teammate. Developing that feeling of commitment is a process which can only occur in a stable, close-knit team where deeper values of trust, loyalty, respect, and love or genuine caring have been established. In 1988 I did a study on Stanley Cup winners in preparation for joining the Minnesota North Stars. Then I found that only six teams had won in the previous 25 years and the leading reason was continuity or stability of core players and management. A quick look at two recent repeat winners, New Jersey (2000, 2003) and Detroit (1998, 2002) shows 10 players from each team playing on both winners.

Another related and potentially powerful foundation for motivation is achieved through selectively shifting the ownership, accountability, and responsibility for motivation from coach to team. Use of core leaders ensuring core values through player-player accountability works in a team which is inclusive and important to each player. Frequently we hear the phrase about a player or team buying in. A coaching challenge is to co-opt and give the player or team a significant stake in the responsibility for team goals. "What's in it for me?" is always present in human dealings. Each coach has to know their comfort level in giving a piece of the pie to players and other coaches on staff.

What about the soapbox speech? Is it effective, and do you use it as a motivational technique in the dressing room?

The challenge for you as a leader is to develop core motivation or sense of mission in each individual so that each player assumes responsibility and accountability for their performance. The role for the coach when delegating or using long-term motivation becomes one of leading, monitoring, evaluating, refocussing, tweaking, and other short-term energizing.

Motivation is primarily a long-term development process because that is the effective type of motivation. Players and others often tend to view motivation, however, as what a coach does in the here and now. Even though blistering, peel-the-paint speeches, cut-to-the-quick strippings, stick-breaking, garbage-pail kicking, punches through coaching boards, and so on normally have a limited impact and very short-term effect, we are nevertheless expected to show players that we are intense, that we care, and that we want to win, so we use them.

We have all used negative comments in short-term motivation, but I never get personal or make comments that attack respect or fairness. Losing one's temper is a non-starter, as it does not lead players toward an effective way of handling pressure in tough situations. If I lose my temper, I am setting a poor example for the player who has to cope with and control much more frustration than I do. Controlling frustration is a constant battle for a player. Unchecked, it is destructive, negative, and draining and can severely limit a player's ability to perform.

My office is the main place for short-term motivation. The one-on-one meeting should not be seen as only a negative get-together, as more of the time it is a session to compliment a player, to discuss his short-term goal setting, to seek a player's opinion and suggestions, and simply to ensure that the lines of communication are open and that there is an open door for every player. All these purposes for meeting fit into effective short-term motivation. We tend to think too narrowly about what motivation really involves. The one-on-one is also the time to address situations or issues that need to be resolved. If that is the case, **I want to ensure that the player leaves the meeting with a clear understanding for going forward, a road map, a video, or whatever is appropriate to guarantee improvement, change, or resolve of a situation.** If it is necessary, this is the place for tough words, demands, hard realism, and so on to change attitude, behaviour, or performance. Regardless of the purpose, every meeting must conclude with resolve of a situation or issue.

Some coaches and players don't like the word "role" because it is too defining and confining. How do you react to that comment?

Earlier I stated that I did not want players to see roles as a straitjacket or coffin. How a player performs in using his strengths and abilities should dictate his use in a game. To state the obvious, some players have offensive ability; others have defensive conscience. Some players want an open, creative opportunity to contribute; others want a clear picture of what is expected of them. **A role, for me, is simply a starting point for performance that is based on a player's strengths. A role defines the starting point for what the player is expected to achieve and contribute to the team.** Players who can penalty-kill, kill; players with offensive flair or gift have responsibility for the power-play role. My view on roles is not as confining or narrowly defined as I think the question implies. My view fits into how I want my team to play.

Overall I want my team to take initiative, be smart, aggressive, to pressure an opponent and put them on their heels, to have the closest man go first into a situation, to go for it offensively but be responsible defensively, and to try to be more active in the game than the opponent. To do this, all lines are balanced. The speed of the modern game dictates a fluid, dynamic approach to the game based on handling game situations.

Three or four times you've talked about core values. Walk us through your core values.

First of all, respect. Respect is both earned and given to recognize the importance and contribution another player makes towards a common shared goal such as winning a game or championship. **Respect begets respect, and leads to trust, loyalty, openness, sharing, caring, sticking up for teammates, co-operation, and other character values necessary for success.**

Second, the underpinning of every successful venture is hard work, persistence, effort. This is also a factor that a player can control. You can control giving your best effort, playing with never-say-die persistence, and outworking and out-hustling your opponent. Hard work, effort, persistence, hustle all form a platform for team success. Respect is earned from teammates and opponents by hard work. You may not be able to control a lot of other game circumstances, but you sure can control how you work and persevere to perform.

Teamwork is another core value for success. Hockey is a team game, so it is critical that all players discipline their individual game towards team success. **Making your teammate successful, giving your gift to the team effort, and practising smart selfishness to ensure team results all contribute to team success.** Businesses and partnerships that fail usually fail because of problems in maintaining sound relationships and/or communication. **Cultivating and developing teamwork seeks to address the relationships issue.**

Integrity has a number of aspects which all contribute to group success. Honesty is a subset that fosters open communication. Being trustworthy means that no player cheats himself or a teammate in the effort he brings towards winning. Integrity means taking ownership and accountability for all performance and behaviour. It also includes setting standards for all players to uphold. There are no shortcuts to championships. Above all it means standing up, hanging together, and remaining steadfast through the tough times.

Success also rests on courage: courage to take initiative, to take risks, to push limits, to stubbornly persevere and keep believing in tough times, as well as to put yourself on the line with physical courage. The NHL hockey style and product in too many teams is stereotyped, conservative, safe, defensive-based, and controlled. Much of this traces back to the insecurity, turnover, paranoia, powerlessness, and lack of support and respect for coaching in the league. Coaches have a short shelf life, so despite the larger reality, we might as well go for it and strike out with courage in what we expect and envision for our team.

There has to be a climate of open and clear communication and an understanding that this communication must be respectful when differences are aired. The importance of both verbal and non-verbal communication cannot be underestimated in a team that includes the diversity of cultures, languages, backgrounds, playing styles, experiences, and so on. Constant attention must be given to fostering clear understanding among the team members. A player must be able to say to a linemate who is not pulling his weight, "We need you on board." Everybody must understand that there is a time to be work-focussed and a time to be social. A pattern of communication stressing respect and the other core values helps point a team towards success.

Pride in yourself, your team, your teammates, in your craft, in what your team values are, and so on is vital for defining who, what, and why the team exists. Building pride and a team ego relates to the other core values. Pride also ensures that a player and a team will never embarrass himself and itself, respectively.

We all have certain abilities, certain strengths, and certain qualities which make us somewhat unique individuals. **Being simplistic, there are givers and there are takers; a team needs givers. Michael Jordan never won a championship until he made Scotty Pippen and his other teammates great. He gave his gift, he built relationships with those players, he made them successful and thereby guaranteed the ultimate team success.** An even better example can be found when you contrast the careers of Bill Russell and Kareem Abdul Jabar. Bill Russell won 11 NBA championships with the Boston Celtics, whereas Kareem Abdul Jabar, who was the pre-eminent offensive NBA player in the same era, did not win any. Bill Russell took pride in making others better; Kareem Abdul Jabar never used his gift to make teammates successful. Passion, commitment, energy, fun, enthusiasm, optimism, and love of the game have fuelled me in hockey, so I want this package to be front and centre as a core value with my team.

How do you do that as a coach? What do you do in practice?

During the warm-up stretch at the start of practice, different players are responsible for the joke of the day, the story of the day, a humorous incident, or if somebody has something spontaneous or just pulled a prank.

Then players have a light moment that sets a good tone for the team. We must make it special to be at the rink and special to practise together.

What do most players miss more than anything when they leave the game? It's the dressing room, the camaraderie, it's the needles, it's all of these little things that are tying in with communication, tying in with relationships, teamwork, bonding, and with having fun, enjoying each other, making your time together special. Now, it seems simple, but you have to work at making it special to be on ice together.

Finding a golden moment in the body of a practice can also be done. When a part of our practice plan doesn't go well, we tend to force the situation, react with anger, perhaps go to a punishment drill in order to refocus to what we wanted in our plan. An alternative may be inserting a competitive drill, a novelty drill, a fun-type drill, or a change of pace before going back to the practice plan. For sure, at the end of the practice we have some dessert by finishing with fun and/or competition, like novelty races, a relay, a little competition, a novelty game, or simply play. Forms of one-on-one keep-away and competitions will often result in much harder effort than a coach will extract through so-called conditioning drills.

Think about business. What do they do? They are focussed on inventing contests, competitions, change-of-pace activities, play, enjoyment, fun, team building. Here we are in an environment where there is fun, enjoyment, play, and we want to go whole hog as a business. We shouldn't do that, especially in hockey. We have to build on what we have, capitalize on it, and make it more fun, because the moment it becomes all business, a drudgery, boring, then we lose our players' spark and enjoyment of hockey. Simply stated, it becomes only business. Players can't wait to get it over with.

This loss of spark, and Florida failing on a promise to build a Stanley Cup contender, soured Pavel Bure. In my first year in Florida, Pavel spent the absolute minimum time on ice, could hardly wait to get off the ice. There was no joy, spark, or enthusiasm. Despite missing on 21 consecutive breakaways, he did not want to spend an extra minute to improve what helped him score 59 and 58 goals in the previous two seasons. When he was traded to the New York Rangers, I gave him a little card in which I said, "I hope that you recover the passion, the love for what you do, the spirit of play, the joy of effort, and good luck." Whereas Pavel scored 22 goals for us in 56 games, he scored 12 goals in 12 games in New York. Pavel is a special artist in our game, and while other factors complicated his attitude, what was clear was that he saw hockey only as a business.

Professional hockey is a business, where we have to make a special effort to build in a balance of play and enjoyment. My concern is that the purposes of hockey for kids have been overwhelmed by too much of the professional and business orientation. There are too many games, too much structure, too much coach control, too much system play, too little play, and too little skill development. Kids' hockey is far too serious a business.

How would you define your leadership style?

"When the job is done the people will say, 'We did it ourselves.'" (Lao Tse) I have always tried to follow this maxim. I have had a variety of leadership roles and responsibilities. Most of my career I have simultaneously held both on-the-job and volunteer leadership positions. Some were based on positional authority such as I held at the U of Calgary. Others, for example in the volunteer sphere, were based on moral authority. However, my leadership style was to make sure that everybody had responsibility, ownership, and was in a position to make decisions and contributions.

When it is appropriate I can fulfill all the roles required of a leader. I have a different background from most professional coaches in that I have been a leader, an administrator, and a manager as well as a head and assistant coach. Having had so much experience in leadership roles, I feel very comfortable in empowering others. I have learned to be "a follower in order to be a leader," because when you lead a team, you are leading through following the play of your players.

You will naturally experience performance cycles in a team in a long season where injuries, drop-offs in performance, especially in goal, and hot opponents cause losses to mount. Insecure leaders too often hit the panic button instead of riding out the adversity and leading when the heat's on. As a consequence, for example, usually one-third of NHL coaches are sacrificed each year. The overall impact of this seriously erodes the leadership that can be exerted by coaches.

As a head coach or assistant, how do you deal with a player who is going through adversity, who's performing below his potential?

The first question I am going to ask is "Why?" I will meet with the player to get his view and possible explanation. It is important to make certain it is not a personal situation, a medical situation, or nagging injury which for reasons known only to the player he does not wish to reveal.

This does occur, so it is important to determine this prior to zeroing in on the performance issue.

A second step for me is to decide if, in fact, the expectation for his performance level is realistic. In an era where high draft picks are hyped and inserted into an NHL lineup directly, most young players fail to meet the hype or expectation. Labeling is often disabling. For example, Rob Niedermayer was hyped as a scoring saviour in Florida. As a result, unrealistic expectations were created, leading to what was labelled underachievement. New digs have allowed Rob to be more who he is: a good player but not the franchise saviour. Recently I worked with Olli Jokinen and Viktor Kozlov in Florida. Like Rob, both were labelled underachievers. Hockey was a very negative place because the label was attached as if it were their first name, as in "the underachieving Olli Jokinen." Olli and Victor, as with all good young players, were not given the opportunity to develop; the NHL is not a development league. **The best organizations are patient and ensure readiness before young players reach the NHL.**

An underachiever is most often lacking confidence, questioning himself, and searching for answers. In the process he is not getting support, probably seeing little ice time and even less success, enjoyment, and optimism in his situation. In total, a very negative place to be.

Step one in solving this and all other performance issues is to focus on what a player can control. A player can control his effort and hard work, so that is the starting point. I have not yet satisfactorily figured out what is fear of failure or fear of success, but I have a better feel for fear and anxiety. At any rate a player must work on mind control to eliminate any fears, anxiety, and negative thoughts. His focus is on a single performance item that he and I identify as a trigger to pull for a small success and confidence builder. Again this must be something he can control. For example, with Olli it was shooting more, and with Viktor it was making only one decisive deke before shooting. Video with previous execution and success, on-ice practice, reminder cards, answers to my questions, and on the bench reminders complimenting success, more positive video, and compliments were used to support and focus the players' performance. During this process the players were cut some slack to ensure more ice time. Later, the ice time was legitimately earned.

Building confidence for a player is always priority number one. This is my focus throughout the struggle to find success and shed the deadly label. Finding examples of success and working with visualization also advances the process. It is, nevertheless, a process and it takes time, support, and success to lift the label off the forehead and shoulders of the burdened player.

How do you balance working with individuals while keeping a team focus?

The saying "You are only as strong as your weakest link" is a useful starting point for achieving a balance point between the team and the individual. Think of the chain as representing the team and the link as the individual. The actual balance point will vary in each coaching situation. Factors such as the age, experience, and the technical/tactical skill level of the players will help dictate how much attention a coach must give to the individual player. To state the obvious, if your players cannot give and receive passes, then you cannot play a team game. My primary focus is on the improvement of the weakest link: the individual player.

Star teamwork is always my coaching goal, but this must always be based on synergizing and showcasing the talents, energies, and sense of mission of individual players. What's important in the NHL at the bottom line? We're in the sport business of winning and entertaining. As a player you're a businessman, you're an entrepreneur, and for you to be successful, then you've got to make sure that you're doing the things to be successful. **My approach to players begins with: "Here's your inventory of what you are doing well now. Here's your inventory of what you have to do if you really want to be successful, if you want to earn more money or get more recognition, or if you want to be a star player."**

As a professional coach, I don't want to know about contracts. I'm not interested in that aspect of the business. I just want to make sure that players are happy with their contracts, and if they're not happy with their contract, I want them to keep it right up front in their mind as a festering irritant or motive for driving personal growth and performance. **I want players to write two daily reminders on their mirror: what they presently earn per hour, and second, what they want to earn per hour. For another player who is complacent or not performing, I also want him to put two things on his mirror: what they're currently enjoying per hour, and second, what their father and/or mother earn per hour.** Something concrete like that often helps a player put things in some perspective. Overall, however, NHL hockey has nothing to do with reality and perspective.

A final perspective for success rests with individual players realizing the ultimate importance of team success and their individual responsibility in making the team successful. From the standpoint of every conceivable personal outcome, winning the Stanley Cup makes all personal discipline worthwhile in contributing to this team success.

In working with players, I try to find a time every day to make

eye contact with each player and have some interaction. The player's demeanour readily tells me his needs. If necessary I zero in for more interaction. Pro hockey is a "now" business, so needs or issues must be resolved right away. This daily communication helps build relationships that have to weather dealing with the pressure cooker of insistent performance demands, and often unrealistic media and fan scrutiny and expectation.

So that's your success process?

As coaches we wish for revolution, but the reality is one of evolution, so we have to be patient when it comes to change and achieving success. It's a development process. For me it has been a very interesting journey where I have been most fortunate in learning from a number of great people and opportunities which have helped me grow. Personally, I know who I am today, but more important, I know who I want to grow to become. My goal has always been to be the best coach and person I can be. I love to pursue challenges, I have curiosity for new experiences, and I set high personal standards. As a result, I apply my expectations for success to my players in a similar growth process. **Throughout my career my curiosity has propelled me to be a student of the game.** Seeking new challenges, new experiences, and opportunities to learn has afforded me a basis to give back to the game by sharing my knowledge journey.

There is a lot of talk in coaching about systems play. I understand you deal more with a structure or philosophy of play. Are you getting away from the word "system"?

Yes, I think that the considerable focus on system and system play misses the target in the game of hockey. This is especially damaging in the case of children and youth hockey, where too many coaches stress team system play to the detriment of developing individual play. Youth is the time to develop individual technique and tactics instead of being limited or shoe-horned into positions, roles, and structured system play. System play is the end product, which is achieved through the means of sound individual technique/tactics, and sound co-operative technique/tactics in smaller-group game situations.

For me the game is too fast, too dynamic, too changing, too fleeting, and momentary for much use of system play. Players can use some structure as a start point to initiate offensive or defensive play, and also as a foundation to rebound from when tough times occur in a game. Beyond these start points, the speed and dynamism of hockey takes over and demands quick decisions and actions. Most game situations involve only one, two, or three players from each team around the puck. Five-versus-five team situations occur inside the three zones, but usually the decisive action centres around the players near the puck. In my view, players must read the game situation and execute high-percentage decisions based upon principles of play and solutions to recurring game situations.

How do you handle pressure and adversity?

I have no pressure other than that which I place on my own shoulders, as I am very demanding of myself. I set a very high standard for myself. I have pressure of conscience on myself to be doing things in a way that I feel is the right or the best way and to make myself useful as a contributing member of society. Controlling the factors one can control has been a guideline for me. I try to remind myself often of this focus so that I don't concern, worry, or have anxiety about things I can't control.

People in other jobs and life situations have real pressure. I have the great, good fortune of "playing" in coaching hockey. **I relish and seek out difficult challenges, tough situations, and opportunities for personal growth. Coaching keeps a person on the firing edge where you have to stand in and lead with conviction through adversity, distraction, frustration, and so forth.** Qualities of courage, perseverance, optimism, trust, loyalty, and genuine caring are all tested in tough times, so it is vital that we challenge ourselves and grow. **Players and coaches will reveal their character and personal resources very quickly in tough times.** You find out who you are, what you stand for, and what turns your crank when you are in a difficult circumstance. Hockey, and especially NHL hockey, reveals a player very quickly, so it is an exciting and fast-track opportunity to help players grow. The bottom line is that often out of keen, to-the-wall competition, pressure, tension, stress, and so forth comes real personal growth. We need challenges to test ourselves and grow.

What effect does adversity have on confidence?

Hockey demands players who have personal qualities of courage, confidence, spontaneity, creativity, discipline, stubbornness, perseverance, and optimism among other things to meet the game demands. Opponents, game adversity, coaches, personal performance results, and at times management and game officials will all challenge and batter the confidence level of a player.

We coaches have no bigger role than ensuring the confidence level of our player. **The most important foundational principle of game play and life is initiative.** For players to play with initiative they must exude confidence, courage, and conviction. Confidence is everything for the player, so that is a daily challenge for us. It seems that everything we talk about comes down to a step-by-step process in which a coach builds up a player. Building and maintaining self-confidence is such a process in which the player must be equipped to take full control of the process.

Growing up in the West I learned to "cowboy up" and take personal responsibility to get up and overcome any circumstance, including getting bucked off a horse. Although the phrase is as old as the hills, I like to think it spoke to the pioneer spirit of my grandfather, grandmother, mother, and uncles. They persevered through much more, saw more change, contributed much more than only having to overcome a down time in a game.

Mike Keenan

"Iron Mike" has won a championship at every level he has coached. A native of Bowmanville, Ontario, Keenan captained his college hockey team at St. Lawrence University from 1969 to '72 while earning his bachelor of science degree in Physical Education. He obtained his master's degree in Education while playing hockey at the University of Toronto, where his team won the CIAU championship in 1973.

Mike Keenan began his coaching career with the Junior B Oshawa Legionnaires in 1977 and took them to two Metro Toronto Junior B Championships. He then moved into major junior with the Peterborough Petes, who won the OHL championship and a berth in the Memorial Cup Final in the 1979–80 season. After one season in Peterborough he coached the Rochester Americans of the American Hockey League for three years, winning a Calder Cup championship in 1982–83.

Keenan's NHL coaching career began with the Philadelphia Flyers in 1984. Under Keenan the Flyers advanced twice to the Stanley Cup finals, in 1985 and 1987. His Philadelphia teams went 32–25 (.561) in the playoffs, winning six of 10 playoff series and reaching the post-season all four years of his tenure. It was in Philadelphia that Keenan won the Jack Adams Award as the NHL's Coach of the Year in 1985.

Mike Keenan next coached the Chicago Blackhawks from 1988 to 1992. His teams made the playoffs all four years in Chicago, winning seven of 11 playoff series. Keenan led the Blackhawks to the Stanley Cup finals in 1992.

Keenan was hired as head coach of the New York Rangers in 1993. The Rangers achieved a record of 52–24–8 (.667) under Keenan in 1993-94, and won a thrilling seven-game Stanley Cup final over the Vancouver Canucks. It was the Rangers' first Stanley Cup victory in 54 years.

Mike Keenan was the head coach in St. Louis from 1994 to 1996, in Vancouver from 1997 to 1998, and in Boston from 2000 to 2001. He was named head coach of the Panthers on December 3, 2001. In addition to his coaching duties, Keenan has been an interim general manager for Vancouver, and general manager in Chicago, St. Louis, and Florida.

His international career includes head coaching jobs with Team Canada at the 1980 World Junior Championships and the World Championships in 1993. As national team head coach in 1987, and in his dual role as general manager and head coach in 1991, Keenan led Team Canada to two Canada Cup victories.

Mike Keenan never had a team miss the playoffs until 1998, and he has won three President's Trophies (1985, 1991, and 1994), six division titles, three 50-plus win seasons, and five 100-plus point seasons. He coached in three NHL All-Star Games and is fifth in the NHL record book for all-time games coached (1,069) and all-time victories (539). More "gold" than "iron," Mike Keenan shines.

The Interview

How did your coaching career start?

It really started when I was a high school teacher. My inclination for the subject area was based on a lot of activity that I had during my university days when I worked at various hockey schools. Even prior to that I ran high school skating programs in Whitby, Ontario. After obtaining my undergraduate degree in Physical Education, I went to the University of Toronto to get my teaching certification. While I was a teacher at Don Mills Collegiate in Toronto, my first assignment was coaching men's lacrosse. We had a very successful run, and really, that's what started to pique my interest in coaching. I also coached female swimming, boys' basketball, and hockey at Forest Hill.

At the same time I was player/coach of the Whitby Senior A hockey team, an interesting combination. I really enjoyed the coaching, so I dropped playing and then went on to coach Junior B in Oshawa while still coaching high school hockey. Next I left teaching to coach the Peterborough Petes, and the following year Scotty Bowman offered me a job in the American Hockey League. I coached there for three years and then returned to the University of Toronto Hockey Club, where I had played as a grad student. After that I was hired to coach in the National Hockey League.

Did you have a background in swimming and basketball, or did you just pick them up?

I played lacrosse as a youngster in Whitby, which is a lacrosse hotbed, much like Vancouver. Swimming was just something that I picked up. I wanted to help the kids, and the swim team coach couldn't make the commitment, so I offered to coach since it was in the fall when I wasn't quite into the hockey program yet. I now integrate a lot of different coaching and teaching techniques from the various sports I have coached. I was also able to integrate some of the strategies that we used between the different sports. The energy systems used in basketball, anaerobic and aerobic, are quite like hockey. Interval training is an important part of hockey, and with lacrosse there is a big carry-over of hand-eye co-ordination to hockey. I experimented a lot too. I moved from one sport to another, and it was quite interesting to see different things evolve in my coaching philosophy and techniques as a result of having a base of different sports to coach. I have found that many coaching principles move sideways across sports. They are fundamentally the same. **The application of strategy and tactics are unique to each sport, but the principles about coaching lie within all.**

What motivates you?

I love the game of hockey. I've always loved the game. When I played at various levels it was never in my mind that I would continue to be involved in the game as a coach. That evolved through time, primarily as a result of my teaching background, which was certainly something that I enjoyed. I enjoyed coaching and I enjoyed teaching. Coaching in high school really perked my interest. I had some success at various levels, and that gave me the confidence that maybe I could coach in the NHL at a top level. It motivates me now to see youngsters share some of the experiences that I've had of winning and the teaching process and being involved in the game. It's highly motivating for me to try to strive to be amongst the best in this industry and to see if I can touch people in a certain way and have them share the same vision and the same motivation that I have.

Do you believe it's an NHL coach's job to motivate a player and keep him at the peak level, or is it the player's job?

I think it's the responsibility of both people. **The coach has to provide an environment, a basis from which to work, and knowledge to help the athlete ascertain his best skill set to develop his best level of performance.** That varies from the youngsters to the most experienced players. I've coached athletes from both sides of the spectrum, and I think it's the athlete's ultimate responsibility to learn how to professionally perform at his peak every night. **I also think the teacher, the coach, has a responsibility to that individual to inspire, care for, and provide a sense of direction for them individually and as a group, because it is a team game.**

In your opinion, does the fear of losing motivate more than the enjoyment of winning?

I understand the question and I understand both motivational aspects. I think when I came into the league the idea of losing was very motivating for me. The fear of losing was something that drove me and made me work that much more diligently at what I was trying to provide for the athlete. I think through some of the experiences I've had with some of the top performers in the NHL I learned to enjoy the winning aspect of it as well. You can enjoy the fruits of your labour. You don't always have to be on the edge of preparing for the next competition; you can let yourself go a little bit and enjoy those aspects. **I would say that the thing that's most motivating for me right now wouldn't fall under either category, and that's the motivation of the teaching aspect as opposed to the fear of failure or the pleasure of success.** I enjoy winning, obviously, more than losing, but I understand the losing process. It is important to develop the foundation for a winning program and get people to understand how that works, as well as getting them to value competition. To thrive on it, to enjoy it, without the fear of losing, and at the same time enjoy some of the aspects that they can be proud of and that they've accomplished, that's the joy of winning.

Can a coach instill confidence in a player? Do you concern yourself with players' self-talk or body language?

You can definitely instill confidence in an athlete. They look for leaders, role models, and support. Most athletes don't mind being challenged. They don't mind being asked to do something that they might be a bit fearful of. You have the vision, as their mentor, of what they might be able to accomplish. Sometimes they can't see it or they have fear that they may not be able to achieve a certain performance level. **You can definitely inspire and provide confidence by integrating the aspects of challenging and supporting an athlete at the same time.** That comes in various ways between ice time distribution or skill development or helping them sort out some of the mental skills that they need in order to be better.

I am definitely concerned with the behaviour of an individual and how he portrays himself. I like to see people feel good about themselves. You can challenge — that's part of the coaching profession — but you have to give the support they need to make them feel good about themselves and give them the preparation process for developing confidence in their teammates, their team game, their skills, and their own individual ability. Give them responsible opportunities to grow, put them in situations from which they begin to get some success, give individuals challenges, and give them assignments that enable them to achieve some level of success. Putting them in situations that they're not ready for can make it difficult for them to develop their own self-confidence. An example of that would be putting a rookie forward into a penalty-killing situation to start the season, as opposed to maybe letting them watch a couple of veteran players do the job. It's better to explain and talk to them as the season progresses, and then give them a little bit at a time until they feel comfortable.

Can you read a player's ability or willingness to perform when you look in his eyes or at his body language?

I'd say yes, just from my own experience and having been around athletes for such a long time. I think that's part of your bench management strength. Another part of my strength is my ability to read the game as it's unfolding. It's unrealistic to think that from Game 1 through Game 82 of the schedule every athlete is going to be at his very best every night. You've got 20 people dressed, and some are going to be on the up-cycle of their confidence levels, physical levels, or how they're feeling about their family or personal problems or themselves, their health, their teammates, their role, or who they're playing against. These are the dynamics of the game.

That's another thing that I love: the dynamics of the game. People can be asked how many minutes are in a hockey game, and the normal answer is 60. Actually there are 720. There are 360 minutes in regulation time distributed between two teams that have 20 players each, so if you give 60 minutes to your goalie (most teams will laugh when I tell them this and say, "You never do that," because I am always pulling my goaltender) then you've got 300 minutes to distribute on your side with no penalties. The other coach has the same. **How you manage this time and who you give it to at what time is an art, and you must be able to read the game and your players as it is unfolding.**

Do you like to change everybody, or do you have one of your assistant coaches do that?

I change all players. Some people don't, but maybe it's an old habit of mine.

I know you've had some great players develop under you. Can you identify players that you challenged to be better?

I've had a lot of good luck in that regard. The first person who comes to mind is Pelle Lindbergh, who was playing in the minors when I arrived in Philadelphia. I gave him a chance to be the number one goaltender, and he won the Vezina Trophy and the President's Trophy because of it. I coached a lot of great young players during my career in Philadelphia. We had four rookies and the youngest team in pro sport. Our best player, Mark Howe, struggled with his confidence at first and then became a superior player in the league. He and his partner, Brad McCrimmon, were plus 52 or 55 one year.

There were a lot of good young players who worked their way through various scenarios, like Jeremy Roenick in Chicago or Ron Hextall back in Philadelphia, both youngsters coming out of the American League, or Ed Belfour coming out of the Canadian national program. Some people were established; some, like Michel Goulet, needed to be jump-started; and others needed a change of venue, like Chris Chelios. Steve Larmer was taught to pay more attention to his personal fitness so he could play at a higher level. A lot of people in St. Louis were wondering about Chris Pronger and Pavel Demitra. Chris didn't have much direction and wasn't trained. Grant Fuhr was a goaltender that everyone had given up on, but he was a Hall of Famer as far as I was concerned.

Do you have a vision for the player, or is it an evaluation process that convinces you a player hasn't achieved his potential?

I'm a firm believer in giving people a second or third or fourth opportunity to discover themselves. I think in a lot of these cases, if you look at them and examine them, these are young people who are put in a pressured situation, and sometimes they are very immature or just not ready. For example, Olli Jokinen couldn't speak much English when he was picked third overall. He arrived in Los Angeles from Finland at 18 years old and probably hadn't spent any time thinking about or preparing himself to be a professional. Organizations proclaim that players like he and Joe Thornton in Boston will be the immediate saviours. Then the media gets hold of this and blows it out of proportion. It's just too much to ask of people like that. There was disapproval of Jokinen in Los Angeles, in Long Island, and in Florida. I sat down with him and said, "We're going to find out, once and for all: Were all the scouts in the world wrong, or should we just adjust the program here for you? You're going to have to train harder. You're going to have to pay attention to what you're doing," and so forth. I think when he was challenged he felt there was an element of fairness and he also felt that there was an opportunity. I think he had squandered it a little bit by his own accord, and part of his maturation was accepting that. He still had an opportunity ahead of him, but the window of opportunity was going to close if he didn't take advantage.

There is an adage that I often use, which comes from my own background: A good teacher is a good teacher when the student is prepared to learn. That is a big plus, but you also have to be inspiring enough as an individual or as a teacher to set a challenge in front of them and give them the support needed because there's going to be a great deal of fear. They've been told for so long that they aren't capable of doing something. If they're on the ice but don't get feedback or support from their environment, they do fail. You've got to provide both at the same time.

Do you ever get a player who goes halfway and you can't get him the rest of the way? If that happens, do you trade him?

Not necessarily. I'll do whatever is best for the team. If that player provides something that the team needs, then that's good enough. **It's not just the coach who can get the other half, but also the dynamics of the group. You have to have sub-group leaders, and they don't always have to be your best players; they can be your best role players.** There's a place for everyone in this culture.

How do you help individual players who are experiencing adversity, and how do you deal with team adversity?

With team adversity you have to try to educate them and build, if you can, a level of preparation for them to know what might be coming. For example, with a young group as you gain a little recognition, other teams are going to respect you and they are going to be more prepared for you. Then you know your effort is going to have to be greater as well. As teams gain a higher level of respect for you they are going to be more competitive against you, so there is a level of adversity you walk your team through, and they build a trust amongst themselves. You reinforce it and teach them. You teach them systems. You teach them what they can rely on, knowing that every level of success is enriched with some level of adversity. What you are going through is of assistance, not a detriment. You're learning from it. You're learning how to deal with certain situations you felt would be very difficult for you as an individual and as a team.

The same thing applies to an individual. **You see yourself in an adverse situation now, but there's an opportunity there for you if you**

look hard enough. There's a window there, something to be found that's positive. You're learning something about yourself. How can you walk through this life and find another venue or avenue or street to walk on that you can benefit from? **You're going to find the journey from the start is not a straight line.** It has its ups and downs going through all the demands and dynamics of what this league provides over a course of 180 days to get to the playoffs. It's not a straight line. It doesn't go straight down, and it doesn't go straight up. It fluctuates depending on where you are, and you will learn through difficult times as well as good times. You're never as good as you think you are, and you are never as poor as you think you are. There's always something there to be found that would be positive in any situation.

Do you have these talks with players individually? Are you a philosopher coach?

I don't know if I'm a philosopher, **but I work to build a philosophy that I believe, and talk about it and try to share it and help them understand it and give them vivid examples of what I'm talking about.**

What types of players are the most challenging for you to coach?

The players who are most challenging are the ones who don't completely subscribe to team skills and the ones who are more interested in their own needs than the team's needs. That is part of what the culture of the game provides, and each team has some members like that, but that's the challenge. The hardest earned respect comes from the individual that you had to work hardest with to achieve the desired result. In the end he is the most revered because it was so difficult for you to get that player to a certain point. Once they get there then they're solid because you had to work so hard on your relationship with them to get them to that point, and if you can do that, then they really believe in you.

Is it a fine line between selfishness and confidence?

Sometimes it's viewed as being selfish, and sometimes it's total insecurity. You've got to read that. Most people in this game are great, so I often give them the benefit of the doubt that they're doing it just to preserve their own ego or their own self-esteem or they're in a situation where they've been rejected. You then need to build their trust in you. They're the hardest ones to earn that trust from, but once you do they are pretty grounded with you.

Is there credibility to a big motivational speech, the locker-room soapbox speech, prior to a game?

There is, and it's timely; it doesn't have to be every day. You speak to your team as a group three or four times a night during the NHL season, so it certainly can't be done all the time, but I think there is a time and place for it. You have to rely on your own experience as a coach and your instincts to tell you what that message has to be at that particular time and when you should deliver it.

Is it a gut feel?

I think it is really from your own experience. After you have coached a number of years you know when it's time to challenge your team or support them. You have to know their development as a group and as individuals to know who you're dealing with, what you're dealing with, and what the circumstances are. You have to understand the cadence of your team in terms of scheduling and in terms of success all year, in terms of health, in terms of the environment they are dealing with, whether you're on the road or at home, what the expectation levels were for the group to begin a season as well as present expectation levels which change during the course of the year. Whether you come from an underdog to a contender or to a failure, those are all different levels of achievement and development, and each of these demand different responses from a coach.

Do you and your coaching staff try to find an angle every night?

You try to find some aspect of their development as a group to give them a reason to reach another level, to inspire them to be better, to build a crescendo from the beginning of the season to the end. You ask them to strive to be a little bit better than they have been in certain areas. Sometimes these are very specific areas and sometimes more general. This may be done in small groups, sometimes individually, sometimes in larger groups, and sometimes with the entire team. Again, it comes in different forms. It doesn't always have to be the same, but you have to know as a coach what it will look like and what it means to the athlete. Another thing I often tell myself or try to explain to those I coach with is it's better to understand than be understood. I have to understand them and they have to understand me, but it's especially important that you understand where they are.

Does the opposition ever play into your pre-game talk and preparation?

It does, definitely. You have to prepare your team. Knowledge is power. There are a lot of keys that come into play that can make a difference. How does your group see themselves with regard to the opposition, as the underdog or as the favourite? This could be based on a hot goaltender or the health of the team you are playing, the health of your own team, the circumstances, the divisional play, or what's at stake. Some of the confidence keys would be your individual self-talk, your visualization, your communication, your knowledge of your system, your fitness level, and your health level. There's always a motivational handle that you can put your hand on before every event and every level of competition.

Have you ever taken one angle and walked it through a playoff series, or does it tend to change with each game?

I know some coaches have done that. They develop a mantra, and it could be you and me against the world, the underdog versus the favourite. In my own coaching experience I've tried to build it into every game in terms of what that series would look like in success or failure, and that really demanded different levels of responses. Sometimes we were the favourite, and that brings a whole different level of expectations and pressures from the public, your teammates, and the organization. Sometimes we were the underdog, and that's a whole different skill of getting them confident enough. Oftentimes it's a misnomer that the favourite may not be confident enough because the expectations are so high. On the other hand, you really have to support some of the best athletes and not put pressures on them because they need a little bit of extra confidence to make the difference. I guess that goes back to your first question when I alluded to teaching. **The most fascinating part of coaching anything, whether it's coaching swimming or lacrosse or coaching in the NHL, is the fascination of the human being because every one of us is so completely different.** You are coaching in a team sport with all those different personalities and trying to make it as whole as you possibly can. It's fascinating for me to coach for that reason. That's what excites me.

What is the identity of your teams? When someone watches a Mike Keenan coached team, what do you want them to see?

I think you look at the development of a personality. The first thing you have to do when you coach is evaluate who you are coaching, their talent, and their experience. You can't go in and say, "I want them to be this." You've got to go in and find out who they have become. For example, I never pretended that the Philadelphia Flyers were the Edmonton Oilers, because they didn't have that skill level and could never become them. I've tried to help teams that I have coached understand what it is like to be a member of a team that is highly equipped with team skills; what it is like to be the best team, not always the most talented team; to be a team that's very cohesive, extremely competitive, proud of what they do together, and a team that will thrive on success as a group and demonstrate that on the ice. I want them to understand what it is like to be a team that would be extremely hard to play against because of the passion and caring they have for each other, to compete as a group and to be the very best athletes that they could be on a daily basis.

How would you keep your players focussed on what's good for the team?

That's the trick of coaching, the art and science of it. You have to find out what the skill set is and what the needs of the individuals are, first and foremost, because they are the sub-group of the large group. **You've got to know every individual's needs to make them feel good about themselves and to make them want to aspire to be better, to improve, to be a part of a society.** Allow them to feel good about their contribution. Give them a role where they feel important. Give them some responsibility. You've got to give them all their own identity, including the sub-groups, whether it's defence pairings, a penalty-killing unit, a forward line, the role player, or the superstar. They have to know how they're going to be part of a large group and how they're going to build their own self-esteem. You collectively work that all together, and that's the fascination of it.

Are there things that you've done to enhance that team cohesion?

I think you have a responsibility in a number of ways: You work together, you learn to win together, and you have to build the socialization of the team. A very interesting challenge for our coaching staff in Florida was having more European players than any other team in the league. We had to be broad-minded, to understand their culture, where they were coming from, where they learned the game, what their expectations were, what their family environments provided for them as developing young-sters, what their country expected from them, and how they were per-ceived in their country. The way you build the socialization of a group is very important so they feel they are a part of something special.

Are there any specific things you have done with teams in the past that you could look back on and say, "This function helped us get to the next level"?

I've done a lot of different things from team parties to taking them to resorts, to taking them out for dinner, to providing opportunities for their wives or families to be together. I call it socialization, which is try-ing to build a better understanding as a group and put them in an en-vironment that is perceived by them to be special. I have taken them to see a world event or to the war memorials in Washington, for example, to share history with them, just to do things that would make them feel that they're learning something about human behaviour, human events, and human development in different situations. I have taken them to a Broadway play, to comedy acts, to completely non-descript hockey func-tions, to places that they've never been before, to give them a broader view of the world. I've given them books and articles to read, brought in special speakers, motivational speakers, psychologists, and other coaches from teams in other sports, anyone that they can learn from. I have used everything from business people to talk about motivational techniques, to aerobic dancing, to female instructors, to skating instructors, to anything I could possibly think of that would broaden the view they would have of the world.

Have you found a pattern to establish a tradition of excellence over the years, or does it evolve? How do you communicate this tradition of excellence?

It's a building block. It's not something that you talk about without subscribing to the ingredients that have to take place for that to happen, which are fundamentally paying attention to details in every way without losing the balance of their own personal enjoyment of the game and their needs as a person, both family-wise and as a group of men. I think that you have to build the process, strive for it, and learn through different situations. Whether it's playing as an underdog against the favourite, or a conference game that could be meaningless in their view, being 2,000 miles from home and nobody really cares, or just giving an incremental objective that they can achieve on a daily basis, it's part of the building block.

I've also used small, segmented objectives to build the process. You talk about setting the big objective. Perhaps with a group you feel that maybe the end is to win the Stanley Cup, but you have to segment that for them, break it down and say, "We can achieve this end if we do these particular things on a daily basis for the next 180 days to prepare ourselves for the playoff game, if we get there." **I like to use five-game segments and then break it down from there to give the players a handle, as they call it, a reason to do something well on a particular day, day to day, and then over groupings of time so that they don't lose track of where they are.** I try to always put these in a context of what their life is, where they were, where they are now, and where they're going. It's funny the way we look at things in this game. **For us there are really only two or three days in a week: It's a game day or a non-game day, or there's yesterday, today, and tomorrow. When people say seven days a week I have no idea what seven days a week means. I don't know what a Sunday is.**

People often define success as winning championships, but not everybody wins, so how do you define success?

I think that in the professional environment, which is completely different from coaching amateur, your success is measured not particularly on whether you've won or lost, but on whether you're winning or losing in the process. If you see your team getting better rather than getting worse, then you're winning. As I said earlier, some of the process is to learn what losing means, that, ultimately, it's not acceptable. People outside the coaching profession don't understand the process. They just see end results, not core results like business people. We get the results that people, including your owners, your organization, and your fan base, are looking for every day. They're in the paper. So the absolute measure of success for you as a professional athlete and coach is measured by whether you win. That comes in different stages and developments: whether you've made the playoffs, whether you've improved your performance over the course of a season, whether you've won a first round in the playoffs, whether you've gone deep in the playoffs, and whether you've won a Stanley Cup. Not everyone can win. In fact, people should understand that there's only one winner out of 30 teams every year, but you can subscribe to a winning formula and see whether you're winning or losing. **A winning program demonstrates that you win more often than you lose over a course of time, and that your program has the opportunity, if things are done well and properly, always to be in a position to be successful.**

Do you evaluate that at the beginning of the season, or is it more general than that?

I think it's a progression. It's also something that's fascinating about sport. The example that comes to mind was in Philadelphia, where the team had not made the post-season the year before, so the expectation was if you made the playoffs it would be a wonderful year. We ended up winning the President's Trophy and going to the finals. How would anyone be able to project that at the beginning of the year? How do you go into a season and say, "This is a non-playoff team that can win the President's Trophy and win the Stanley Cup"? It's only happened twice in the history of the NHL, so you go in with an expectation that you want to continue to see improvement. You want to see the team getting better, and that's how you describe it, whether you're winning or losing, not necessarily whether you have won or lost. **If you're winning you see improvement. You see individuals and every aspect of the team getting better.**

You are responsible as the leader and coach to improve skill development, team development, your defensive system, your offensive system, your special teams, your goaltending, to see them play at different levels at different times, and that progression both fascinates and motivates me. I go back to the individual. Who's to say what the limitations are at a given time in our life? If we knew the answer to that we'd take a lot of fun out of living. It's always open-ended because you forget not only what your group is going to do but also what another group is going to do. The team that's supposed to win might have injuries, their chemistry might not be right, they might have lost interest or motivation, or whatever the case might be. Something totally unpredictable might happen to either you or your opponent.

What was your most memorable coaching experience, your greatest accomplishment?

I've been fortunate to have had a lot of them. One was winning the Canada Cup in '87 when we played an incredible series with the Russians.

The entire country focussed on that particular series. I was very young. I think I was 35 at that time, and the expectations of a country were placed upon me! Another one was winning a championship at the University of Toronto as a player and a coach. I think there were only two or three people, Tom Watt and perhaps Lester B. Pearson, who had done it, and that was exceptional. Winning the Calder Cup with an all-rookie defence core was another, to go to the Stanley Cup with the youngest team, and finally to win the Stanley Cup in New York. I've had a lot of great experiences so I can't say one was greater than the other. I enjoy being part of a group that learns to do something that may be a surprise for them. For example, in Philadelphia, they even surprised themselves. It was fun to be around people who said, "You told us we might be able to win. At the beginning I thought you were crazy, and at the end we won." It was a lot of fun.

What did all of your successful teams have in common? Is there something there you've seen over the years?

I've played for a couple of championship teams in the minors and at the University of Toronto. The one thing the teams I coached or played for that won everything or went to the finals all had in common, **the one thing that stood out for me more than anything else, is that they absolutely cared for each other more than they cared about themselves. It was not always having the most talented people but having the best people. The best teams for me had the best people.** They wanted something, not for themselves, but for their teammates.

As a coach are you in that group, or are you separate and forcing that group together?

Sometimes you're a part of that group, and sometimes you're not. Some coaches who may be described as players' coaches would probably like to find that solution. I would say, personally, I think it's pretty obvious that I'm not necessarily a part of it at all times. I might be the catalyst that forces that group to be that way, which is also enjoyable. In the end most of those people will come to me and say, "I didn't understand it at the time but I do now, and I appreciate it." Some of my veteran players understood what I was doing, but for a lot of youngsters it was a leap of faith. You're getting them to do something when they have no knowledge of where they are going or whether they can do it. You're telling them they can do it, but they have to overcome the fear of whether they can or can't.

They have no real basis to say, "I can" or "I can't." "I don't know, and I'm going to have to develop a leap of faith with this group or this coach to try to get me from a certain level to a point that I've never experienced before." That's one type of group.

Then you've got a group like New York, where a lot of guys from the Edmonton Oilers and the Chicago Blackhawks had walked that journey before. Although the journey is always different, they had that sense that they could get there somehow through their own experiences. The group in Philly, particularly in the first year, and Chicago when we finally went to the finals, or the championship winning one at U of T, or the one in Rochester, had no idea whether they could arrive at the end result that we were striving for.

So you don't always have to have a group who knows what the end is?

That's the surprise of it. Every team has to learn. The New York Islanders had to learn through some devastating failures in their mind: losing to the Toronto Maple Leafs and the Oilers, losing to Los Angeles, or going to the finals and getting beaten four straight before they could learn and gain the confidence that they could get back to that certain spot that they were striving for.

Do you win at all costs?

I'd answer that with mixed feelings. Today no, but close to it sometimes when I was younger. That drive was also again the fear of failure, the fear of losing versus the enjoyment of success. As you know, it's also the process that every man faces in this league. The average length of your career is less than two years, so maybe at the beginning that fear is really going to be strong and you might push the envelope a little bit. **If I had it to do over again, sure, there are times I wish I had done it a different way.**

Do the successes you have spill over into everyday life?

You try to live by the principles you teach. You've got to walk the talk and you try to be consistent, but you're human and we all make mistakes. Those things are fundamental in you if you're honest, you have a level of integrity, and you're fair. The way you try to live your life will definitely spill over into your coaching. **The one thing about athletes**

**is that good athletes are committed and invest a lot of their time, so
you have to be real to them, completely real, and if you're not you lose
them.** They appreciate it if you are real to them and fair and honest and
forthright. Some may ask if I have changed. **I have definitely changed
my methodology, but I haven't changed my principles, and that's a
big difference.**

How do you handle pressure?

Personally, it's something I have learned to deal with. Over the 27
years I have been in the teaching and coaching professions I have been
trained to deal with it. An important reminder is to maintain your own
health, exercise, eat well, sleep well, spend time with your family, and get
away from the game. As much as you find it difficult to separate yourself
from the game, it is important to do other things to broaden your interests
in other areas. Sometimes this is possible during the season, but it's mainly
done in the off-season. It is important to take time to recharge your own
enthusiasm and energy levels, to be able to step back and draw perspective
on who and where you are and what you are doing. I think those things all
help you handle the ever-increasing expectations, pressures, and demands
of the profession, driven primarily now more than ever before by the eco-
nomic needs of each franchise. That's how I try to deal with stress, and I
would suggest that most of us, if we can, pay attention to things that are
important.

What was your worst moment?

The absolute worst moment was the phone call at 4:00 in the morning telling me that our goaltender in Philadelphia, Pelle Lindbergh, had
broken his neck and was on life support. I went to the hospital and had to
deal with the death of an individual who I cared a great deal for, and tell
his mom and dad who had just arrived from Sweden the day before, and
tell his fiancée, and tell the team that Pelle had died. That was my most
difficult coaching moment and the subsequent time that surrounded that
tragedy. Anything that you do in hockey is not tragic. If you lose a game
it's not tragic. Tragedy is losing loved ones or someone in your family or
something way beyond the game. We often lose perspective about that.
**The game is very important to us, but there are things in the world
that are a lot more crucial than the game itself.** That event was the most
tragic and difficult to deal with in the context of the game for me.

When I was going through a scoring slump in Montreal, I'd go over to Children's Hospital, and that would help me keep things in perspective. Are there things you've done over the years that you could pass on to coaches that would allow them some perspective?

That's a good example, and we do that, and I've been able to do that pretty much throughout my life. I know my persona is that I'm intense, tough, and demanding, but I've been able to keep things in perspective through my own life experiences. I lost a brother when I was young. In my first marriage I lost five pregnancies. I lost some family members who were close to me, and I had to separate this in my own mind because I went through some things on a personal basis that were difficult. As a result, I didn't feel a lot of empathy for players who complained about having to work too hard. In the back of my mind I'm thinking, you really could have a problem. Having to work hard and subsequently getting paid a lot of money for doing it is not a problem. **I've always demanded a lot of players because I felt that was their responsibility to themselves, to their families, and to their teammates, and I had very little room for anything less than that and probably still don't.** I tell them, "If you really want to have a problem lose a child or lose a family member or lose one of your team members. That's a problem." There's a fine balance but I think sometimes we get caught up and lose a sense of reality in the NHL. Remember: We fly first class, we stay in first-class hotels, our nutritional standards are way beyond the average citizen in the world, our lifestyle is very demanding, yes, there's travel, wear and tear, and a lot of time away from our families, but it's something we chose to do, so we should live up to that responsibility. We chose to do it. We have to accept the responsibility that comes with it all when we are treated exceptionally well and are recognized publicly and get privileges. With that, it takes a lot of work. There's a balance there as well.

When you are challenging athletes, are there different standards for elite players?

It depends on where that player is. I have no problem giving privileges to players who have dedicated their lives and proven things to the league and have earned special attention. There are others that you have to teach how to earn it. You have to have an innate ability to feel where that threshold is at that time for that individual. How much can you ask of them? How much are they ready to give? **When is a teacher a good**

teacher? When the student is ready to learn. How much is he ready to learn right now? You take him to that point because he's overcoming fear, he doesn't know if he can do it or not, and then he says, "Yeah, OK, now I get it a little bit more, a little bit more, a little bit more." Somebody calls it a horse whisperer.

What are your most valuable skills as a coach?

I think my best skills are motivating the athlete, setting a stage, setting an environment, setting an expectation that will make them move to a higher performance level. I think those are my strengths as a coach.

Do you like the technical side, or do you typically delegate it?

I pass a lot of that off to my assistants because I think you need to empower them, make them feel responsible, and more a part of it. If, as a head coach, you are focussed on motivating the team, then you have to empower your coaches and staff. When I was a young coach, like most young coaches I was the video man, the technical man, and I did the x's and o's, going right back to junior in Peterborough and Oshawa. I had no assistant on a regular basis in the American League, and I had one assistant at the University of Toronto. You have to do a lot initially.

After I arrived in the NHL I moved through different phases of development and brought other people in to handle specific parts of the coaching responsibilities. Initially we didn't even have video set up in order to get every game or time-on-ice stats. If you know your strengths then you should use them. If you want a technical part of the game covered or video work done, then you hire capable people as part of your coaching staff. From my perspective, the NHL coach is more like a football head coach who has the offensive coordinator, defensive coordinator, and special teams coordinator. It's broader now because the demands and needs of the players are broader among youngsters who have gone through a variety of programs from Russia, Finland, Sweden, Czech Republic, Switzerland, the United States, Canada, Poland, Germany. You need a broader base of skills, and you need to empower your staff to provide you with more information.

How do you handle the responsibility of a head coach? It sounds as if you delegate a lot now.

In the beginning I was very demanding, and because of my personality I always seemed to be out front, but I've always given a great deal of responsibility to the people I'm working with. I give even more today than ever before, because, as I said, those needs are really broader based now. We don't have 15 or 20 Canadians to deal with whose culture and background you know because it's your culture, whose lifestyle has been ingrained in your life. Instead, we've got a whole series of nationalities to deal with, and it's better and more productive if you let others assist with the demands of the athlete. The athlete wants to be well fed. He wants to know about nutrition, massage therapy, aerobic training, strength training, flexibility, plyometrics, skating skills, on the ice with parachutes, and weight training. Therefore you need people who can assist in providing it for him.

Do you feel that the dressing room environment influences team success, and what do you do to influence a positive environment?

It definitely influences team success to provide a clean, dynamic, and up-to-date environment. You have to provide all these things. **You have to give players the resources that help them to feel good about what they are doing so they can be at their peak performance levels. You have to provide an upbeat environment.** I don't know of any other team in the league that has done this, but I put a kitchen in the dressing room to give the players a nutritional center in Florida because we had the youngest team in the league. I wanted to feed those kids breakfast and lunch every day to make that kind of investment in them. That's just another aspect of trying to make the dressing room a positive environment.

Eisenhower said leadership is the art of getting someone to do something you want done because they want to do it. Would you agree with that?

I think that's a pretty good explanation. They finally will want to do it. You can take the horse to water but you can't make them drink. That's exactly right. You have to get them to a point where they want to drink.

How do you define and develop your captains?

You develop them by giving them responsibilities and watching how they respond. Some people have more intrinsic values for leadership than others. Some are more comfortable and confident with it. Some can pull out their past experience which they have learned from, and some don't want the responsibility of leadership. They find it a burden rather than a privilege, and you have to set an environment for them.

Define your leadership style.

I think my leadership style is based on my personality. I focus on developing an expectation amongst the group that there is a higher level of performance that we're capable of achieving.

How do you kick back and relax?

I don't relax as much in the winter as I'd like because of the preoccupations. Coaching is very demanding, and I really struggle with that balance. I've gotten a lot better as I've matured, and I believe it has reflected in my coaching. Sometimes, because of the focus on achievement, I have been too impatient for the development that needs to take place and have been very hard on myself and consequently difficult sometimes with the athletes. I think I've learned. I started out a little more patient, but as you know, you get involved in this and have some success, and people become impatient with you. They forget about the process. They just think that you can turn things around right away and then you end up putting those expectations upon yourself.

The off-season is very important to me. I'm with my family and spend a lot of time away from the game, as much as I can in Canada. We live on a lake. We also spend some time in Maine, and outdoors to get away from it. During the summer my down time really is just my family, time spent relaxing with my wife, because during the year we have very few off days. I talk to my players about this often. If you're committed to an NHL program you only have time to deal with your family and your team, and that's it, nothing else.

Andy Murray

A ndy Murray, with his 30-plus years of coaching experience, is widely respected for his coaching philosophy and reputation of preparation, commitment, and accountability.

A native of Souris, Manitoba, Murray's first head-coaching position was with the Brandon Travelers of the Manitoba Junior A League, from 1976 to '78. He moved on to become head coach at Brandon University for three seasons; he led the Bobcats to the league championship and number one ranking in Canadian university hockey during his final year. In 1981 Murray moved to Switzerland, where he successfully coached several Swiss Division A teams over seven seasons.

As an assistant coach, Andy Murray helped guide the Hershey Bears of the American Hockey League to the Calder Cup championship. He then received his first NHL job as an assistant coach of the Philadelphia Flyers, remaining from 1988 to 1990. He reached the Stanley Cup finals in 1991 as an assistant/associate coach of the Minnesota North Stars. He was an assistant coach for the Winnipeg Jets from 1993 to '95.

Andy Murray was hired as head coach of the Canadian National Team in 1996 and guided them to a two-year 77–29–14 record. He collected silver medals in 1996 at both the World Cup of Hockey and the World Championships as an assistant coach of Team Canada. In 1997 he captured gold as head coach of Team Canada at the World Championships in Helsinki, Finland, and in 2003 he became the first Canadian coach to win a second World Championship following the team's victory once again in Helsinki, Finland. He also served as an associate coach for Team Canada under Marc Crawford at the 1998 Olympic Games in Nagano, Japan. Additionally, he has a record six gold medals as a coach for Canada at the prestigious Spengler Cup Tournament in Davos, Switzerland. In 2007 Murray led Team Canada, as head coach for the fourth time, to the IIHF World Men's Hockey Championships.

Prior to making the final step to the NHL as a head coach, Murray led the Shattuck St. Mary's Prep team to a National Championship in 1999. Later that same year, Murray became the Los Angeles Kings 19th head coach. During his tenure behind the bench, Murray guided the Kings to three playoff berths and three 90-points-plus seasons. In 2001–02 he became the second-fastest coach to record 100 wins in Kings' history, earned the fourth-highest points total in team history (95) and accomplished a franchise first of losing less than 30 games for the second straight season. He currently holds the Kings' all-time record for wins (215) and number of games coached (480). After a stint in 2006 as a playoff commentator for *Hockey Night in Canada*, Murray once again accepted the challenge of turning a losing team around as head coach of the St. Louis Blues, midway through the 2006–07 season.

The Interview

What is your hockey background?

I grew up in Souris, Manitoba, a town of 2,000 people. I had a passion for sports, and my father was so inclined as well. In our community if you didn't play a sport, then our town didn't have a team, so everybody in town played all the sports. As I advanced in hockey I had to make a choice between university and junior. I chose to play university hockey in Brandon. At that point I realized that my aspirations of becoming a pro player were not going to be realized, but I enjoyed coaching. Even though my family is in the automobile business, I had a passion to coach and teach.

I taught school for a couple of years and played senior hockey at the same time. We had a really good senior league in the West. My uncle was involved in the ownership of the Brandon Wheat Kings about that time. They had fired the coach of their Tier II Junior A team, and two days before the start of the regular season, after encountering problems in exhibition play, they asked me if I was interested in the job. So I started coaching Tier II junior in the Wheat Kings system. After a couple of years I was approached about taking over the head job at the university. I coached at the university for three years.

In my last year my father passed away. I had some decisions to make because I had stopped teaching and was running our car dealership with him. I took a leave of absence from the university and our automobile dealership and went to Europe. I thought I needed to get away for a year and ended up staying seven. During that time I coached professionally in Switzerland. I also had the opportunity to coach a number of Canada's Spengler Cup teams and was involved with the Olympic national team evaluation camps.

During my tenure in Switzerland I worked with John Paddock, who was coaching in the American Hockey League. My season in Europe always ended in February, we would come back in March, and I would work with him in Hershey with the Hershey Bears. I got to know Bob Clarke through that connection since Hershey was the Flyers' number one affiliate. I then went to Philadelphia to be Paul Holmgren's assistant coach. From there Bob Clarke went to Minnesota, and I went with him to be an assistant coach with Bob Gainey. I was there two years and went to the finals in '91 with them. I returned to Switzerland for a year, but it wasn't the same feeling after having coached in North America. We came back after a year, and I coached two years in Winnipeg and then was given the opportunity to coach the national team.

I loved it. It was probably the best job anybody could have. I tried to make a bit of a difference in that program, but once I thought I had done all I could with the National Team, and wanted to spend more time with my family, I went to Shattuck St. Mary's Prep School and coached there. It's not the normal stepping-stone to get to the NHL, but Dave Taylor from the LA Kings called and asked if I would be interested in that job. I was excited to talk to them and fortunate to get the opportunity. I was also fortunate to have coached in the World Championships as both head and assistant coach, and in the World Cup and '98 Olympics as an assistant.

What motivates you?

I don't want to let other people down. This may seem like the glass-half-full approach, but whether it's the players I work with or friends and family who are enjoying what I'm doing right now, I want to achieve because I feel that a lot of people are identifying with what I'm doing. I think to be a good coach you've got to live it, and they are living it with me. I'm living it right now, but I know everybody back in my hometown and all my friends and associates are living it with me. They're up in the morning checking the papers or staying up late to watch the game. Although this may sound like a negative, it really isn't. It's something that drives me every day. We've got to get it done. We've got to get it done because there are people pushing me who are enjoying what I'm doing.

What are the things that allow you to be on top of your game every day?

First of all you have to love what you're doing. I don't ever feel sorry for myself; I recognize how privileged I am to be doing what I'm doing. I also realize that out of 2,000 people in my hometown of Souris, there are 1,999 who would change jobs with me any day of the week. To me, that's an energizer within itself. Whether I'm coaching Canada's National Team or I'm coaching the LA Kings, I feel so fortunate to be doing what I'm doing.

How do you keep your players at their peak level?

I believe the biggest part of motivation is preparation, giving the

players a feeling that they are well prepared for the next battle and that if they execute the game plan in place they have a good chance to be successful. They need both mental and physical preparation. Part of my methodology is to make the players recognize how fortunate they are, that it's a privilege to be in the National Hockey League, but also a responsibility, and there's a lot that comes with that. My wife says that I have the ability to make people feel guilty if they are not taking a seat at the table with everybody else. I have an inability to understand why people won't buy in, and I never want to get to the position where I understand, because I think then maybe your expectations drop. I believe you get from people what you expect of them. If you have high expectations for people, that's normally what you get in return, so I hold people to high expectations.

Do you adjust your motivational approach to different players?

There's no question you have to treat each player as their own individual person, because that's what they are. I think you have to be consistent in your approach but not predictable. You have to get to know your players as individuals. People have heard me say at coaching clinics, **"Before people care how much you know, they want to know how much you care."** You have to show that you care for each person as an individual, recognize that they all bring special ingredients, and treat them accordingly.

What are you doing with them or for them to get that "extra" out of your players? How do you get players to go through the wall for you?

It's an association between getting the players to recognize how fortunate they are and that **there is no gratification or satisfaction that comes with individual success if the team doesn't have it.** Individual recognition and gratification come through team success. When you see guys sacrificing and doing that little extra, for example a top offensive player like Ziggy Palffy backchecking and stealing pucks from behind and closing the gap from behind, that's as inspiring to our team as when Ziggy Palffy scores a great goal. I know I've noticed it and everybody on the bench has noticed it. It's that ability to get players to do things that you want them to do because they want to do it. You've convinced them that this is the direction they need to go, and they've also recognized that hey, that's the way it has to be done, and that contributing to the team or helping our team have success is the way that everybody gets recognized.

How do you build confidence in your athletes?

The word confidence is kind of taboo with me because I've heard it used so much. In fact, for a number of years now I have not allowed our players to use that word. I don't allow them to say, "I didn't have confidence today," or "My confidence is not great." They'll say it at times and catch me looking at them, because I have yet to hear anybody define confidence.

My responsibility in the coaching profession is to eliminate excuses, and provide reasons for success rather than failure. Lack of confidence is the biggest excuse in the world, in my opinion, because you either play well and you feel good about yourself, or you play poorly and you don't feel good. What comes first? Do you have confidence and then play well, or do you play well and then have confidence? Confidence to me is playing well and feeling good about yourself.

Players often say, "The coach didn't give me confidence." How does he give you confidence? He can provide opportunities and he can be a facilitator of performance, but he can't go and grab something and say, "This is confidence." Once when I was coaching I gave everybody an envelope and put the word "confidence" on a piece of paper. When I handed it out, I said, "Guys, we've got it now. This is what it is, and we've got it now, so let's not even talk about it."

Is there credibility to the big motivational speech just before a game or in between periods? People outside the game will often say that the coach must have really given it to them, when the team has played well.

There's an edge that can be brought to every game, an emotional point that you can tap for each particular opponent. There's always a specific thing, either your position in the standings on that particular day, or the way that an opponent treated you last game by maybe not showing the level of respect that they should have. **There's always a reason to win, and you can always key in and focus on that.** It's primarily about preparation, but there is an emotional stimulation that can be tapped there, and I think it's important to do it. If your team is not well prepared it doesn't matter what you say, they're going to have the feeling, holy smokes, who's he trying to kid? If your team knows they're well prepared for this opponent and that when they step on the ice and execute there's an opportunity for success, then you're going to have people listen.

What angles or edges have you brought to the game?

I can remember our young National Team playing the Swedish National Team before the Sweden Games, a big annual tournament in Europe. We were playing the Swedes, who were loaded, in their building, and Canada had been blown out of most games in the tournament for the last couple of years. I can remember the president of the Swedish Ice Hockey Federation coming up to me before the game and saying, "Andy, we know you can't beat us tonight, but we need a good game for the fans." Obviously that was a rallying point for our team.

You always have to respect your opponent in this business, and there have been times when a team has not respected us and maybe taken us for granted and taken some liberties. You would remind your players of that particular fact. I constantly remind them that in Los Angeles we're playing for the Stanley Cup too, because it's almost as if the perception is the LA Kings don't play for the Stanley Cup; only teams like Detroit and Colorado and Dallas and New Jersey do. What it comes down to is that in every situation you're appealing to their sense of pride. You do it in different ways, but the bottom line is you're appealing to their sense of pride. Hockey players have a lot of pride.

Most of us believe the team tends to take on the identity or a piece of the personality of the coach over time. What would a player that Andy Murray coached 10 years ago remember?

I would like to think that the first thing that players would say is, "He cares and he's a good person." **In this business, or in anything you do in life, it's more important to be known as a good person than a good doctor or a good lawyer or a good player or a good coach.**

The day I got hired for the job in L.A. one of the stations sent a TV crew out to Faribault, Minnesota. They interviewed a bunch of the kids who had played for me on the prep team. They would play part of my press conference where I talked about intensity and then play a clip asking one of the young guys, "When you think of Coach Murray what do you think?" "He's intense." I think people recognize that I work at the job I've got and I'm an intense competitor, as we all are in this business, and I think people would associate that with my profile as a coach.

It's a journey to get there, obviously, but winning a championship is only a fleeting moment. The most gratifying thing in this business is the feeling that you've made a bit of a difference. When a former player calls you for advice, it's because of the relationship that you forged with them. I started coaching when I was pretty young, and I've got guys who are over 40 now, and they still call me Coach. I've told them for years just to call me Andy, but they call me Coach. It's the feeling that you made a difference in their lives.

How do you keep players in today's game focussed on what's good for the team when there is so much attention on individuals and their accomplishments?

I've never made any decisions with players based on their contracts. It's a matter of appealing to the fact that the only success that one has is in the recognition and gratification the team has. It doesn't come individually.

I try to recognize everybody's contributions, things that maybe some players, some people, some fans, some media, some management might not notice. Then I have made the unnoticed noticed. That enhances everybody's profile and makes the star player who is not doing some of those things realize, "Hey, the coach identifies with that as much as with some of the goals I'm scoring." It enhances everybody's profile so you become a better team.

You always see the things that players don't do well very quickly, but I want our coaches to make sure that we catch people doing things well. Emphasize that, and it will help emphasize the team concept. You have to work at catching people doing things well.

What have you and your coaching staff done to enhance team cohesion?

We emphasize "green-light level of communication" in the sense that everybody's got a green light to come in and talk to us whenever they want to. As long as it's not going to change the world, don't worry about issues that tend to bother some people by making them big issues when they don't have to be. Do whatever you can for the players. People will sometimes ask me if I have an itinerary. I'll change it by 15 minutes if it gives the players more time to do something. I think it's a matter of doing whatever you can for the players to help them in their profession.

Can you remember implementing something in particular?

One of the things that I like to do is involve the wives and the family out of a sense of team pride and to recognize them. Quite often we will bring the wives into the dressing room and have a talk with them about how important they are to the team. I always send the wives flowers on the day of our first regular-season game. It has been three years now; maybe I need to do something different! It's a way of saying thanks to them, and it brings them into the team mindset. I think we've all tried different things like that for bonding, whether it's bringing in special speakers or other different things.

Are there things that you can do to establish a tradition of excellence within the organization?

I think there are. There's body language and the way you carry yourself. First of all a coach has to live by those standards, to make sure that the players identify that he's the first one at the rink and everything's organized when they come in. Everything's in its place. This is the way we do business here with the Kings.

In practice we blow the whistle once we complete a drill, and the last guy into the coach usually has to skate a lap. I've done it all the way along in my coaching, not to punish anybody, but to say, "Hey, we're intense. This is the way the LA Kings do things." As soon as the players step on the ice the helmets are buckled up and we're ready to go, we're going to work. I don't stay on the ice at the end of practice and fool around with the guys afterward; that's their time. When I'm out there, it's all about adherence to our concept of excellence, and then I get off the ice and deal with the media, and the assistant coaches go to work in the individual areas.

Everything you do as a coach helps define the standard of excellence that your team is going to have. One of the most important things is your first impression, the impression that you make on your team right away. I had the good fortune to coach a number of players like Rob Blake and some of our leading players before in international tournaments. When I came in the first time in L.A. and said, "This is the way we're going to do it," and walked out the door, I believe that Rob would have said, "He knows what he's doing, and that is how we are going to do it." Everything you do as a coach has a bearing on that standard of excellence.

Why do so few organizations ever reach that so-called level of excellence?

I think one of the reasons is a lot of organizations don't allow their people to fulfill their specific responsibilities. There is not the support level that is required and there's interference, but the bottom line is that not enough organizations have had success, and excellence is based on a pattern of success. When you're struggling all the time, you're always saying, "If we could just get a win here we'll be all right," but those are tough to find, and some organizations always seem to be in a state of flux. The problem when you are in a state of flux is that you can't look at three- or five-year plans. Your plan becomes how you approach that next game. In a lot of cases individual interference inhibits teams from being able to go to work on a daily basis and get the job done.

Is success goal driven? Many people define success as winning championships, but how do you define it?

I want our players to have no regrets when they hang their skates up for the last time in a season. That would be something, if we can hang our skates up at the end of the year knowing we laid it on the line and played as hard as we could. I battled as hard as I could individually and as a team, and there are no regrets. I don't know if you necessarily get there, but for me as a coach it's the fact that **I want to do it my way and not look back and say, "If I'd only done it this way, the way I wanted to." Do it the way you want to do it and have no regrets.**

What would be your most memorable coaching experience, your greatest accomplishment?

There are special feelings when you win a championship. My most memorable experience, though, is the knowledge that somebody appreciates what I've done every time I am hired for a new job. This may come back to what drives me, trying not to let people down who have expressed a level of belief in me. The best part of being an NHL coach is the day you get the job. The best part of being the National Team coach is the day you get the job. When somebody said, "We'd like to have you," there is a sense of accomplishment.

What have all your successful teams had in common?

I've never been blessed with teams that one would consider to be talented, with a lot of star players. **The teams that I consider to have been successful, and we're talking about winning teams, were the ones with a level of resilience that enabled them to overcome obstacles.** We recognized there would be ups and downs, but we battled our way through them. We were resilient and kept working. We didn't make excuses; we just went out and performed.

Which is more motivating for you as a coach, the fear of losing or the enjoyment of winning?

I am still tough on myself. When we win, I do believe it's the players, and when we lose I believe I could have done more and I need to do more, so I guess it's the fear of losing a game. To qualify that, it's more not wanting to let the people and players I'm working with down. I feel that if we don't get the job done, then I have let them down as well as the people identifying with our team, our ownership and our management who have given me this opportunity. I almost take winning for granted. That's what you're expected to do. **When we win that's what we're supposed to do, and maybe the high isn't really high, but when we lose it's not supposed to happen, and I never want to get comfortable with that feeling.**

Do you win at all costs?

I would say no. **My coaching is still based on respecting the game, respecting your opponents, and most important, respecting your own players.** I would never want to do things that would interfere in any of those three areas. Does to win at all costs mean that you send your tough guy out after the star player and you set out to hurt him? Those are things that show a lack of respect for the game, for your opponent, and for your own players, and I don't believe in those things. To me there is still a respect level that you have to have for all three areas, and if you are saying that you are prepared to win at all costs, I think in some ways you'd be tampering with that mindset, and I'm not prepared to do that.

What are your most valuable skills that make you a successful coach?

I think I'm detail-oriented, and I believe that I set an example for our team and our players about how we're going to work. I'd like to think that the level of communication is such that I can have relationships with players. **The toughest thing for me in my coaching is to tell a player who I know cares and wants to be in the lineup, that he's not playing. It will never get easy for me, and I never want it to get easy.** So I consider compassion a key. I care a lot, and I also think attention to detail, being an example for the players, having compassion and the desire to succeed and not let people down are important skills of mine. I think I live the life. I don't just talk about the way we should conduct ourselves, I try to live that way, and I'd like to think that inspires players. Everybody is unique and everybody has to be treated differently, but consistently. I think my ability to know people and to know what they bring to the table and to surround myself with good people have all contributed to my success.

How do you handle pressure, deal with adversity, and face failure?

I believe in déjà vu coaching. I've told a lot of young coaches, "You've arrived as a coach when you've been there before." You come to a certain situation in a season or in a pressure situation in a game, and you know how to react because you've been there before and you know when to call that time out. You know exactly what you're going to say. I always take time before a season or before a game to just sit and think about the way things are going to develop: If this happens, how am I going to respond; how am I going to react? In a lot of cases that feeling of déjà vu is there because it has been prepared for and it's part of my coaching repertoire. Everything I do is based on preparation, but I would say I deal with it because in most situations I feel I've been there before.

A gut decision is the key to coaching. You have to be able to make that decision. "I've been there. I'm not just making arbitrary decisions. I've made this decision before." We've all had a déjà vu feeling, and I like to think that all my gut decisions are calculated.

What was your worst moment, and how did you recover from it?

I don't know if I could isolate one thing, but it may be when I've said something to somebody that I think about afterwards. I wake up in the middle of the night and wonder why I said that. **It's very important for coaches, and there are probably going to be young coaches reading this, to be very careful about what you say to players because you can leave scars that last a lifetime and affect a relationship.** Everybody has them in their life. I try not to say something to a player that's too personal. For me it's when I swear at a player. I've tried to maintain a situation where I don't swear at the players, but there's the odd time I have for whatever reason, and I kick myself afterwards and ask, "Why did I do that? That's not the way I do it." That feeling that you've said something or done something that wakes you up in the middle of the night in chills may be something small to everybody else, but it means so much to me. Why did I conduct myself that way? It's not so much one thing, but things you look back on that you regret. In a lot of cases things that you've said to somebody that could leave some scars.

What do you do in that situation?

Usually, if it's something that I can deal with right away I'll talk to that person and try to handle it immediately. So often we avoid communicating with people because we're afraid of reactions. It's important for me to deal with things right away. I'll call the person the next day and say, "I apologize. I was out of line. That's not the way I want our relationship to be, and I shouldn't have said that."

I'm pretty careful in what I say. **In this business I'll never question a player's pride or his courage, because if players didn't have pride and courage they wouldn't be where they are.** I'll appeal to their pride and I'll appeal to their level of courage and I will condemn their lack of commitment or their lack of work ethic and I will challenge players, but I'll never challenge pride and I'll never challenge courage. If you haven't done those things yourself and particularly for me, not having played in the National Hockey League, I don't know how I can question a player's courage or pride. I can't challenge those, and I don't think even if I had been an NHL player I would have challenged them.

How do you deal with team adversity?

During the course of a National Hockey League season there are new experiences every day with a team. I don't call them dilemmas, they're just new experiences that you have to deal with. **To me the best way to deal with adversity is to deal with it before it becomes a problem.** As soon as you see the symptoms, start to deal with it right away, rather than allow it to fester and become a major problem. In terms of dealing with something that you perceive to be a problem, the first requirement is immediacy. Don't let it go until tomorrow if you can deal with it today is the bottom-line philosophy. Don't put it off because then it just becomes a bigger problem. Deal with it; certainly don't sweep it under the carpet. You've got to bring it out and deal with it; it has to be talked about.

It's just like when you sell a car to somebody. A lot of things I've done as a coach are related to my family's association in the car business, and this would be a matter of follow-up. Is your customer who just purchased that vehicle satisfied with the delivery and how it's operating? Go up to a player and ask how things are. "How are you dealing with this new experience?" **Part of my basic philosophy as a coach, and I want our assistant coaches to adhere to it as well, is to make contact with every player every day.** I think if you do that, then some of the adversity that might come up is easier to handle. You have a relationship you've developed, and a person feels comfortable talking to you about it.

The bottom line in dealing with adversity is that players hear more when they know you've been listening, so listen to them. Don't jump into a situation; don't accuse anybody of anything ("What's going on here?"); just listen for a while. Some of the GMs I've worked with, Bob Clarke, Bob Gainey, Dave Taylor, John Paddock, guys of that nature, have been very good listeners.

How do you help individual players when they're experiencing severe adversity?

It depends on what the problem is. You must first of all make sure that life is kept in perspective, that hockey is not the most important thing in their lives. If it's a personal family situation, then you give them the time and space that they need, whether it's missing a practice or doing whatever you can for that individual and caring for them. If it has something to do with the way that they're performing in a game, I think the bottom line is that the players want to be told how to do things, not why they can't, so give them the information that will allow them to correct the problem. Be of assistance to them; give them an outline for success.

For example, I've given a lot of players a little one-page thing that says, "When I play well I ..." and then there's a list of things like "I finish my checks" or whatever you have for that particular player. You give that to them, and then you sit down with them and talk about it before the season. This is the kind of player you are, and this is what is expected. When he's struggling a little bit it's a matter of reminding him to take a look at that and review what he does when he plays well. It's telling them how to do things, not why they can't.

What type of players are the most challenging for you to coach?

For most coaches it's the players who have the ability but not the commitment. It's very frustrating because you have one player who is totally committed, totally focused, does everything he possibly can, but couldn't score a goal if he tried, and you've got somebody else who has the natural ability but doesn't work at his game and maybe doesn't have the right level of team commitment. Those are the most frustrating players.

How do you challenge an athlete who is performing below potential?

The first thing is to let him know what's expected of him—"this performance level has to be there"—and to hold him accountable. Then you have to be prepared to follow through on what you say you're going to do. **That to me is a real key in coaching: Never, ever say or do something to a player that you're not prepared to follow through on. Never say anything to your team that you're not prepared to follow through on.** You have to make sure that you are believable and that people trust you, so you have to find guidelines that you can follow through on. First of all you let a player who's struggling know what's expected of him, and then, if he needs to work on certain things, you make sure that you provide the right level of information to help him get through the struggle.

How about a lazy player?

With lazy players again the problem is accountability, what you expect. Normally they don't last too long with me. It's a matter of showing him, making him try to understand that he is a lazy player and what his potential would be if he just achieved. "What are they paying 40-goal scorers right now? You're a 20-goal scorer. You've got the ability to be a 40-goal scorer, a guy who is making $7 million a year. Are you as good as this guy?" I think it's showing him real-life examples of his capability.

How do you challenge your star player?

You have to let your star players know how important they are to the team and how important they are to the overall success of your team. In my opinion you have to establish a guilt level about how many people they are letting down if they aren't doing it. You want to drive your star players with the same thing that drives me, in the sense that people are depending on them, and they picked the life. **"You were given the ability, you worked at your game, your agent came in at the end of the year and said, 'This guy's a star player,' so it's part of what's expected. You're expected to be a star player. That's what you are."**

Can you read a player's ability to perform by looking in his eyes and at his body language? Do you know if a guy's going to have a good game on a certain night?

I think we've all tried. You look at a warm-up and think, we had a great warm-up and we're flying out there, and then you go out and play poorly. It's very difficult, but I am big on body language. Whether it's in practice or games I am always saying, "Get your eyes up." I hate poor body language, and I'll remind players that it's not so much how it affects them but how it reflects on our team and the message that you're sending to the fans and to your teammates and to your opponents. You never, ever want to show weakness in any area.

How do you handle the responsibility of a head coach? Are you hands-on, or do you delegate?

I'm a big believer that you are only as good as the people you have with you, and I've been blessed throughout my career by associating with good people. I firmly believe that this comes from having been an assistant coach for a lot of years. I know I have to make my people feel appreciated and that I have to delegate and let people do their jobs. I have to give them a sense of empowerment, that this is their role and they are going to be allowed to fulfill it.

How do you manage your time as a coach?

It's an area that I can improve on. I probably work too hard and spend too much time on certain things, but it's just the way I am. I believe in checking and re-checking and making sure that things are in order and probably go a little bit overboard that way. I think my time management could be better.

How important is building an environment to the overall success of your team?

There is no question that environment is everything you do as a coach to set a standard of excellence: the way the dressing room is set up, the way that the trainers conduct themselves, the way the assistant coaches conduct themselves. Every little piece has to be in its place. You can't have any dissenters. Everybody has to totally believe in the program. They have to believe that we're the best team, we've got the best trainers, we've got the best coaches. If anybody wants to talk negatively about anybody in our organization, it better not be to anybody on the outside, because if I hear that people are talking about our people or our players to other people outside, then those people will be eliminated. We deal with our problems internally and that's all about creating the environment.

Describe leadership.

I believe leadership is believability. It's not trying to fool anybody. It's being the person you are, not the person other people think you should be. It's who you are with no false illusions. It's being of strong conviction and knowing where you are going and how you plan to get there and having the ability to convince people of the same thing. It is a matter of having a plan. To me it's all about your profile and the way that you conduct your everyday business.

How important are leaders within the room, and what qualities do you look for when you are selecting captains?

Your leaders have to be an extension of the coaching staff. You have to know that when you walk out of the room your leaders are saying, "He's right. That's the way that it is." **I've always believed that you have to have a minimum of seven strong leaders on your team.** The way that life works there are going to be certain days that someone may not be as capable of leading as he would like to be. You've got to have other people ready to step in.

What do you do to get away from the game?

I don't do a very good job of it. It's something I tell myself I have to work on all the time, and obviously the last few years in L.A. have been tougher because my family has been in Minnesota. Normally in most situations I think family is the best way to get away from the game, but when you're living by yourself there's a tendency to be there all the time. I don't feel sorry for myself because my passion, my work, everything I enjoy doing is related to the game. Certainly family would be the main way to relax. There's nothing I like more than going to my kids' activities and watching them participate in things.

Do your sports principles follow you in other areas of your life?

I'd like to think so. I think most people would view me as a person who is approachable and that I don't have a particular ego about being a coach and that I have time for everybody, and that's important to me. I'd like to be even better in my family situation but it's difficult because of the distances when we live apart. I'd like to think that for the most part the values that I have, I don't just do them in the hockey arena, but I adhere to them at all times.

At times I have a tendency to be a coach at home, and with my level of intensity I think I make it more difficult on my family members than I should. It's something that I'm working at. **When I had my brush with death during my car accident and came back, I realized that although it's nice to be known as a good coach and so on, it's important to be known as a good dad and a good husband.** I think I can be better in those areas. Most people know how much I care for my family and the things I'm prepared to do for them, and would see me as being a pretty good family person, but I think I can be better. I would never want to say there's not room for improvement, and I am aiming at not bringing home the level of intensity that I have in the game.

Who influenced your philosophy and development as a coach?

There are so many people: players, business leaders, and family members. I've been a sponge. It would be very difficult for me to name one person except of course my mother and father. My father Ewart for his patient demeanor and my mother Florence for her passion.

Who has been your mentor?

My father was a real people person. I don't think I recognized how good he was in that area until he was gone. It's something that you are around and take for granted. I've had so many people who knew him tell me about how he treated them or the things he did for them to help them, so there's no question that my father was a real coach in his business setting and in many other ways. I don't think I recognized it until it was almost too late. When you're young you don't take time to recognize those things.

I have also learned from all of the coaches I've played for and coached with, as well as other business leaders. My uncles are involved in business and very successful, and I have learned from them too. I think it's from being around good people.

Dave King

Dave King has earned a reputation as one of the game's most respected figures at every level that he has coached for more than 35 years. King was born on December 22, 1947, in North Battleford, Saskatchewan. He began his coaching career at the University of Saskatchewan in 1972–73, one year after receiving his bachelor's degree in Education. He went on to coach the Saskatoon Junior B Quakers, the Junior A Saskatchewan Olympiques, and the Western Hockey League's Saskatoon Blades and Billings Bighorns. In 1978 he was voted the WHL Coach of the Year. He returned to the University of Saskatchewan in 1980 and led the team to a national title in 1983.

In 1982 King coached Canada to the gold medal at the World Junior Championships and served as assistant coach with the bronze-medal-winning Team Canada at the World Championships. He then spent nine seasons, from 1983 to 1992, as coach and general manager of the Canadian national team. It was here that he became known as one of hockey's brightest teachers and tacticians. In 1983 he led Canada to a bronze medal at the World Junior Championships and a year later coached in his first Olympics, finishing fourth in Sarajevo. In 1986 he helped Canada win the silver medal at the prestigious Izvestia Tournament and a year later captured gold at the same tournament, in Moscow, Soviet

Union. King returned to the Olympic Games in 1988, guiding Team Canada to a fourth-place finish in Calgary, Alberta. He coached Team Canada in the World Championships from 1989 to 1992, capturing silver medals in 1989 and 1991. He enjoyed his greatest Olympic success for Canada at the 1992 Games in Albertville, France, where his team won the silver medal.

King next spent three seasons as head coach of the Calgary Flames, posting a 109–76–31 record. During that time the Flames captured two Pacific Division titles in back-to-back seasons (1994 and 1995), for only the second time in their 32-year history.

King spent three seasons with the Montreal Canadiens serving as assistant coach and director of European scouting, from 1997 to 2000. The expansion Columbus Blue Jackets then hired King as their head coach on July 5, 2000. In 2000–01 he led the Blue Jackets to a 28–39–9–6 record and 71 points, which ranked second among NHL expansion franchises.

Dave King accepted a head coaching position in Hamburg, Germany, in 2003. When he was hired by the Metallurg Magnitogorsk of the Russian Super League, King became the first North American ever to coach hockey in Russia and led his club to a Regular Season title in 2005-06. In 2006 King became head coach of the Malmö Redhawks of the Swedish Elite League.

Dave King received the Order of Canada in October 1992 in recognition of his contributions to Canadian hockey, and was inducted into the Canadian Olympic Hall of Fame in 1995. In 1996 he joined Wayne Gretzky and the 1972 Team Canada squad as recipients of the inaugural Canadian Hockey Awards. A recipient of the Father Bauer Award for leadership, Dave King was inducted into the International Ice Hockey Federation Hall of Fame in 2001. His reputation spans the world.

The Interview

How did you become the coach you are?

I was very lucky to be able to coach in some great situations. I worked with a lot of great coaches at summer camps and have attended many coaching clinics, so I've really been open-minded trying to learn from others. I have always been very attentive to detail. Even when I watched NHL games while coaching at the University of Saskatchewan, I would always see things and then jot them down. I would see a guy make a play and I would make a note of it, and then I'd look at it again. I watched lots of video, and that really helped me to understand the way some things are reoccurring in a game. I learned to rehearse and improve those things so that they can be done more consistently. I can remember defensive zone coverage in the mid-'70s. I was starting to think about how you work in your own zone. My teaching background as a physical educator with degrees in both Physical Education and Education helped me to understand that things can be broken down into steps.

I coached football, basketball, wrestling, and track and field before I coached hockey. From those sports I learned how to take things, analyze them, break them down, and then teach them. There were no books then; there were no coaching clinics. People give me credit for this cycling stuff in the offensive zone! I saw Lanny McDonald, Darryl Sittler, and Errol Thompson horsing around in the Leafs' practice one day, taking the puck up, passing to the slot or throwing it back behind them. They were just horsing around, but I thought it was an interesting concept, you know, like the space behind the puck is a valuable space if somebody can anticipate it. If you can make a play inside, make it, but if you can't and you're under pressure, don't throw it away. Use the space behind. I was able to examine that concept and come up with the term "cycling." I've always been very much a student of my game, and I am changing all the time.

Because athletes are different now, has coaching changed over the years?

That's the key. **Everything evolves. Whether you are talking about technology or about yourself as a person, you are always evolving. Your level of expertise is always developing.** At the start of your career you may be a bit of a control freak because you haven't got all of the answers, and you know it. As you get older and you get more coaching experience, you get more confidence and you change accordingly.

Guys who fail don't change. They have a style that they are just going to stick with and, come hell or high water, that is how they are going to coach. The most successful guys in enterprises try to get some feedback from the people they are working with. Then you have to digest the information and be honest with yourself and admit: This is a comment that I'm hearing consistently from people. Maybe people say that I'm too focussed and therefore not a good communicator. I then have to be willing to spend a lot more time on relationships with players. I have to make more time for players and give other people more of the technical stuff to do. If you seek out feedback and you are not afraid to admit that sometimes you aren't perfect, then you start to evolve and suddenly become better and better.

Is it difficult to listen to feedback on your abilities?

The other thing you learn after you have coached awhile is that expression "Perception is reality." At times coaches tend to be in the spotlight and on the stage so much that when they get a chance to get off the stage a little bit their personality tends to come out. If you are a quiet person who generally is fairly reserved, which I am, and fairly humble at times, people may think you are aloof. That's the assumption; that's what they see. You may really question their perception, but then you realize if that's what they're thinking, you have to deal with it. You have to consciously become a little bit more outgoing. That means, when you are in a social setting, more small talk, more social talk, don't always go to hockey, go to something else, and try to diffuse that perception of being aloof.

And then the media enhances that sometimes because they can create the image.

Yeah, they always do. The media is famous for putting labels on players and coaches, and that is one of the things you always fight. When you get into professional sport, people cover you on a regular basis, and they start to label you. They have to slot you in some category, and it may not always be correct. There are also a lot of good things said about you that are not always as true as you would like to think they are!

In addition to the things players may not have liked about you early in your career, what else did they see in you as a coach?

We had some successful teams. At the University of Saskatchewan I was a hard-driving guy, but that group loved it because they had had coaches who didn't care before, who didn't work hard, who didn't push them, so I was the right guy at the right time for that team. It was amazing because I pushed those guys relentlessly; yet of all the guys I have ever coached, those guys from that three or four years at Saskatchewan continually call me, and they embellish all the stories about how tough I was on them at all the barbecues. They love telling all the stories about the way it used to be and how tough it was, but they needed and wanted that.

Don't you think the players have changed and maybe you've simply changed along with them? Maybe your early style was the right style.

It was a style that was prevalent. That was the way coaches were; it was almost the expectation. I remember when I coached major junior that the guys wanted to get yelled at sometimes. The captains would say, "You've got to yell at us more. Give us hell more."
Coaching has changed. People have changed. Now you have to have a lot more skill in terms of dealing with people to coach, because now people are much more independent. Your players are well coached along the way, and they know the game better than before. Coaching is becoming a bigger challenge now. Before, so many things were automatic. You had a position of respect automatically, but now you've got to earn it, and not just with the tactics of the game, but by the way you deal with people.

What are some things over the years that have kept you focussed and driven to continue coaching?

I have always tried to be a student of the game and the profession. I have always looked back at the end of every season to analyze what I have done and learned. I have used feedback from the players and information from other coaches to make me realize that although what I was doing may have been correct, it could still be changed or altered. I have always felt everything is changing and there are people inventing new technologies and improving things, so in my coaching career I continue to try to improve. I look for better ways all the time without departing from things I really strongly believe in. You can get to a point where you are always looking for new ideas and you are all over the place, so I look at other options, but I have got to be really convinced they're better. Even though we have had teams that have won, I have never felt like I have absolutely done the best possible job coaching. There are some areas of my game I know I can improve, and I have always just been focussed on trying to get better.

I have gone to enough coaching clinics and seminars over the years that I have started to look at what I do, check it out, maybe even second-guess myself a little on some things, but ask questions. I look for a different way of doing things. Is there a better way? Is there a better way to communicate? **I don't change what I believe in, in terms of how the game should be played, but I have been motivated to find better ways to teach it.** I try to find cues that explain it better. That's how I can clarify what I mean to a player. That's part of what I have really enjoyed in the game. I read hockey, I enjoy it all the time, I think of it all the time. Even when the season is over, every day I find lots of time to think about hockey.

Do you believe coaches have a responsibility to motivate players, and if you do, what are some things that you would do to keep them at their peak?

We definitely have a responsibility to motivate. The players also have some responsibility. If you have a guy who lacks a great deal of self-motivation, your chances of getting success from that player are probably limited. **I believe that there is a continuum in everything. There is no such thing as a guy who is totally not motivated, and there is no such thing as a guy who is completely 100 percent motivated in every area of his life.** We have a role to motivate, and I think that's part of our job.

Some players require more time than others, and that's one of the most challenging things in coaching: Sometimes you spend a lot of time on very few people. It's really important if you are going to motivate people that they see that you are always making an effort, always well prepared, always open to suggestions. **If you are asking them to be open-minded and you are not at your end, then I don't think you are going to be very successful.** They have got to see that you are striving to improve your part of the game, which is coaching, and the spinoff is that they are going to respond.

At the same time motivation is an over-used term in the game. Often the real reason why guys play well or poorly is courage. I really believe that. **I believe that some guys play very well consistently because they have more courage than others.**

Courage, as in the physical courage to play the game?

Yes, courage to go into the corners, courage to take the punishment, courage to win the battles, courage to play the inside game. A lot of times we mistakenly call that motivation. Why does a player one night really play inside and the next couple of games he won't do it? More times than not I don't think it's motivation at all. It may be an aspect of motivation, but I think it's courage. **This game is hard to play. Instead of talking to a guy face to face about courage we say, "You have got to be more tenacious, you have got to be more competitive, we need more drive from you," when we really mean courage.** If you are going to play this game well every night and be a very consistent player, then you are going to get banged around more than somebody else, because you are going to be in the action, and when you are in the action, you are going to find body contact. Some guys enjoy it and some guys don't.

Some players have to work to overcome the fear of that type of game, and that's why they are inconsistent. They can do it for phases of a month when things are going well, they are feeling good, and their game is at a good level. **For four or five games they will play very well and really compete, and you will say, "Wow, he is really motivated." No, he's not. He is just in a cycle where his courage is up.** Then it will drop along with his confidence, and all of a sudden you say, "The guy's not motivated." A lot of times it's not motivation; it's courage.

What do you do if you see your players' energy levels dropping through the season?

It's really important that players understand that there are definitely going to be fluctuations in energy. It's human. It happens to us all. There are times when we are going to be more energetic and therefore accomplish more and compete harder. There are also going to be times when energy levels are going to be lower, and all of a sudden that edge that we need to play is not going to be as good. It's important for the players to understand that is a natural thing, that we all have that, that it's not just them. Once they understand this, I think a lot of times they catch themselves and admit, my energy is not good enough, I have to pick it up, I have to address that.

The variation you have in your practices, maybe changing the focus of what you are doing on the ice for the players, and your off-ice variation, can all help to kick-start their energy levels. You can adjust the type of drills you do and the type of atmosphere and tempo you create in a practice. **If your team is more energetic than somebody else's team, there is usually a pretty good opportunity to win those games.** That's where you rely a lot on your leaders, because you need guys who have more natural energy.

Energy and motivation are a closer concept than motivation and courage. That's our job, to somehow find a way to give our guys energy, and I think the key is variation. Sometimes just a different voice makes a difference. That is why you have coaching staffs of two or three because then somebody else can take a different angle with a player. Change of pace, variation — those are the ways you deal with fluctuating energy levels, which usually drop because things get the same. Players can kind of get into a routine, and we all fight routines. It is important to give them something that snaps them out of it a little bit and makes them think about something else. There are all kinds of ways to do it. Sometimes I just tell the guys, "Every time we go by a bus stop have a good look." You'll see a lot of people catching buses to go to work, people who are probably in their 50s and 60s, still catching that bus to go to work the same way every day. Keeping in touch with reality is a great way to upgrade your energy levels.

I am going to get off topic a bit here. **I have coached for a long time, and I have always seen two categories of players: There are carriers and there are guys who have to be carried. I have always tried to surround myself with more carriers.** I have gone back and looked at all my team pictures and asked, "Why is this team better than that team?" Usually I realize I had more carriers that year, more guys who could carry other people, who had more natural energy, who had more natural courage, and that's why they competed the way they competed; that's why they influenced the rest of the group. **If you have too many guys who need to be carried, you are in for a long darn season.**

Can the carriers influence the motivation of the guys who need to be carried?

Yes. They were guys on our team in Columbus like Tyler Wright and Lyle Odelein who came on the ice and loved to practise. They set the tone, and I let them know that I really appreciated the way they did that. Once they realized Coach King liked something, they brought it all the time.

They would naturally do it even if I didn't say anything, but because I had acknowledged something that they may never have thought of themselves, they learned that they could set the tempo. They set the stage and they seemed to kick-start the team to practise better.

Talk a little bit about players who struggle with or lose their confidence. How do you address body language with your players? Is it important?

Oh, it's really important. Your observation skills are very important because some players don't talk a lot. They won't come see you. There are guys who don't like to admit they need help, so you have to be really alert to their body language, to their demeanour, because it tells you that they are percolating inside and something is on their mind. That's why our coaching staff tries to be really alert to how our guys are feeling and to the talk in the dressing room.

We watch guys in practice to see if a player looks like he's got more frustration than normal, if he misses the pass, if he is upset about his play, and we take note of that. We check to see how he has performed in his last few games. Maybe his game marks are not as good as they were, his ice time might be a little bit lower, so you try to be preventive. You try to get to the guy early and then diffuse it early.

Dealing with confidence is hard because most players are confident when you play them a lot and use them in situations that they sense are important. Their confidence will grow accordingly. As a coach there are times when you have to have the ability to say that at this point in the game I'm going to take this risk, I'm going to play this guy in this situation, even though I know right now he is not playing very well and his confidence is low. I'm going to play him here and hopefully he is going to perform, and then I can then use that to kick-start him again. I want to be able to say, "Hey, I played you against their top line tonight, and you played well and did a good job." **In coaching there is risk all the time, and you have to be prepared to take it. I really believe in that theory to have the right guys on the ice, but there are times when you have the wrong guys on the ice because you are taking a chance to give their confidence a boost.**

... for the right reasons.

Exactly. You are saying to yourself, "I am playing him and I am holding my breath, but, boy, if we can get him through this game and situation, give him this role tonight, give him the feeling of importance tonight, then we are going to get a huge gain out of it." Sometimes you put a game at risk because you are willing to do that, but if you don't do that, I think you are going to have a difficult time with your players. The guy with the low confidence level or low motivation knows the score and the time on the clock. They all know the game scenario. They know that if they are on the ice against a top line in the last two minutes of a period, the coach is showing some confidence in them. **I believe it's really important that we take some risks to help some players gain confidence. If we don't, we are going to have a lot of guys who aren't very confident and have to be carried.**

What do you think of the big soapbox speech?

If I coached football I might want to use the emotional part of the game a bit more because I have only 16 to 18 games. We play 82 games plus pre-season and playoffs, so I think you've got to pick your spots. Sometimes it's not that your speech is so motivational or inspirational, so full of fire and brimstone, it's just that sometimes you get on the right theme. You make the players acknowledge that, yes, they can play better. You are honest with them and deliver the message, but it's how you deliver the message that counts. Your team can be having a bad game, and you can go in there and insult them, rant and rave, and it may shock them out of it, but sometimes it will go the other way. I think it's important to be honest and very straightforward. **Most players don't mind the message; it's just how you deliver it.** Most guys want to acknowledge that they are not playing hard enough and well enough, but you can't insult them every time. There are times when you use that a little bit to create an edge, but not all the time. We deliver a pretty good message but not always full of fire and brimstone every night. I don't think players are going to buy that.

Did you try to find an angle for your university, national team, or NHL games to get that edge?

Sure, you can do all the tactical and video preparation you want, but I think at times you have got to find the angle. I will look at stats to see if there are some angles that we can work with to get a little focus for our team. I always have our media guy go back two or three days to see if the press discussed our upcoming game and whether there is anything they've said that might give us a bit more of that edge to play. I use that all the time. I am always trying to find ways to create an angle to make every game a little bit unique.

If our 82 games just blend together, we have no chance of being successful. It's really important that every game is a little different. You've got to create some little scenario with that game, whether it's the use of stats or the underdog rule. Whatever it is, you are looking for ways to create an angle, to create an edge, to create better performance.

At times I will address our team with, "Guys, it's the third game in four nights. A lot of teams can't do this. This is going to be a real challenge." I'm not even talking about the other team; it's our circumstance, our travel. I'll say, "A team that's not strong mentally is going to have a tough game tonight and probably not do very well. You guys can do this. You guys can deal with this. We can deal with this." You are just looking for some way to attack that game. That's all it takes some nights, just a bit more of an edge, and suddenly it's not just another game; you're competing.

Are there any other examples of things you have done over the years?

Oh, yeah, I can go back to very crucial games. I remember at the '92 Olympic Games in Albertville, the Czech national team was very, very talented, and they tended to draw a lot of penalties. We had played them a lot that year, at the Sweden Games, the Izvestia Cup, and in the Czech Republic. We knew them really well. At the right time they found a way to get the power play, and that always made a difference in the game. So at the Olympic Games I told the coaching staff well in advance that if we ever meet the Czechs in a crucial game we have to make sure we get both our guys and the referees ready. I looked at the schedule and the referees were practising right after us. I knew this was a great opportunity to influence the referees as well as our team.

We did a couple of checking drills where the offensive man who had the puck was going to be checked by the player behind him. The player with the puck was supposed to take a dive and try to draw the penalty, just the way a lot of teams do. We did a couple of drills where there is a puck carrier and a chaser for warm-up; you do a little hook and the puck carrier takes his flip and flop. The referees had just come in and were getting ready for their skate. I could see all these guys watching us, and I thought, good, we've got all the referees watching the acting display. It was good for our guys because they were amazed at the way you can make something appear, and how carefully and smartly you have to check. It set the stage for our team because they realized they were going to be playing against guys who draw a lot of penalties with theatrics. It set the stage for the referees a little bit too. In the actual game we were very disciplined. We beat the Czech team 4–2, and it wasn't even close. The power play didn't even become a factor in the game, and I really believe it was because of tailoring and timing our practice to the circumstances.

What's the identity of a Dave King team?

Everywhere I've coached I have always tried to create hustling, hardworking teams so that people see energy. We are well conditioned so we can do that. My teams have always been identified as disciplined. The teams I've had have never been highly penalized. There have been some really aggressive teams. I had really good, tough teams, when I coached in major junior and in Calgary, but I just channelled it right. We have been really tough and courageous, but not stupid. **We don't beat ourselves very often; somebody else has got to do it to us.**

Maybe it's a good thing, and maybe sometimes it's a bad thing, but you can see that we do a lot of things consistently. That's good in some areas of your game, for example your breakouts, but in other areas of your game it might make you too predictable. You want your players to consistently be able to find more than one option, find the middle as much as the wide play. On the power play, though, teams can take things away from you when you are too consistent. People tell me they can see that my teams are well coached, that they know what they are doing, that there is a plan, but in some areas there is a danger of becoming too predictable, and that's the one concern I always have.

How do you establish your team identity?

Part of your identity will be totally dependent upon your team and the skills that they bring to the table. I don't think you can impose a complete identity on a group because sometimes you just inherit a team that's already got a skill set or a number of people with skills in certain areas and deficiencies in other areas. So the balance might not be exactly what you'd like to have, but things like effort and hustle, hard work, conditioning, attention to detail, those are things every team can do.

Most of my teams play the game with a lot of energy, a lot of tenacity, and some have played at a fairly physical level. Our team in Columbus was very tenacious, but not very physical. Tenacity doesn't just mean you're going to be physical, you're going to be strong, and you're going to bowl people over. It can also mean being tenacious on the puck.

I always make sure, at the first meeting we have at the start of the season with every team I work with, that I talk about our identity and what we're going to achieve. Some of these things are going to take more time and they're going to come with the evolution of our people, but a lot can be achieved very quickly. Players have to sense that there's an identity you're driving at, and they have to see that identity.

Do players have any input into the look of your team?

I think they do because once you get a few guys turned on to the identity you're trying to create, then they create some peer pressure that helps you achieve that. They have to be part of the process. When I talk about being an energetic team, it's really important that I talk to my leadership group so they understand why I think it's important. They need to understand what I'm thinking, my vision, and hopefully they see the sense in it. They are the ones who apply some of that peer pressure inside the room. You have to give them that type of input.

Our carriers are the guys who love to have an identity. If I have more carriers than you do, I've got a good chance to beat you every night. Skill is important in ice hockey, but skill is more important in basketball. In basketball the most skilled team is probably going to win. You can hustle all you want in basketball but I still think skill, because of the nature and rules of the game, is still predominant. **In hockey, skill is very important and you want to have as much as you can—don't ever downplay skill—but hustle and effort can definitely, definitely level the playing field in our sport.**

How do you focus players more on the team and less on themselves?

Well, I think the number one thing is to understand that at times they are going to be thinking a lot about themselves, especially when things aren't going well. When it's going very well I think it is easier to have a wider view of the world. **It's the same with all of us: When things are going well we can see a wider picture, but when things don't go well, we all tend to focus on a smaller picture.** If you understand that's a human trait that we are all prone to, then I think you understand that this is not unique to a certain player. It's unique to all of us.

There is a continuum, not a selfish guy and a selfless guy at either end of the scale. They are all somewhere in that middle area. Some guys are certainly more self-centred, a little more selfish than other guys, and then there are guys who are always a little bit more selfless. They seem to be more compassionate toward their teammates, to always see a bigger picture of the game and of their teammates, and have a sense for more than just themselves. You have to understand that teams are like that. It's really important that guys know that when it's not going well we can understand why they are a little more selfish. When things are going very well for them they have to understand that they need to be more selfless.

I wish there was some magic formula but a lot of it is just not being afraid to be honest with the guy. I have no problem saying to a player, "I think at times you are a bit selfish. I recognize I could be wrong, but that's my perception." Players don't like to hear that, but if you deliver it right and make sure the meeting is open and admit that you yourself as a coach aren't perfect, and make sure that the player coming into the meeting understands that he is a good person first of all, I think you can deliver those messages to players. **Boy, if you are afraid to deal with some of those topics with those guys face to face and one on one, you can't coach.** That's the hardest part of coaching; you just can't candy-coat everything.

What have you done to increase team cohesion?

The nature of the game of hockey is co-operative and collective. You achieve more when you collectively work with others.
I took the guys in Columbus to the high ropes course at Ohio State University. When you get on those ropes you've got 10 or 12 guys going from station to station. Everybody's got to be on the same page because you work in pairs, but you still have to rig to the other pairs on the course and, boy, do you learn the importance of dealing with others, communicating with others, and supporting others! Even though you are strapped into a harness and you can't really fall and hurt yourself, you are up high, and some people are not very comfortable up there. You quickly learn you can accomplish very little in some of those situations working by yourself. There are times when you've got to take your teammate's ropes and provide him with the physical support to make that manoeuvre to get to that next platform. You learn that if you support a guy and help him through it, when he gets done he'll provide you with the same thing. There are lots of team-building gimmicks that are very effective and very illustrative to the athletes that teamwork makes a difference.

The other thing we've done with every team I've ever been with was to have our video guy shoot us on the road. He takes footage getting on and off the bus, on and off the planes, at our team meals, and then puts together four or five minutes of funny things like watching different guys eat at the pre-game meals. If you've ever done it, it's the funniest thing you've ever seen. Some guys have their faces in their plates, you know, and the guys laugh like crazy. I've always asked my video guys to be very attentive. If there's something we're going to do that I think is going to be funny I'll warn them, "At practice today I'm going to do a drill that's going to be really funny for the guys. They're going to screw it up. Get it on tape for me."

One of the most important parts of cohesion is encouraging the characters on your team. We had the phantom in Columbus who was always putting shaving cream in shoes. No one knew who he was, but we finally found out. Tyler Wright set up his video camera, put the shoes around the camera lens, and finally, after about two days of filming, caught the phantom. Then the players held court to nail the phantom. You've got to utilize these moments.

Sometimes it's the way you react when something happens that brings everybody together. You can plan and schedule things if you like, but there is a lot of spontaneity that just happens, for example, when the coach takes a big fall on the ice. Use it. Laugh at yourself sometimes. The guys like those kinds of things. There are times they'll play pranks on you, and if you don't react well, you can diffuse what could have been a great situation.

As you look back on your teams that were really tight and close, do you think it was a lot of those things that helped bind them together?

That's why I've always tried to have some characters on my team. I like to have a few guys who are phantoms in the room, guys who do that kind of stuff, because I really find humour is a terrific thing for a team. **I've heard the expression "Humour is a great team lubricant." Well, it really is, and I think a lot of that is spontaneity. You can't plan it; it happens. It's then all about how you capture it.** We've had guys come on the bus sometimes, and they look like heck, and you can tell they have had a good time on their day off. If you get angry it's a very negative atmosphere, but if you make a joke about it, it can be very, very effective.

There are always a few guys who like to draw humour on themselves. Their dress code is always a little lower than everybody else, and you can give them little hits and all the guys appreciate it. You plan as much as you want—it helps—but you've got to capture the moments when they happen. That's spontaneity, to grab that moment and make it work for you. That's huge.

How do you establish and communicate a tradition of excellence within an organization?

Tradition comes from being successful, and there are a lot of organizations in hockey that have a tradition of lack of success. You don't want that, so I think it's really important that you are able to achieve a certain amount of success to help you to instill the tradition you are looking for. **Tradition and identity are inseparable. I think when you create an identity it generally gives your team a consistency that, over time, leads to a tradition.**

Tradition is built day by day when you have good attention to detail. People can always see that you are well organized. People can sense that you know where you're going and that there is a vision to what you are trying to achieve. Tradition only comes if you have disciplined people, and it is difficult to achieve because it takes so much mental and physical discipline.

A lot of organizations can't achieve a strong tradition because they don't have enough strong people. They have too many people who have to be carried. I'm talking now about management and coaches. There is a relationship between identity and tradition. It's really important to acknowledge what past people have done, whether they are players, management, trainers, coaches, or whatever.

There are teams that will go up to the top and drop off, and there are a few teams in every sport that somehow keep their programs up there year after year. What separates those teams?

Great leadership from the staff is a very important part of it. There is a vision. People can see that there is an expectation and a good atmosphere. Many subtle, small things, like dress code or deportment, establish expectations. All those things relate to establishing identity and a tradition. I think it's really important that your staff, whether management, coaches, or trainers, clearly understand where you are trying to go, so they are always trying to get there too. They are creating that tradition by their performance. You've got to have the right people to do that. It takes time.

It's an evolution. When you get good people, don't lose them. Unfortunately this is much more difficult with salaries going up. We are seeing so much change in our team's personnel from year to year because we can't afford players. Sometimes we lose key people who really are part of our core group. We try to keep our core, but our core is now becoming very, very expensive.

The most important thing in professional sport is to recognize that some players bring cohesiveness and chemistry to your team, and they carry a price tag that's worth something. We've got to acknowledge that some guys do bring more for your chemistry than just goals and assists. There are times that you can let some of those guys go because they get too expensive, but are they? They make a difference; they set the tone. You can tell that the good organizations really know their core guys, the guys that really, truly make a difference. Sometimes you'll see a team let a player go that you thought was one of their core guys, but they know he's not. They know he's a pretty skilled player, he brings pretty good numbers, but they know more about the person than we do because they have had him. They are letting him go because they have a tradition they are trying to maintain.

A lot of tradition comes when you have continuity in coaching, continuity in management, and continuity in vision. Coaching staffs change a lot now in pro, but in college and junior you get a chance to stay with a team a little longer and put your blueprint on the team. Hockey organizations that stay with coaches through the good and bad times have a better chance of attaining a tradition.

When visions change all the time, it's because coaches and management are always changing. You then establish a tradition of inconsistency. Everybody who comes in seems to have his own idea, and there is no direction. Consistency in people leads to consistency in performance, and that leads to tradition. That's why I like it when teams recognize that they may not have had a great year, but it had nothing to do with the coaching. Maybe it was injuries or other things. The trouble in professional sport is that if you have a poor season you have to show the season ticket holders that somebody has paid the price. Otherwise they're complaining, "What the heck is going on? They had a bad year and they haven't changed anything?"

What would you consider your greatest accomplishment?

My greatest accomplishment has nothing to do with championships;

it's the fact that a lot of the guys that I have coached have gone into coaching, either full-time coaching or in youth hockey. I just think it's terrific when I see a lot of guys I've worked with now coaching. I know for sure then that I've done something right, and it makes me feel good that they must have enjoyed the atmosphere and environment with me.

Clare Drake should be very proud of his coaching. He won scads of National Championships with the University of Alberta, and I am sure they were all very good, but I'm sure Clare would look back on how many coaches he has influenced and how many players he has influenced as a coach. That is a really nice feeling. That is a great satisfaction.

How do you define success?

Well, the media will define success as winning and losing, your record, your winning percentage, but you yourself know that you coach in different circumstances. Sometimes you coach really good teams that are favourites, strong teams that should win. Sometimes you coach teams that are going to struggle, and you are going to have a heck of a time getting wins. Every year you redefine success based upon what you think you have to work with, and sometimes that doesn't jive with what the fans think or what the media think. **It's important for every organization to define what success should be for that group.** They might not be public goals. We defined success as the level of performance that we felt was achievable with this particular group.

We won six games the first year I coached the University of Saskatchewan. I think they had won only six or seven games in four years before I started, so I didn't walk in and say, "Guys, we're going for the gold here. We're going for a National Championship." I dealt with the process of trying to improve. That year I talked about only one thing: Let's improve; let's get out of the basement. That was going to be our goal.

It took us till the last game of the year to beat the University of British Columbia and escape the basement. It was like we won the championship. We were pumped; we were almost 500 and we were out of the basement, and they hadn't been out of there for so long. It was a great feeling. And then next year that same group of guys, with a few changes, got to the National final and lost in the last minute. So you define success every year depending upon your personnel, the strength of the other teams, and where you're going. Then it's important to let the players know what you expect.

What did all your successful teams have in common?

Lots of character and a lot of guys who didn't like to lose. **I look at all the pictures of teams I've had that won more games and were more successful, and clearly there were a lot of guys on those teams who were carriers and a small number of guys who needed to be carried.** They were guys who had a lot of pride in what they did and hated to lose—I mean, hated to lose. That's why they were so hard to play against. It sounds so simplistic but that's what it is. You need more guys who are carriers.

What are your most valuable skills?

I think they are simple things. I work pretty hard; the players sense I'm well prepared. The players know they can talk to me. There was a time when guys felt that maybe I wasn't very approachable and I intimidated them with what I was doing. I honestly feel now that there is so much good coaching going on, that when players come to me they are not as intimidated by me because they've played for good coaches. There was a time, back in the '70s, when guys would come to our program with the national team or the University of Saskatchewan's team, and they couldn't believe I taught forechecking and defensive zone coverage. No one else had ever done that, so they were afraid to ever second-guess or talk to me because they thought I obviously had all the answers. Now more and more kids come to me who are well coached, and they aren't afraid to ask questions or ask for clarification.

If a player asks a question I try to never put him down or embarrass him. When a guy asks me a question I never, ever want to give anybody the impression that I'm questioning his hockey sense. I believe my players feel safe when they ask a question. They know I'll take it seriously. I think I am more approachable now.

I have changed so much since I started coaching. I've gone through phases. When I started out I was a little bit insecure and much more of a control freak. As I've become more secure that I know the game, and am doing a good job, I am more confident in my work. I was able to recognize, around the middle of my coaching career after so many people had said I was very technical or aloof, that I didn't mean to be that way and I could change. Sometimes you don't like to do that, but you have to because, as I said before, perception is reality. I know what I am doing now makes sense. I know it's the way to do it. I'm thinking more and more about player relationships because I'm more secure with other parts of my game. I've become more and more a player's type of coach.

Are you the same away from the game?

Not quite the same. When I'm coaching I'm performing. There are times when I have to keep people really focussed. I'm very much in a leadership role. With my family the same thing exists but I'm more relaxed. I am much more of a marshmallow! I have to lead and push so much all day that when I come home I try not to coach as much, even though parenting is coaching.

At one time there was a big difference between how I was with my family and how I was with my teams, but that's starting to shrink. I am more and more the same person, which is a big surprise to me because there used to be such a distinct difference. A couple of my players said to the media this year, "It's really hard not to play hard for Coach King because he's like my grandfather." They obviously enjoyed having me around. More and more I find myself becoming the same person as a father and as a coach. I guess it's because I have become more comfortable with myself.

What do you do to relax and get away from the game?

I am a daily runner. My run is as important for my mental state as for my physical state. I like to get away early in the morning. It gives me a chance to think about some of the important decisions I've got to make that day like my lineup, or what I can do for a guy who's not playing well. Then I come back, have my cup of coffee, and arrive at the rink very early because I like the feeling of being well prepared. I have to have that. When I feel rushed I am not as good, but when I feel well prepared and ready and have had a chance to think, I am better. Routine is very important for me and relaxes me.

Secondly, I really enjoy going for a walk in the afternoon on game days. I don't nap. I don't sleep. I do my work, and then I always go for my walk, no matter what the weather is. It's another chance to have some time on my own with no one interfering, and not always to think about hockey, just to relax. Sometimes when I jog by hospitals in the morning, I think, boy, there are a lot of people in there who can't do what I'm doing. Or I will go by somebody at a bus stop and see a person who hasn't got very much, a disadvantaged person. It keeps me in touch with reality.

Of course my wife Linda is terrific too. She really enjoys hockey, but she knows there are times when I need more relaxation. She will suggest we go to a movie. In fact, she will read our schedule and create a few things for me to do that are good, but relaxing enough to keep recharged.

And during the off-season?

My wife says I don't relax enough. In the off-season I really enjoy things like canoeing and swimming. I love the water. I'm a tremendous gardener. I love planting and tending a flower garden, which amazes some people, but I really enjoy it. My flower garden is a form of relaxation, and it's a little like coaching.

In the off-season I find it's important to get away from the game a little bit. I still think hockey every day and read hockey almost every day, but it's more relaxing because I am more into what other people are doing every summer. I always take notes from five or six old coaching seminars I have attended with me to the lake and go through them again, and it's amazing how I will highlight four or five things that somehow I missed. It just keeps me thinking, and then I also enjoy reading what other coaches do. I like books by other coaches. I find it very relaxing to get a book by another coach in another sport and read it.

How have you recovered from a bad situation?

I think one of my worst moments was when the Calgary Flames didn't renew my contract. They said that they wanted to make a change. That was the first time a team ever told me, "Thanks, but no thanks." At first you try to be positive and deal with it. You know you want to work, so you don't say too much. You feel you did a pretty good job, but you realize you've got to find another one, and the main thing is not to burn a lot of bridges.

I dealt with that part of it, but then when that's all said and done there's a period of time when it's like somebody in your family has died. There's a time of mourning, and you really feel bad about it. You shouldn't second-guess yourself, but at times you do, and that's not fun.

You start to think, where am I going from here? You critique yourself and your performance, without pointing fingers. You might disagree with the decision but you should look at what you did well and what you didn't do well. Analyze it a little bit, talk to a few people who have gone through it, which I did, and find out what they think about it. What was their reaction? You start realizing other guys have gone through this, and they start giving you a few tips on what they did. I called guys like Pierre Page and others for advice, which was funny because Pierre ended up getting the job!

How did you get back on the upswing then?

I just started to exercise more. I went for two runs a day instead of one. Linda was great. She encouraged me to take an inventory of myself. She said to me, "Look at your resume. Look at all the guys you got into coaching." So I went back to my resume and realized it wasn't too bad. I realized there were other opportunities. She asked me questions like "Do you want to coach in Europe?" and "Are you still pretty healthy?" So you start to take stock and build back your confidence, and it takes other people sometimes to help you with that; you can't always do it by yourself. The one thing I can be guilty of is refusing help. When things aren't going well I often want to do it myself. At first I was like that, and then I realized others have gone through it, so I talked to a lot of people and started to heal.

Was there anything else in your career that you would say would be one of your worst moments, when you thought the world was caving in?

I was very disappointed in the results of the 1988 Olympic Games. We finished fourth and were 5–2–1. In those days the format was unforgiving, and we lost the wrong game. Finland beat us 3–1, and that bumped us out of the chance for a medal. We had done so much work for that particular event. I was never disappointed in the players, but I was disappointed in myself. As I look back, **I feel that at that time in my coaching career I was way too focussed. I didn't enjoy the trip nearly as much as I should have.** I pushed and pushed and pushed. I was almost relentless, and I think that was a turning point in my coaching career because I realized I've got to ease up here; I've got to see a bigger picture. I was very disappointed, but I told myself I was going to stay until '92 and do it differently.

So you enjoyed '92 a lot more than '88?

Absolutely, because I mellowed. I started to find more time for the players. I started to enjoy the trip, the process of getting to the Olympic

Games, having more fun with the players. It just became much better, and I enjoyed that quadrennial more. I changed the way I did things. It was really good for me to become less focussed and more aware of other things. **I thought more about my players as people and what they were going through. I got into their skates more than I was in my own skates.**

In '88 I was far too focussed on the fact that we had to get better, we weren't good enough. It was tougher too in '88 because the NHL was untouched. There were few Russians and Czechs in the NHL, so those national teams were tough. By 1990 suddenly there were some Russians in the NHL, so I knew the teams we were playing weren't going to be quite as good. Eighteen of the Russians went to the NHL, and most of them are still there.

I decided to just widen up and enjoy the process a little bit. I looked at the situation and asked, "What is success?" From '88 to '92 my view of success was enjoying it. I wanted to develop players, and hopefully they would stay with us, but they might go on to the NHL. I wanted to have a good and competitive team, and as long as we played really hard and we played every game the best we possibly could, I was going to be satisfied. I can honestly say I went into the '88 Olympics thinking we had to get a medal and into '92 thinking we just had to play well and see what happens. I knew I couldn't control all the factors.

We got into a shootout with Germany, of all teams, and we could have been knocked right out. We might have finished fourth again but a puck went through Sean Burke, dropped down, and stopped on the line. We scored on the next shot and won the shootout. There you go. Now all the heat was off and we were gone, we just took off. We played well and won a silver medal.

How do you deal with team adversity?

At some point in the season on every team there is some adversity, so don't think you're the only guy it has happened to or it's going to happen to. Every year in coaching there will be some points of adversity, when your team is not playing well, they're not playing together, or something has happened in the team that caused a controversy.

I just use the common sense approach. If we're in a situation where our team is experiencing adversity and I sense we're not on the same page, I talk to the other coaches. I talk to my captains. Do they see that there is a problem, and how big is it? **When you see the problem as a coach, you can make it bigger than it is.** So I usually try to find out from the assistant coaches and from my captains and from other people around the team, the trainers for example, what are we dealing with here? How big is this? What do they see? What's the scope?

Then I try to clarify what it is, without making assumptions. Never assume it's because one guy is causing a problem. I try to get an opinion from everybody in our organization who's closely involved with our team, and if I get enough people saying, "Yes, I think there is a problem," then we'll sit down with the team. That's when you have team meetings. You'll bring in some food after practice and sit down and just talk through it. "Our observation, guys, is that we are not playing really well together right now." Usually you gain some information. You know that something has happened. Either the team is losing its confidence because they're not getting enough wins—that happens, that's just slumps, that's adversity— or there can be internal problems.

Before I do any team meetings I always call my captains in. There is never a surprise team meeting. I've called them in, said, "Guys, this is where we're at right now," and asked for their reaction. After they give me some feedback, I'll ask if they think this warrants a meeting, or whether there's another way they can deal with it. Usually I have the players help me with the strategy. They may say, "Coach, you've got to come in. We've got to talk about this," or one of the guys will say, "Coach, I think this is the way we should be doing it. This is what I would do." So I don't surprise them with a team meeting. The captains know it's coming; they'll keep it to themselves, but they know it's going to happen.

The other thing I've done by giving the captains some advanced warning, is given them a chance to think about it too. And very often they do step up to the line and say the right things because they've had a chance to think about it. It's not a surprise like, "Whoa, where did this come from? Out of left field?"

How do you handle confrontation?

Confrontation is really tough. There are times when you can sense a player does not like you or the way you coach, and you are not really enamoured with him either. First I make sure I really check it out. I ask the other coaches and maybe the trainers how they read this guy. I don't want them to be afraid to tell me if I'm wrong.

I don't like to talk to the captains much about other players because that's awkward for them, and I don't want to compromise them. At times I will talk about a player without telling our captains who it is.

Before a confrontation I will ask my assistants to spend more time with the player, on and off the bench, to see if we can diffuse this thing without it starting to fester. I use the old train, transfer, terminate thing. Termination is the meeting. If the guys are saying, "Coach, right now you've got to meet with this guy," that's when you have your meeting.

In your meeting you have to make sure the player understands right away that you don't think it's just him. "Obviously we are having difficulty, and I recognize that some of it could be me and some of it could be your responsibility. I'll bet you it is a bit of both of us." Right away I make him feel like we want him and that I know he's a good person and I know that some of this could be my misunderstanding, that my perception of reality might be wrong, but I do think some fault is his too. Then we start to get into the conversation, and when it's all over I just make sure I thank him very much for coming in, that I appreciate his candidness. I tell him I was trying to be candid and honest with him, that I might not particularly like how he's playing for us, but I know he's not a bad person; he's just not doing what we want him to do right now. I tell him I'm glad we had the conversation and that I've learned a little bit about him and his thoughts on the situation. I respect that and say, "Hey, tomorrow is a new day. Let's go."

I've learned so much from those confrontations. It's easy to start to get into a contest with a guy, so I never, ever go into those meetings emotional. I always take time to think about it, ask other people, plan what I'm going to do, and I'm ready and relaxed and I know we can get something done. I've been pretty successful, I think, in getting a lot of guys turned around. Even though they think I'm a hard nut at times, they're surprised that I've done my homework and they're surprised in a one-on-one meeting that I'm willing to admit that, "Hey, I'll bet you part of the problem is me."

What type of players have been the most challenging to coach?

The guys who have to be carried are always the most challenging players to coach. Sometimes it's lack of motivation, sometimes it's lack of courage, and sometimes it's laziness, or lack of fitness. Of the categories mentioned, the most difficult guys to deal with really are the guys who lack the motivation, even though I have found that term to be overused. There are guys who, for some reason, care sometimes and don't care other times. They are just not courageous enough and can only deal with this at certain phases of a year. Particular teams intimidate them. I guess guys who seem to lack that second effort and drive are the hardest to coach. Those are all intangibles that are hard to create. You can deal with a guy who's got limitations in his game skating-wise, but a guy who hasn't got enough courage to play the game, that's real tough. Those problems are hard to deal with, and my recommendation to all coaches who read this book is: Don't have too many of those guys. You're going to have some, since there are no perfect teams, but don't put up with too many of those guys.

How do you deal with an athlete who is performing way below his potential?

I've always taken the positive approach. If I think a guy is underachieving, I'll say to him, "I'm going to challenge you. I'm going to put you up with the best players. Maybe you're thinking in your mind you're not playing with good enough players, so I'm going to answer that for you by putting you with the top people so that there's no possible way we can have our next meeting and you can say, 'I'm not playing with good enough players.' I'm going to take that and diffuse that, so there's your challenge. To play with those guys you're going to have to compete. You're going to have to hustle."

You've got to give a guy at least one or two chances in a positive vein, and then after awhile you may have to get to other strategies like "I've given you all kinds of opportunities. Now I may have to reduce your ice time if this continues. We've tried. You can see we played you for four or five games here. Here are your ice times. Here's the amount of power play opportunities we've given."

I like to follow the old train, transfer, and terminate theory, the three Ts of business. Train is used when you've got a guy who has a problem; give him extra training with video or conditioning, whatever it might be in our sport of hockey. Then transfer: Change positions, change lines, transfer the communication with them to another coach. Finally, terminate. You get to the point where you say to the guy, "It's not working, so that's the best thing for both of us." Termination can be just a temporary benching or it can be a permanent termination. Sometimes the press box is the best place for a guy to re-evaluate where he really is and whether he really wants to play. Again, it can be really negative if you deliver it that way, but it can be done positively, if you say, "The best thing for you right now is to go to the press box and watch us play and think about your situation. Watch some other people and then re-evaluate where you are." Those are the three Ts of business, and I think they are pretty applicable to coaching.

How do manage your top players?

There's a misconception that your top players always have to have a lot of exceptions to the rules. Top players, top performers sometimes do things on the ice that aren't quite what you believe in. They may not be the complete player you'd like to have. Some of your top scorers score because they cheat a little defensively, but you have to look at what they're doing for you. There are certain times in the game where they should cheat—maybe you need a goal—but there are times when you hope they're thinking more about the other side of the game. With star players you can't have huge double standards, but sometimes there are some double standards that exist because if they were playing 100 percent the way you like defensively they may not be as good offensively. They may tend to leave the zone always a little bit ahead of the puck, but their judgement is pretty damn good, and eight out of 10 times they're right because they anticipate a bit more offensively than somebody else might. You have to live with some of that because that's what makes them good. All players can't be the same; all players can't be good in every area. As a coach you learn to live with that and understand that they bring something special to the table.

How do you get the most out of your players?

I work really hard and pay attention to detail. It doesn't mean I'm programmed or over-focussed any more than I used to be, but I just think the guys see that we are a well-prepared team. We try to make sure everything in practice makes sense so there are few surprises. I make sure the guys understand why we're doing something. I've always said to myself, if they know why they're practising it, there's a pretty good chance they're going to do it in a game. Then guys start to understand that you know what you're doing, and you care about performance.

I believe the coach sets a standard. We set a standard by our deportment, the class we have, even by how much we laugh. All those things can affect your environment. I really believe if players are having some enjoyment they're going to play better. It's an old cliché that players like to have fun, but I really believe more and more that's a huge factor. The season cannot be a torture test.

In my first year in Columbus we sat down and said to the players, "We're going to go through some tough times. How are we going to deal with that? What if we get out of the gate and lose our first 10 games?" We only won one of our first 11, but we were so prepared for that. We said we weren't going to change, we were going to stay positive, and we talked about growth and discussed all the possible problems we could have and how we were going to deal with them. I said to the guys, "We're not going to do anything to de-motivate this team. There will be enough of that with the level of teams we play against. We can't be a burden to this team. If it's a bad game, we'll show them a few clips maybe, but our script will be positive. It will be that we can rectify these things. We'll also show a couple of things where we can see some improvement." It's really important not to de-motivate your team. We had problem times and had some team issues sometimes, but we never let it get to the team. We always made sure that we could have a laugh through it. I asked my trainers to smile every morning. **We hired a lot of staff who are energetic, upbeat people because we wanted to create that environment, and your environment is everything.** It helps your team prevail. We had so much fun together and we had such a good environment that when we were struck by injuries guys would step up and fill the hole.

How do you handle all of your coaching responsibilities? Do you delegate or take on certain loads yourself?

I remember coaching with Guy Charron, a terrific person with great people skills. With the national team leading into 1988, I tended to do all the technical, tactical stuff, and Guy did most of the relationship building. I was in that phase of my coaching career. He had more time for the players because I didn't burden him with too much technical preparation because I did most of that myself.

Since then I've changed. Now I still do my preparation the way I want, but I find a lot more time to be part of the environment building. I don't delegate that to anybody else. I've taken much more responsibility for working on the environment for the last six or seven years of my coaching career, and my other coaches have worked on the video and game preparation.

How have you dealt with your assistant coaches, trainers, equipment people, and people who work in the office?

In some cases I inherited staffs, but in most cases I've had a chance to build my staff, and I've always tried to find people who complement me, who are different from me. They bring other things to the table. I've always looked for people who I know are upbeat, with lots of natural energy. I don't like a lot of people who are going to whine, complain, and get weary of the whole thing. I like guys who get up in the morning and get going, so I've looked for those things. We ask all those people, even the doctors, to be upbeat and positive. Our staff is very much that way. They are asked to be that way all the time.

I've tried to employ the right people, and I've always had meetings with the staff in the summer time. We have lots of meetings about the environment in the room as training camp approaches. We set the tone and review some situations that could happen, making sure we know how we are going to deal with them.

Talk about the dressing room environment.

There are a lot of things about the dressing room environment that are controlled by its actual construction: the amount of light, the type of furnishings, the set-up in terms of the players' lounge, where the weight room is. We have one bulletin board for family notices and one that is more the NHLPA stuff. We acknowledge birthdays for everybody, births in the family, even difficulties with the family. If a player gets his 100th assist we make sure all the guys know. It's in the game notes, but some guys don't read those things. Those are all the little things that make the environment effective.

I like to have lots of banter in the room. In Columbus I encouraged my assistant coaches, Newell Brown and Gerard Gallant, to get out in the mornings on a regular basis, get into the players' lounge, have coffee with the guys. I can get coffee in the coaches' room, but I go down to the players and have my coffee down there. We always go for strolls through the weight room and to the physio area. We're visible every day. We have our area down here at the very end of the dressing room, but I think we spend more time out in the players' area. Players want some separation at times too, but it doesn't mean you can't be in their territory at the right time doing your thing. We're visible; we talk a lot to the guys; it's upbeat.

How do you manage your time?

I'm a list maker. I make lists every day. I have a list right now on the bulletin board in my office of what I've got to do after you and I are finished. Then I just prioritize the most important things. I like to do the most important things early in the day as much as I can and then do the things that don't take as much time later. I tend to be better the first half of the day; it's the best part of my day for doing things on off days, non-game days. I'm a list maker. Otherwise I overlook things; I forget.

What is your management style?

It has changed. I'm more a facilitator coach than I was before, but that changes throughout the season too. You start out with, "This is the way we have to do it, guys," not dictatorial, but you're very firm. You've got to train and retrain your guys that this is what is expected. It doesn't mean you've got to be a hard-ass or impolite, but in a very enthusiastic way you are very demanding. You're selling, but as things get better you become more the facilitator.

What do you look for in your captains?

My captains are very important because there are times when I don't like to have a lot of team meetings. **The captains can often set the stage for you if they're informed about what you're thinking.** I meet with the captains every week to discuss what's going on with the pulse of the team.

I look for stability in my captains. I like them to be very talented too, but more than anything else I look for a player who I know is stable and whose teammates recognize that trait in him. He's a guy you can count on; he's one of your carriers. Some coaches slap As and Cs on guys because they want them to change. I don't like doing that. That to me is not a good place to experiment. I would like my captains to be respected by other players for the way they compete and play and practise. I always make sure the captains know they set the tempo.

I make sure that they know that I trust them. I talk to them about issues without ever compromising them in front of their teammates. At times I will ask them how the players are feeling. Your captains have to know you respect what they say, but that doesn't mean they dictate what your team is going to do. You have to ask their opinion. When you do that and you trust them I think that they feel good about coming to you again.

You establish a relationship where they know that at no time are they the messengers. I tell the team at the start of the year that I will meet with the captains once a week, so if you see them down with me, it's just a regular meeting to discuss where things are going. I don't want to compromise the guys.

I like the captains to feel like I trust their judgement, and at times I'll ask them what we should do, for example, "Here's our schedule for the next week. Here are our games. Is there a day you want off?" We also set a monthly schedule that the captains help us with. They get some input into our schedule for every month, and once we give days off we never change. Even after a stinker of a game we never change. I have never gone back on that since I began coaching pro hockey. When I say it's a day off, it's a day off so the guys can plan with their families. I want them to know well in advance that they could possibly babysit the kids or take their wife and kids out to do something on that day. The captains like that. They feel like they're guiding the ship a little bit.

How much of your top teams' success can be attributed to leadership?

A lot of success is leadership because you only achieve as a coach as much as you can get out of your players. If you want to get more out of your players you have to have a good relationship with your captains. They are the guys who can establish some peer pressure. I have had captains say and do things that were huge. I got the credit for it but I knew the captain did it. It's really important to acknowledge that. I try as much as possible to acknowledge our leaders to the media. I don't so much pick out one guy, but I'll very often say, "Our captains really want to do this tonight." I try to use the media as much as I can so that when the guys read the newspaper in the morning they can see that I do acknowledge what they bring to the table, that their opinions count. When we give them a day off and they play well, we say that the day off was the players' decision: "They told us as a coaching staff to give them that day off, that they would play really well, and they delivered." I try to use the media as much as I can to make the guys feel good.

Do you trust your instincts?

Totally. I love that part of the game. **If coaches ever become afraid to trust their instincts and second-guess themselves, they're crazy.** There are many times in the course of a year when I know I'm taking a chance. I know it isn't the highest percentage play, but I get a feeling that this is the right thing to do. I know that I can get that player on track. I can give him a boost that may be huge for his career. I used guys killing penalties last year who have never killed penalties before in their lives!

Some coaches will always play the percentages. I know in baseball there are stats on this guy batting against that pitcher in this circumstance. That's good, and in my coaching I try to play percentages too, no question. **I'm not a Mississippi gambler, but there are times when I'm going to say, "Uh-uh. I'm going with this, and this is the way it's going to be, and if it doesn't work out, not a problem, I'm accountable for it. I'm prepared to take the heat."** There are times too when it really backfires and that guy really doesn't come through. Those are tough times because you've given a guy a real vote of confidence and he didn't come through for you. I'm prepared to take the consequences; it doesn't bother me a bit.

Describe your leadership style.

I strongly believe that I'm much more optimistic than I used to be. I really work at being the optimist: "It's not that bad, guys. We can play better. It was an awful period, yes, but I know we can play better. I've seen you play so much better. Shake it off. Let's turn the corner here." **I don't like to grind salt into the wounds. I've given up that strategy. I stay away from de-motivating my team.** My leadership style is to find some solutions, turn the page, and stay positive. The guys are surprised sometimes after stinker games how I'll come in and just talk common sense to them. I do that, and then I leave the rink.

Do you talk to your team after every game?

Every game. I do it even if it's a stinker. I'll say, "Guys, that was not good enough, and I think you know that. We can do some things to improve it." They are never surprised by what I talk about the next day in the paper because I've basically told them what I'm going to say! I never drag it through the newspapers. I refuse to let a newspaper reporter drag me down a road I don't want to go. I'll just ignore the question he is asking and answer another question, and he'll look at me like I didn't ask that question. "I don't care. I'm giving you this answer. My job is not to write stories for you." I never let those media guys take me down an alley anymore. I've had it done to me, and I've been reeled in by a few of those guys, but now I refuse to do that. I'm not going to single out people in bad games at all, and I always make sure in the paper that I'm telling people that our guys know we didn't play well, and I'm really happy about that. I know our team doesn't feel good about the way we played so they'll find some solutions for it. I've taken the approach that you've got to be really positive.

I guess when I got fired from Calgary, and rehired, I realized that generally I'm a very positive person but when I get into coaching mode situations sometimes I get so focussed and so intense I lose the positive aspect of my personality. I decided that I was no longer going to lose that in a coaching situation. I stop myself now, better than I ever have before. I tell the players that getting angry is easy, and, "even though it's hard for me to talk to you the way I'm talking, this is what I'm going to do. We can play better. I know that you know that."

What are your thoughts on team vision?

It's interesting that you talk about vision because it's one of those buzz words now, but it's a pretty accurate buzz word. **With every team I've ever coached I had a picture of how I wanted the team to play at the end of the season, and I made sure that the players knew it at the start of the season:** I would like people to describe our team this way at the end of the season. I would like them to say that we never quit, that even when we were down we sure were working and hustling and giving a good effort, that we were obviously a team in very good condition because we could work like that. I'd like them to say that we were a team with speed. I'm really a big fan of speed in my game. I love guys who can skate. I'll forgive some guys if they can skate and change tempo. I tell the guys this is what I want when the season's over, that if people said this about our team I would be really happy.

Everything we do in practice is related to that, and I will continually talk about that in practice. I don't like to do a drill if the guys don't understand why they are really doing it. "We're a speed, tempo, and pursuit-of-the-puck team, and that's what we want in this drill." You don't just say it once either; you repeat it. After awhile the guys know this is what I want, this is what I expect, this is where we're going, this is the kind of team we are, and there's your vision. You have to impart your vision to your people in terms of day-to-day coaching; it's not just a big meeting at the start of the year. That is where you paint the picture, but then you've got to work on it every day. **Vision, after awhile, leads to an identity, and after awhile identity can lead to tradition; that's the sequence.**

Do other people help shape your vision, or do you shape it and then others help define it?

Other people have to help you shape it because in professional sport, where you have a management team that's going to have scouts identifying and drafting players and signing free agents, you all have to be on the same page. In Columbus our vision and identity was struck by our group, including management, because there is no point for me to have a vision if they don't help me get the players who can create that vision of our team, that identity, and hopefully that tradition.

This is where difficulties occur in some organizations: The coaching staff may have a vision, which the management may not share, and they never really find time to discuss it.

I made sure our trainers were part of the process with the University of Saskatchewan Huskies and the Canadian national team. Our board, with members like Sam Pollock, knew what we were trying to accomplish, the type of team we wanted to get, and the identity we were trying to create. They were all onside and were given a chance to provide feedback. I believe your core group has to understand the vision. They see it, they understand it, and you hope they buy into it. All players won't fit the vision, so that's why there's change; that's why there's a termination.

Do you have a unique awareness or creativity that allows you to observe something and bring it into a drill or strategy?

Yes, but I don't know why I have that trait. I can see something and realize that it is something we could have some fun with and could add to our game. I see it, and then ask, how do I get it across to my players? That's why I have so many key words, cues and stuff. People call them "kingisms." I'm just trying to find descriptions so that the listener can say, "OK, I've got you now." Because of my experience and background as an educator I have been able to make things simpler. Some people think I am making the game complicated. I don't make it any more complicated; I'm making it simpler. If you're organized in your zone, is it not simpler to play?

When I used to play we had the wingers cover the points, and then it was mayhem down below. We had no idea. You'd leave a guy and stay with a guy, and you didn't have any idea what you were doing. We were just taught one defence. We had no guidelines, no advice. Today we simplify the game for the player. It doesn't mean you have to restrict them. **I have always told the guys that basically I'm asking for one-third of the ice, maybe half. Give me half the ice and we'll call that the coach's game. The other half, the offensive end, can be more your game.** People often say technical coaches make the game so complicated, but I can remember when the NHL teams started to hire the college coaches as assistant coaches because they wanted that information. They knew it was going to make their teams more consistent.

Do you teach life lessons in addition to hockey lessons?

More and more I'm totally that way, although at one point in time I don't think I was at all. When I first started coaching I just coached. Winning games was everything. The more I coach I realize there is a lot to learn from the game that can help with life skills. Since the '88 season I have been continually looking for those situations and pointing them out. They can easily lose touch with reality because their standard of living is huge, and a lot of people cater to them. I want to make sure that they are always in touch with what's going on out there.

How important is it for minor hockey coaches to teach those lessons to their players?

I think it's absolutely important to teach those lessons to kids. There are so many parallels with what is going to happen to them in life, things like dealing with adversity, or having to get things done that you don't like to do, or the feeling of working together. There are moments when your team knows. When they come into the room you can just sense a satisfaction that they did it tonight. It wasn't a great goalkeeper or this or that; they all did their job. Those are great moments. I'll say, "Guys, that was a terrific collective effort tonight. That was unbelievable. We had so many guys deliver their game tonight, and that is really impressive." You've got to capture those moments.

In the university textbooks it always said that you could teach a lot of life through sport, but it's amazing how you get so immersed in the sport that you forget the life lessons you can teach. The more you coach, the more you realize that when you do that for the guys they become so much more rounded, they see a bigger picture, they are just better competitors.

Who shaped you as a person?

My parents, for sure. My mom and dad were just terrific people. They both died at age 71, very young, five months apart, but they were both wonderful. My dad was a really terrific father, a really hard-working guy. I can remember him always having time to play catch with me, or coming out to the rink. He always had time for us. He was an insurance man, and when he became what they called a field-training instructor he worked western Canada, so he travelled quite a bit. As busy as he was, he always created time. I'm always appreciative of my dad. My mom was a great lady. She was very ill for most of her life, but I remember one time when she took me in a toboggan. My little brother was about three or four, and we had to play a game in Saskatoon at Victoria School. My dad was on the road and my mom couldn't drive, so she put my little brother, in his snowsuit, on the toboggan, put my hockey bag in the back, and walked down to the rink with me. It was about 20 below. In those days you played until 20 below. She stood in the snowbank and watched me play. I often tell that story, and it gets my emotions up every time. That was my mother, and she was a great lady.

Was there anybody else in your younger years who really had an impact on you?

I had a lot of trouble in school until my Grade 5 teacher, named Helen MacMillan, told me, "Until you get organized, young man, you'll struggle with your school." I was very disorganized. She was the one who got me into making lists. Helen MacMillan helped me to understand that if I was organized I could achieve more academically. She was one teacher who really affected my development. She got me on track. I was probably going the wrong direction in terms of school because I was always in trouble. I didn't really care much about it and didn't see any reason to work hard at it, but she had a way.

She was also a very athletic lady, and she was the first person to ever acknowledge that strength in me. She would say, "I see you scored two goals last night," and boy, she caught my attention! She had read in the paper that I scored two goals in a hockey game the night before! Well, I was motivated. I wanted to perform in school for this lady because she was taking the time to find out what I was doing. She knew that I was a good hockey player, that I played ball, and boy, did she flip the right switch for me. I've never forgotten that; she took an interest in me beyond me as just a student. I wanted to impress her.

Who influenced you as a coach?

Clare Drake and George Kingston come to mind. They're right up there at the top of my list because when I was a young college coach in Saskatchewan they were very established coaches at the University of Calgary and the University of Alberta. Boy, do they know their stuff. I was in there with some guys who knew what they were doing, and that made me realize I had better work because these guys were smart hockey coaches.

George had so much European coaching experience. Their power play was so impressive. It was new to all of us because George had brought it over from his European experience. Clare's teams were just so good at every aspect of their game. They were so consistent, they worked so hard, they were everything you want in a team, and you could just sense that they were all on the same page.

In 1978 I was a young pup at the Olympic camp with Father Bauer, Tom Watt, Clare Drake, and George Kingston. It was unbelievable. It lasted two weeks, maybe the best two weeks of my life as a coach because I discovered that there was so much to this game. They made me realize that I should look at everything, that I should study the game. Clare had some progressions for things I thought were so simple, yet so effective. To this day I still use Clare Drake's drive skating progression all the time. It's a classic, a work of art. They really affected me a great deal.

Whom do you turn to when you need advice, help, and opinions on things?

Linda, for sure, is a good resource for me in so many ways. Professionally, George Kingston is a guy I talk to a lot. He had a great influence on me because he was a great coach, he enjoyed music, art, drama, was a fabulous carpenter, a father who raised great children, and Wendy, his wife, is a fabulous girl. They had a great lifestyle, this family. George made me realize there's a lot more to life than just coaching, and that coaching didn't have to mean you had to be in a rut. I did get caught in a lot of that for a few years from '84 to '88, that rut of just hockey, hockey, hockey. George made me see that there's a lot more to the game.

I also call many of my coaching comrades and ask their opinions. People like Wayne Fleming, Wayne Halliwell, Clement Jodoin, and the late Roger Neilson all enjoyed sharing and helping. We all realize after years of coaching that we still don't have all the answers, and we may at times be too close to the situation to see the obvious. For these reasons I have never been too proud to seek opinions from others.

Scotty Bowman

Scotty Bowman, the "winningest" coach in NHL history, was born in Verdun, Quebec, in 1933. Although readily acknowledged as one of the NHL's most superb coaches, Bowman's original plan was to play professional hockey. An injury changed all that, and when the Montreal Canadiens sponsored minor hockey teams in his hometown, Bowman decided to begin his coaching career at night while selling paint for Sherwin Williams during the day. In 1956 he was offered an assistant coach/assistant manager job with the Montreal Junior Canadiens. The team advanced to the Memorial Cup finals in consecutive seasons, winning the championship in 1958. Bowman moved on to his first head-coaching job with the major junior Peterborough Petes, an affiliate of the Montreal Canadiens. He took the team to the Memorial Cup final in his first season and never looked back.

When the NHL expanded in 1966–67, Lynn Patrick hired Bowman to be his assistant coach with the St. Louis Blues. Patrick relinquished the head-coaching role to Bowman on November 22, 1967, and the expansion Blues went to the Stanley Cup finals in their first three seasons, winning two division titles along the way.

In 1971–72 Sam Pollock convinced Bowman to return to the Canadiens organization, and the Montreal Canadiens won the Stanley Cup after his second year. It was the first of nine Stanley Cup celebrations for

Scotty Bowman as a coach, and the beginning of a particularly success-ful time in Montreal's hockey history. After winning the Cup in 1973 the Canadiens missed the finals the next two seasons, but then proceeded to win the Stanley Cup for the next four consecutive years. During that run Montreal won six divisional titles in eight years and scored more than 100 points in seven of the eight years that Bowman coached. The only year they failed to score 100 points, they scored 99 instead. The team lost only 11 games in 1975–76, eight games the next year (a record that still stands for the fewest losses in a single season), and 11 in 1977–78.

After coming off a Stanley Cup victory, Bowman left the organiza-tion and joined the Buffalo Sabres as coach, general manager, and director of player personnel. He remained with the Sabres for eight seasons before leaving in 1987. In 1989–90 Bowman was hired by the Pittsburgh Pen-guins' GM, Craig Patrick, to be director of player personnel. Under coach Bob Johnson, the Penguins won the Stanley Cup in Bowman's first year. The next season Johnson became ill, and Bowman took over the team on an interim basis. Sadly, Johnson did not recover and passed away that year. Bowman continued to coach the Penguins to another Stanley Cup victory in 1992.

Scotty Bowman was hired by the Detroit Red Wings in 1993–94 and spent the next nine years establishing them as one of the NHL's best franchises. In 1995–96 Bowman coached Detroit to 62 wins, setting an NHL record for most wins in a single season, which surpassed his own re-cord of 60 wins, set in the 1976–77 season in Montreal. Detroit also set a new franchise record by reaching 131 points that year. Prior to Bowman's first Stanley Cup celebration in Detroit in 1997, the Red Wings had been without a Cup since 1955. The revitalized franchise energized Detroit, and the team went on to win Cups in 1997, 1998, and 2002. The 2001–02 season was Bowman's last as a head coach, though he continued as a consultant to the organization. He finished with a league-best 51 wins, 116 points, and Detroit's third President's Trophy and 10th Stanley Cup.

Scotty Bowman's all-time coaching record is 1,244 wins, 583 loss-es, and 314 ties. His winning percentage is an astonishing .654. He has 233 playoff wins and has coached a record number of 2,141 games. He has coached four teams (St. Louis, Montreal, Pittsburgh, and Detroit) to the Stanley Cup finals 13 times with a record of 36 wins and 22 losses in 58 games. He has won nine Stanley Cups as a head coach (surpassing his hero Toe Blake's record of eight) and one as a director of player personnel, and he is the only coach in NHL history to have won Stanley Cups with three different teams.

Scotty Bowman has also coached in 13 All-Star games and won the Jack Adams Trophy as Coach of the Year twice. In 1991 he was inducted as a builder into the Hockey Hall of Fame. He was inducted into the Michigan Sports Hall of Fame in 1991, the Buffalo Sports Hall of Fame in 2000, the Michigan Jewish Sports Hall of Fame in 2001, and the U.S. Hockey Hall of Fame in 2002. In 2001 Bowman received the Lester Patrick Award for outstanding service to hockey in the United States, and the Wayne Gretzky International Award in 2002, given annually to an international citizen who has made a major contribution to the growth of hockey in the United States. In 2003 Canisius College granted him an honorary doctorate of humane letters. While other coaches can be measured in games won and lost, Scotty Bowman is measured in Stanley Cups won and lost. His dedication, longevity, passion, and pure results are second to none in the sport of hockey.

The Interview

How did you start coaching?

I had a passion to play hockey from an early age and wasn't interested in very much other than the time from mid-December to mid-February when we had outdoor ice. I was one of those guys who had skates on at 8:00 in the morning and never came back for lunch. I made a good midget team, and we won the Provincial Championships. I played in high school and made a junior team at a young age.

Although there were only six teams in the league, I never once thought I wasn't going to be an NHL player. My only dream, to be in the NHL, was shattered when I was in my late teens. When I got injured at about age 17 I knew I wasn't going to be able to play anymore. I don't know if I ever wanted to be an NHL coach; I just wanted a job in hockey.

Still, at the time I was pretty fortunate. Montreal had tabs on me because I was a junior in their program. Mr. Selke told me, "If you want to go to school we'll look after your schooling, and we'd like you to coach a minor team in your hometown." That's basically how I got started. I got a job working in a paint company full-time. I'd finished high school, went to my business course at night while I was working, and coached the bantam and midget teams. I was only a few years, maybe four or five, older than my players.

When I was about 21 I got an opportunity with an independent Junior B team that was looking for a coach. I just happened to know the guy who was hiring; his parents and my parents were in the same church together. He told me there was no money involved—I think it was about $450 overall—so I never thought of it is a job. It was a great opportunity to be coaching at such a young age. We had some good veterans, our team somehow clicked, and we got into the league finals, beating some sponsored teams on the way.

After that the Montreal Juniors were moving to Ottawa and were looking for some young guy to learn the business. I got a call from Sam Pollock asking me to come to Ottawa, and that was my first full-time job. It was 1956 and I was 23.

The underlying factor with me is that I have never gotten up a day that I was thinking I should do something else. Only once, when I was in Montreal and had a young family in the late '70s prior to going to Buffalo, did I get a call to see what my interest was in coaching Michigan State. The job didn't pay very much but you start thinking about sending your kids to college. They told me, "If you come here you will get tenure and your kids will be able to go to the school." In those days NHL coaches were not making terrific money. I think when I was in St. Louis doing two jobs I was making $37,000. Then after I left St. Louis, Montreal offered me a coaching job for $30,000. After that I just kept signing and never really thought about the money. They never offered more than a one-year contract, and I never asked for more than one year. It was automatic, first year $30,000, next year $40,000, $50,000, $60,000. Finally I got to $90,000, and that's when I went to Buffalo because they were offering me both (coach and general manager) jobs. When I was in Montreal with my young family I gave college a little bit of a look, but Montreal was such a good team to be with, I couldn't leave. I didn't have any ambition to do anything else.

Over the decades that you coached at the NHL level, did you see a real change in your responsibility to motivate the player?

My first start was a good start. When the league went from six to 12 teams we got a sprinkling of players who had been on NHL rosters, but most of our players came from the minor leagues. They were players who just couldn't crack the nut of the six teams, fringe NHL players. In St. Louis most of the players were coming off minor league contracts of between $6,000 and $8,000. It seemed that the normal salary in the NHL was about $15,000. A lot of our players were in their mid-20s, some even older, and they were given an opportunity to double their salaries. So the players were very motivated. Players who had been in the minor leagues maybe three or four years were finally getting an opportunity to play in a league that had looked, for a while, more like a place where they might only have had a cup of coffee or short stay with an NHL team. That was a big part of the motivation during the first three or four years that I spent in St. Louis in the late '60s.

When I went to Montreal of course the motivation for the players was different. In Montreal it was really a strange start because they had a big upset in '71. The Canadiens won the Stanley Cup; Dryden just came out of nowhere. Boston was really building a winning program when Orr went there in '66. The Bruins won the Cup in '70 and '72, and they should have won it in '71. If you look at the standings during the regular season they wiped up most teams, but they found a way to lose and Montreal found a way to win.

I was starting with a team that was getting a bit older. The motivation to try to win in Montreal was huge because of the people. **I always felt that the pressure in Montreal brought the best out of good players.** Having come from there and having lived through the eras of their big '50s when they won five in a row, and the five more they won in the '60s, and into the '70s, I know first-hand it is a terrible disappointment for the people that you meet during the off-season when you don't win the Cup. That was the big motivation for that team in the '70s.

Later in your career in Detroit, after things had changed a bit and salaries had gone up, was it more difficult to motivate players?

I think the correct term would probably be to "integrate" some high-profile players into a team. Trying to stress that they take the individuality out of their game was not easy, especially as more players came in during the late '80s and '90s. With free agency came the ability to earn a good salary, but it was predicated on their own performance rather than that of the team. **The motivation was to get them to think as a team, as opposed to individually, and that's not that hard. You'll run into the odd**

player who swings more the other way, but most players want to be in a good program.

Over the last couple of decades, with a lot of Europeans coming in, how has that integration worked?

I've always thought the players from Sweden have been brought up in a more team-oriented environment. The Russians, unless you've got them at a young age, come over and have to be integrated into the team because they play a little different style and have a little different mentality. For the most part I found that most of the Russian players have never taken a back seat as far as contracts are concerned. I think you just have to know who they are, how to handle them, and that their mentality is a little bit different. The Czech Republic players have yet another mentality. I always wondered if those players would be able to integrate with the North American players, especially come playoff time. The whole thing of growing up as an American player or especially a Canadian is that the Stanley Cup is the end result, and nothing else counts.

Guy LaFleur once said to me, "I lost my confidence for scoring goals." Can you sense how confident your players are?

I think it depends on the relationship that you have with certain players. Obviously players you've had for some time have confidence in the coach. One of the most humorous things that ever happened to me occurred when I was coaching in St. Louis. We had a team that battled pretty hard. I had coached Barclay Plager in junior, but he was a player who bounced around a little bit. When he was 17 he came to me in Peterborough, and I knew he was going to be a good player, even though he didn't make it right away. He was just a special player who had a lot of character and a lot of try in him. I could pretty well do with him what I felt. I could push him to the limit because he had that kind of mentality. One day I was upset with him because he hadn't played up to the mark for about a month, and I called him in. I said, "Barclay, you haven't touched anybody in a month. Look at your record: You've got three assists. Even your penalty minutes are down." I just gave all the bad things that I felt he was doing. I finished it off by saying, "Besides that, you have no confidence." My point is that you treat a lot of people differently, and I think it's important for a coach to know there are fragile egos on the team. I really think that is probably one of the things that has changed the most in my coaching over my time.

How do you and your staff handle team preparation?

When I first started there were a lot of group sessions and meetings on strategy. You still have some meetings now if you want to address the whole team, but I started wondering why I was sometimes addressing the entire roster on the power play when there were only eight guys on it. I'm not sure when we started it, maybe in Detroit, but these meetings that you have with a team are not as effective unless you bring in two lines at a time or maybe the penalty killing group.

It's a lot of preparation. At first we had meetings in the mornings at 11:00 a.m. You'd have a quick rundown, and that was it. Now it seems that for a 7:30 game in Detroit we jam in 45 minutes of short meetings, from 5:45 to 6:30. When we want to change things up we bring in one line at a time for about five minutes each. Now it's become more individual. I don't know how the other teams do it, but I don't think team meetings are as effective for strategy sessions as smaller groups are. In Detroit we used to zero in and show any video we felt was necessary. That's when Barry Smith and Dave Lewis would generally handle some of these things. Even in the last couple of years, when we would have the defence and the goalie come in, I often just left the room and left it up to both Dave and Barry to handle the defencemen. They would go over with them what I thought we should be doing better or what we should be trying to look for.

How do you evaluate performance?

We had a system in Detroit where the three coaches would rate the players after each game. The system we used to rate the players was accumulative between the three of us. Then after 10 games I would give the players their ratings. We changed it a little bit later, but this didn't work as well. I didn't think I was getting the right reaction, so I decided to let the players rate themselves. I tried a lot of things as a coach.

The ratings started in Montreal when I did it for the general manager so he could look up Game 9, for example, because when you're coaching and playing you don't remember games two months ago as much as the one last week. Claude Ruel and I would rate players and then give the results to our general manager, Sam Pollock. We had ratings categorized from 1 to 5. I picked the number system up from the late Bob Johnson, who was interested in golf, so the lower the number the better your performance was. It was like a 1 to 5 but we kind of zeroed in from 2 to 4. If a guy had a horrible game we gave him a 4. We didn't give a lot of 4s, and there were some players who never got a rating lower than 3. It was based on your ability to perform. We very seldom gave Doug Jarvis a poor rating because he worked hard every night and he was not an offensive player. Maybe it's a little bit skewed, but I think you gain the most when you have some players who are not always as consistent as they should be.

In Detroit it was a lot of work getting the numbers tabulated, so I had a guy who was big in computers print a graph. This might show that the team's norm was 3.2, and all of a sudden you have a good game but you were 2.8. This showed where you stood individually against the team. I don't know how much that really plays into it, but it made the players aware.

When I got to Detroit I made a big production out of posting the league standings. I put the power play and penalty killing on the board and listed the top 10 in each category. If we weren't in the top 10 there was a space at the very bottom for Detroit that showed our place. They were posted near the shower so the players would pass by them often. I was very emphatic with the guy that I held responsible for keeping the records. We had a third guy in the dressing room, and it was his duty every morning to go to the front office before the players came in. Realizing how important it was, he would get the numbers and different percentages from the PR department, and then come into the room and post the results. I would get upset if it wasn't accurate. I wanted it up-to-date. The odd time I would quiz the team. I asked them not to look at the board and tell me how many points we were ahead of the next team or what our record was in the last 10 games. Those were times when we talked to the whole team. When I wanted to zero in on strategy, we generally did it individually or in a small group.

What happened when the players rated themselves?

It lasted about two segments. They didn't really think it was beneficial, so I said, 'Fine, then, take my ratings."

How important to you is the big soapbox speech prior to the game or in between periods?

I think it could be effective occasionally, but when it's done a lot maybe players come to expect it and tend to tune you out a bit. In Detroit every year we had a guy over from Windsor who was good at taking very high-profile movies and doing voiceovers. We did *Patton*; we did *Gladiator*; we did *Braveheart*. I would spring these on the team prior to a big game. I picked the seventh game or when you needed to win a game on the road or just for the playoffs. It was a humorous tape with a message. We were going to do this, we were going to do that, and it had the voiceover. The players are big movie buffs. They know movies, especially some of our guys, so they would get a kick out of this. They were short, just five, six, or seven minutes, but that was only once in awhile.

I think you could arouse their emotions with a certain speech, but the important thing was finding the right time. Is it before they go on the ice for the warm-up or before the final suit-up? You know the players have a routine. I did make a rule a couple of years ago. I said, "You can do anything you want, but before you go on the ice for the game, at five to seven, I want those five minutes. I need them, and you'd better get in the habit that those are my five minutes." Sometimes you felt obligated to say something. Sometimes you weren't going to say anything.

Are you a philosopher coach who tries to teach your players life lessons?

Sometimes I bring up things that are not related to the game like why someone is successful and others are not, but I'm not big on that. I don't make big speeches. I try to make fewer with more substance. You are better to make a couple of points than ramble on.

Did you feel the dressing room environment influences team success?

Yes, very much so. I think it's important to have the players respect each other. That's important for a team because they spend a lot of time in the dressing room, a lot of time.

I like the history of the team's tradition. I feel it is important to make them aware of their surroundings so they can sense what that tradition is. If there are some good traditions, you want to make the players aware of them. I really think the right dressing room and the right equipment and training facilities go a long way.

Did you approach certain games with a specific angle for the players?

Basically, if we were playing a very competitive, comparable team,

I very seldom wanted to praise the other team. I remember when Roger Neilson worked with me he would be saying, "Don't let him shoot. He shoots bullets." We knew he did but I didn't want to make our guys think about that if we were playing against a good team. If we were playing against a lower-level team or a team that was out of the playoffs, and those games are dangerous because you might not be ready to play, then I was more apt to exaggerate the opposition's abilities. I would put the team on record and say, "Yes, they've only got 32 points after 40 games, but I'll tell you what: They got 10 points in their last 12 games." Often I found it a little more meaningful to talk about our team. You still have to make reference to the other team, and we used to do that with videotapes. If you're playing Vancouver you've got to have some good tape on what they do on the power play, it's been pretty effective, or if you're playing Detroit the same thing. I didn't like to spend a lot of time on the opposition because I didn't want our team to be in awe of them, but at the same time you don't want to underrate a team that is over-performing.

What were the identities of the teams that you coached?

I think I'm like most coaches. Even in Montreal you wanted them to have pride in their defensive game and work ethic. **On a really good team the role players—the foot soldiers—stand out to me. You can't have enough of them.** Game in and game out their performance is very level and their work ethic is good. I've always felt the most important thing is to have role players who accept their role. Sometimes it's not an easy role. It means no power plays, and it's usually crunch time when they have to perform. **Role players are the most important component of good teams.**

When I first arrived in Montreal the one thing we used to talk about was that come the playoffs you can never tell who might be going down with an injury, or might have just gone dry, and that's when your other players must be ready to come in and perform. Some are players who could have performed but hadn't been given the opportunity. I tried to stress that you can never tell who might come through if your top guys don't play. You're probably not going to be successful, but a lot of players can rise to the occasion.

Everybody strives for the Stanley Cup, but only one team wins. Did you have a vision for each team that you coached, a sense where each of your teams fit, and particular expectations for individual players?

One of the things that used to bother me was when people thought we had an automatic win coming up and I wouldn't feel that way. It's kind of a funny feeling, but when people overrated your team you couldn't hide behind the fact if you had all the tools and weren't performing. You just can't say, "Well, you didn't win." **I always took this theory as a coach, which I think is important, that if Ryan Walter scored 50 goals last year and now this season he's on target to get 20 or 30, I felt my job was to get 50 goals out of him. If he's not getting 50, only 30, then it's also my responsibility.** I don't think a coach can say, "We didn't win this year because last year he got 50 goals and this year he got 30," because now you're talking about yourself. There are some players you can't get through to, but you still have to take part of the responsibility.

I think as a coach I used to try to make it as comfortable as possible. You have to give your top players protection from pressure. You have to give them the nod when there is an opportunity to really make up ground. **If a coach isn't on target with all of his players and if your lead dogs ever think that you're not in their corner for them to perform to the best of their ability, you've got a real problem. I think that's a creed that a coach has to take.** It's his responsibility if a guy's got the numbers. I know that coaches sometimes get a guy who's a goal scorer, and even though he's got a high number of goals, suddenly they're not happy with his defensive play. I think sometimes it might be better to try to get them to score 60 rather than try to play defence. Otherwise the player gets confused. You don't have to play that player in certain situations if he can't come through, but he scores 60 goals.

How did you keep players focussed on what was good for the team?

It's not as difficult when you're doing something for the first time, but it comes into play when you have maybe won a Cup or two. You see the players' focus changing a little bit, and that's the toughest time to bring them in. I don't think it's difficult to focus them when you're on the rise.

When you have a team on the rise it's important to bring in a few new players, but it's also important to have a strong core. We were fortunate in Detroit because we had the same coaching staff for nine years. I was there with Dave and Barry nine straight years, and that's kind of unusual. The nucleus of the team, if it's on the right track, should stay together. That's a really important part of it because with the exception of Dallas in 1999 when they won the Cup—I looked it up the other day—

no team since the '70s has won the Stanley Cup that didn't have a minimum of 10 players who came up through that team's system.

Lately it's a little more difficult. We played the Islanders in Detroit last night, and it was amazing that with all their poor teams of the last decade, they had only two players on their roster who have played their career as Islanders. Other than DiPietro in net and a player named Martineck, every other player came from somewhere else. You have to have some players who come from within. It's a little different now because you have to go out and get players, but it was very much the case until about three or four years ago. That is an important message to your team. I don't think that it's difficult to keep them focussed when you are on your way up.

When I first went to Detroit I was told how good Steve Yzerman was. I only knew Steve Yzerman as an opponent. Detroit had never really done great things. I called him in, and he was very quiet. I told him what I thought was going to be important for him to do: "You scored 65 goals. You've got 160 points. You feel all the pressure on your shoulders that if you don't score every game we're not going to win. This team is getting better so it's important for you to do a lot of other stuff." I tried to tell him this wasn't unusual by recounting the following story about Jacques Lemaire. When I coached Jacques Lemaire in junior hockey in Montreal he was a shooting winger. He had a tremendous shot, but he wouldn't play any defence for our team. I used to get upset with Jacques when we were playing against some good teams and I had to use a younger kid instead of him in some situations. I once told him, "Jacques, if you keep playing the way you are, you aren't going to make the NHL. They're not going to pick you up because you don't play defence." He was tabbed as a future Canadien, and he took it so seriously. His dad had died when he was quite young, and his mother brought him up. She actually called the Forum and said Jacques was devastated because I told him he wasn't going to make the NHL. He didn't do much in junior, but I turned him around. He was a scoring winger, and then he became a thinking centre. He turned into a very valuable player, and now he's one of the better coaches in the game because he stresses discipline.

Why do so few organizations reach that level of excellence?

They might break down in their philosophy. Eventually you realize you've got to stay with it for the course, despite the many factors that can happen. Maybe you're losing patience with a young player, for example.

Every time you change, someone else is coming in who infiltrates through the team. **I really think if you get into a swirling atmosphere of constant change, that's what hurts you the most.**

How do you define success?

I became a firm believer that you don't have success overnight unless you've had some adversity, and that goes back to the time that I first started coaching. My very first year in St. Louis we had a rivalry with Philadelphia. We were coming home to win Game 6 in a bitterly contested series, and all of a sudden with 15 seconds left in the game they scored a fluke goal to tie the game 1–1 and then won it in overtime. That was the lowest I've ever been. I remember going into the dressing room, and Glenn Hall, our goaltender, said, "Well, things are dark right now, but when we get up tomorrow the sun will probably be shining," and we took that adversity into Game 7 and won. You're going to have adversity. There are very few people who haven't had adversity before they had success. Teams stumble a little bit and they come back with a better game. That's one of the most important things about success; it doesn't come without a price.

Over the years did the fear of losing motivate you more than the success and enjoyment of winning?

I always thought that the fear of losing only surfaced when our teams got into the final. You play games in your mind about how close you are to the end and yet how far. It is true, especially in hockey, that the team that loses in the Stanley Cup finals hardly ever gets regarded as the second-best the way the runner-up in the Super Bowl does. Maybe it's because I started with three years in the finals, being a big underdog, and not winning a game, going 0 for 12, and wondering if we were ever going to win a game. When you're in the finals you're always thinking, we're this close, we're not going to drop it now.

What do successful teams have in common?

In our sport goaltending is a big factor, but for the most part the ownership of the team was huge. I've been close to some of the owners. My first year in Montreal, Molson sold the team to the two brothers Edgar and Peter Bronfman. They were around the rink, but they never interfered. They played hockey on Sunday mornings with friends before we practised. I think the team got the feeling that they would do anything to win.

In Detroit Mike Ilitch is the same way, and that feeling was there even in Pittsburgh with Howard Baldwin. In my first three years with St. Louis our ownership did things that were unheard of. We lost four straight games in the finals but they happened to own a hotel in Florida where for three straight years they brought all the players and their families, as well as the scouts and the coaches.

Success comes from ownership, goaltending, and I've always been thinking that you can have a fire-wagon type of hockey but your ability to play good defence has got to surface. **The thread that ran through all of my success was undoubtedly ownership's commitment to win.** I've been quite close to some of the owners, and the Bronfmans' passion for the game as owners in Montreal and the Ilitches' commitment to create a winning team in Detroit contributed greatly to our success.

What would your most valuable skills be in developing a successful team?

I believe my ability to stress competitiveness and concentration are really valuable. Concentration to me is huge because you go into the game with factors that could take your mind off the game. I was involved with the scoring of the U.S. Open when Tiger Woods was playing in it. I had met Tiger Woods about six months before, and he's not a huge hockey fan, but I was within 10 yards of him for a four-hour round and he never even saw me. He was totally focussed with his caddy. When it was all over he turned to the lady who was also scoring and to me, noticed my name tag, and said, "Scotty, what are you doing here?" There are hockey players who have that intenseness about them. I try to keep calm on the bench but at the same time give them the feeling that they know what they're going to do. **That's so important as a coach: getting the team focussed and in the zone.**

Do you trust your instincts or gut feeling to make decisions?

Usually when I had a decision to make and something else ran through my mind, I would try to get back to the first thought I had as quickly as possible.

Do you or your coaching staff win at all costs?

I don't know about winning at all costs. **You have to have the mentality that you're going to do everything you can to win. I always felt you leave no stone unturned.** You can't magnify the smaller things, but Kenny Holland likes to tell this story that happened when he first took over as general manager after we won the Cup in '97. The next year, in '98, we were going into the finals, and I told them that I thought it was wrong that ESPN was putting a camera on the clock. I was concerned because if we happened to flip a puck and it hit the clock in our defensive zone, we would have a faceoff in our defensive zone at the wrong time. Little things like that would bother me. I wanted the game to be won on the ice, not on some ESPN camera. Ken agreed to go to the guy who put it up there and say, "I'm sorry, but it's got to be changed."

I don't want the playing field to be uneven. The photographers' circles, which are cut out in the glass for them to shoot through, were getting bigger and bigger in the corners of the arena, and that's fine for them, but what if we're defending a lead one night and we shoot the puck off the glass and it goes through the hole? Now we've got a faceoff in our zone. Some rinks don't have them, some have them small, and ours you could put two pucks through. I would be conscious of that stuff. It bothered me that when we went to Colorado their bench was a lot different from our bench. So we made a small bench and brought it with us. **I want the edge; I don't want the other guy to have the edge.**

How do you handle pressure?

Initially when you first start it must be huge, but it's so long ago for me to remember. At the later stages of my career the pressure didn't seem to bother me as much, maybe because I had been through everything, so what else could happen? What I did do is stick to a general routine. I think the one thing that you should do is stick to your routine. I'm a stickler for that.

Did you try to focus on solutions or any sort of method to get you out of pressure situations?

It's important to try to analyze and be darn truthful with yourself, what really is taking place, rather than complain about it when it's happening. You've got to take it, break it down, and have a counterattack plan. I was more focussed on what we were going to do and naturally what we couldn't do as a result of the other team. You've got to focus on them somewhat.

How did you recover from your worst moment?

I think the worst moments are when you get to the end and you don't make it. You try everything that you think might change things, and then it just doesn't function for you. My first year in Buffalo was tough. We had good teams but we didn't have the right mix and we didn't have any good, solid veterans. We were up against some pretty good opposition.

It takes time. I bought a small farm down in Baltimore, and my kids were young enough that they weren't in school yet. As soon as the playoffs were over I stayed down there until September. I think the worst time as a player or coach is when you get eliminated. The first week or so is tough, and after that as time goes on and you get closer to the next season, that's when you have to change things.

How do you deal with team adversity?

The good teams know when adversity is facing them. Keeping them abreast of how you feel is important. **I don't like to sugar-coat much if things aren't going our way, and that's one thing players get a feeling for. Players want to know when I say something that I mean it and believe it.**

Which types of players are the most challenging to coach?

Generally players who come in from somewhere where they didn't want to buy into the program are always a challenge for you, but I've had all kinds. The guys are a lot different now from when I first started. I look back on it now and realize how good these guys were as players and how good the teams were. When you're doing it and performing you never really get a chance to tell them. I could have, but it really wasn't my style. If I see them now, like a Dryden or Savard, even if I had an average rapport with them when they were playing, I often comment that I didn't realize how good they were. When I watch games now that Serge Savard played in I know I never realized how he made very few errors. He played something like Nickalus Lidstrom, who never makes mistakes, never gets caught, and doesn't take a lot of penalties.

How did you challenge an athlete who was performing below potential?

You can do it a lot of ways. I think if it's a young player and he is struggling, you have to make him aware of what's happening but at the same time you've got to give him the opportunity to get out of it. Some people don't do that. They get upset or they get mad. I never really got upset, but obviously if he does it over a period of time you have to get him back on track as fast as you can. They have to be informed of your expectations. I think that's the toughest part of coaching.

How would you get the most out of a lazy player?

If he's lazy, somehow you've got to get him over the hump. Actually there were a lot of players I suspected weren't in as good shape as others. Trying to get them into shape is always a big challenge. Just keep after them; don't let them drift; it's not going to go away. Wishing is not going to solve it; you've just got to keep after them.

How do you deal with confrontation?

I didn't mind a confrontation with a player. I observed, when I was in Pittsburgh, that the late Bob Johnson was a very non-confrontational person, but he wasn't a softie. I couldn't do that. I observed what worked for him, but I think you have to do what you feel you can to change or improve, so I didn't mind confronting a player at the right time. There's a right time and a wrong time. Those times are very individual and you have to be prepared.

From an environment point of view, if you have a bad apple do you move him?

Sometimes you have to explain to your training staff that a young guy coming in may have to earn his stripes, but all the players have feelings. If he's going to be there for the long haul, at least let him get his foot in the door. That's when you have to be hands-on. There are a lot of decisions that are made for you, but if you can somehow get involved in them, it's better.

How close, Scotty, did you like to get to your players?

When I first started coaching I had a lot of veteran players. Some were a lot older than me so I had to try to find solutions to accommodate that. Claude Ruel, in Montreal, was more of a player's coach than I was. He was a good friend to some of the players, but he had a good attitude and he would either tip me off or warn me if we needed to do something with a certain guy. Every place I go now there are two or three assistant coaches. I think they can be the ones in the position to be there on a daily basis with the players. I always had a core of players that I could talk strategy or just generalize with about the team. You are always closer to a few than many.

Could you look in a player's eyes or read his body language to know that he was ready to play?

I don't know if I could do that. I guess I knew when something was bothering him. You could tell from his body language that he was not satisfied. Hopefully they are going to be focussed before the game is close to being started. From the bench the coach has to notice if he's got a hot player who is really in the zone.

I also think you have to have your next plan of attack because the original one can go down the drain pretty quickly. It's important to somehow get key players who are in a funk out of it, whether it's by changing a player or two around or putting them in a position where they might succeed. **I don't think you can coach the team routinely. You're not going to be able to succeed unless you try things. Some aren't going to work and some might be goofy tries, but it's better to do that than do nothing.**

What qualities do you look for when selecting captains?

There are two different kinds, and I've had both. **I always found the captains who said less and did more were better than the ones who said a lot and did little.** Some guys do a lot of talking, and the next thing you know the game is on the ice and what they said not to do happens. **It's important for the leaders to be very respected by the group and to accept the leadership of the team.** If they're going to be a high-profile guy there's a bit of a responsibility that goes with it.

What are your priorities as a coach?

I was a stickler for dotting the i's and crossing the t's. **I always felt that coaching had three categories: the practice and preparation, the bench management during the game, and the conditioning of your team mentally and physically.** It's important that you are on top of things that are important. There are some things that aren't as important as others, and in time you get to know that.

Do your principles of success spill over into other areas of your life?

My wife is the same kind of person as me. She pays attention to detail. She doesn't make our five children toe the line, but they are well aware that she expects them to do certain things. I think that's what you try to do; you try to get them to live up to your expectations.

How did you relax? Was there anything you did to get away from the game?

I relax most by watching other teams play. I just love to watch games. I would watch a game or I'd tape another game. Later on, after I started coaching again in Pittsburgh and my family had grown up, my wife came down from Buffalo for some games, but I had a lot of time in the last 10 years that I coached. I had no other hobbies during the season. I didn't even want to go out for dinner because I wanted to watch games. If I went for dinner, it would be early. I didn't enjoy taping a game and then watching it later; I had enough of my own tapes to look at.

The time that I enjoyed not coaching was at the end of the season. That's why I enjoy coaching better than anything; once you've coached your last game you are sort of free and clear until the next training camp. There were a few times you might go to the odd meeting, but that was the down time, the time that coaches get to do other things. I had some hobbies. I have a couple of antique cars, and in the summer I used to go to a lot of car shows. I had some friends who weren't really involved in hockey, and the last couple of years I got involved in the summer in a few golf tournaments. I like that, and travelling, but during the season I was big on routine: Get to the rink at a certain time, the players are gone early to mid-afternoon, and then go into the dressing room and put some tapes on. The next thing you know, it's 5:00 p.m.

I remember we had a poor start in St. Louis, but then began to have some good endings for the first two or three years of expansion. Guys got carried away looking at how well they were doing, and then we got into a terrible slump one year. I scheduled two practices a day and made both practices during the rush hour. For the first one they had to buck the traffic coming down into St. Louis from the West County to practice at 9:00 a.m., which meant they had to be there at 8:00. Then I had nothing until about 4:00. We did this for about five days in a row. I don't know if you can do that now, but we did it then just to get their attention. I said to them, "Now you know how the other side of the world lives. Would you like to do this for 50 weeks of the year?"

In the beginning, Scotty, where did you get your advice?

During my early days in Montreal the person I talked with the most was Toe Blake. He had had enough and retired. He was wonderful to have around the team because he knew exactly when to talk to somebody, when to seek somebody out, and I asked him a lot of questions. I found him to be a good source of experience. He used to tell me every player was my friend, and I got a kick out of that. Every coach is going to have somebody he calls for advice. I was fortunate to have somebody who had been through everything, so Toe was the man.

How is it, now that you are retired from coaching and the one who can give advice?

I was hired in Detroit to coach for two years. After two years I asked what the plan was, and they said, "We'd love to have you stay with the team." So that two years became nine. Now I like what I do. I go to NHL games with the manager, Ken Holland. He appreciates what I've done. He allows me to make my own schedule, and I can help the team in my own way. I'm pretty careful to stay out of the way, because it's their team. I talk with Dave and Barry, and I keep telling them I'm not there every day; there are some decisions they have to make themselves. I can only put in my two cents' worth when I feel it's time. I think it would be tough to be a coach or general manager, and then all of a sudden you're finished and you're just a spectator. I don't consider myself just a spectator. I knew it was time to leave, so I never sit here and say, "Gee, I wish I was behind the bench." I'm going to stay a couple more years and make my own schedule.

Roger Neilson

Perhaps no other NHL coach elicits more affection from fans and players alike than Roger Neilson. Loud ties, a sense of humour, an intense devotion to the game, and a man of faith all spring to mind when his name is mentioned. Roger was born on June 16, 1934, in Toronto, Ontario. He began coaching minor hockey as a 17-year-old student at McMaster University in 1951–52, and won the Bantam B Championship in 1952–53 and the Toronto Hockey League title the following season in 1953–54, while continuing to coach the other sport he loved and excelled at: baseball.

After 15 years coaching minor hockey Roger jumped to major junior, where he coached the OHL's Peterborough Petes from 1966 to 1976. During this time he taught high school Physical Education as well, but in 1973 he decided to devote 100 percent of his time to coaching junior hockey. Under Neilson the Petes finished in the top three in the league standings eight times and reached the 1972 Memorial Cup final after capturing the OHL Junior A crown.

In 1962 Roger received his first NHL job, a part-time scouting gig, from Scotty Bowman, who was the Montreal Canadiens' eastern scout at the time. Roger stepped behind the bench as head coach of the Toronto Maple Leafs in 1977 and coached the team to 44 wins and a first-round playoff upset of the New York Islanders that eventually advanced Toronto to the third round. After two years behind the Leafs bench, including the time that he was fired and rehired by owner Harold Ballard, Neilson was once again hired by Scotty Bowman to be his assistant coach with the Buffalo Sabres. In 1980–81 Roger took over as head coach, guiding the Sabres to the second round of the playoffs.

He was hired as Harry Neale's assistant in Vancouver in 1981, took over as head coach mid-season, and helped the Canucks give the highly touted New York Islanders a tough run before encountering defeat in the Stanley Cup finals. It was in this playoff year that Neilson originated the "white towel affair" in defiance of a perceived bias against his Canucks by NHL on-ice officials. He was ejected from the game after waving a hockey stick draped with a white towel, but at the next home game and for countless playoff games around the league since, fans appeared in the stands waving white towels of their own.

Roger became the head coach of the Los Angeles Kings in the 1983–84 season and was hired as a video analyst by Edmonton during the 1984 playoffs, where he helped the Oilers win their first Stanley Cup. He became the New York Rangers' head coach in 1989 and won the Patrick Division title in his first year and the President's Trophy for first place overall during the regular season in 1991–92. He became the first-ever head coach of the Florida Panthers and was an assistant coach in St. Louis from 1995 to 1998 before moving on to be Philadelphia's head coach until the end of the 1999–2000 season.

Roger was always recognized as an innovator and tactician of the game over his 26-year NHL career. He took such advantage of existing rules that he forced changes to the rulebook in junior and became known as "Rulebook Roger." He was one of the first coaches to conduct on-ice aerobic training and develop an extensive off-ice training program. He designed systems and strategies to give his teams a competitive edge at the professional level. He spent endless hours, often all night long, analyzing game videos to pick apart opponents' weaknesses, and to see where his own players might improve—pioneering work that earned him the nickname "Captain Video." He established the Roger Neilson Forever Hockey Fund to bring children and hockey and fun together. His Roger Neilson's Hockey Camp, established in 1977, and Coaches' Clinic, running for more than 20 years, continue on as he wished.

Roger Neilson was an NHL head coach for parts of 16 seasons, 11 of them with a winning record, and achieved a career total of 460 wins and 159 ties. He also has the distinction, welcome or not, of having been fired from more NHL coaching posts than anyone else. Jacques Martin stepped aside as head coach of the Ottawa Senators to allow Roger, then his assistant, to coach his 1,000th NHL game on April 13, 2002. Roger was runner-up for the Jack Adams Award for NHL Coach of the Year in 1992, and was inducted into the Hockey Hall of Fame as a Builder in November 2002. He received a Doctor of Laws degree from McMaster University in 2001. On January 19, 2003, Roger Neilson was awarded the Order of Canada, his country's highest honour for lifetime achievement.

On June 21, 2003, Roger succumbed to a long and hard-fought battle with cancer. In 2003, the City of Peterborough changed the name of George Street South, opposite the Memorial Centre Arena where he once coached the Petes, to Roger Neilson Way, and the Ottawa Senators now call the coaches' booth in the press box at Scotiabank Place Roger's Room. In September 2004, the Roger Neilson Public School opened in Peterborough, and in 2005 the Ontario Hockey League created the Roger Neilson Memorial Award, to be granted to the top academic player attending college or university. On April 21, 2006, the Ottawa Senators Foundation opened Roger's House, a pediatric palliative-care facility located on the grounds of the Children's Hospital of Eastern Ontario. All honour the memory of the colourful, selfless, humble man who enhanced the lives of his hockey family. We miss you, Roger.

The Interview

You've been coaching for a long time. What drives you?

The love of the game. Not just the love of being on the ice, or in a game, but the whole deal: the practice the day before, the game-day skate, the game-day routine, the pre-game, showing the power-play and penalty-killing tapes, and then analyzing the game. I've been doing it for so long, and I feel so grateful that I've been able to work in a job that most people would do for nothing.

Do you believe that a coach has a responsibility to motivate the player, or is the player on his own?

The coaches always say you have to be a teacher, a strategist, a motivator, and certainly the most important of those is being the motivator. You do have a responsibility to provide an environment where players can be motivated. I don't think that you have to talk to players all the time, but you've got to provide the environment. They have to know that the practice is going to be good. They have to know that the pre-game talk is going to be a decent talk, and they've got to know that you're prepared. They have to know what their role is. **That's how you provide motivation: Set the environment so that they have a chance to be their best.**

Do you have different strategies to motivate different players?

Within that atmosphere that you are creating, which is a team thing, you have individuals, and it's the same old story: You treat them all differently. You may want to be a little friendlier to some guys to get them to perform. You have to bring in other guys and tell them off.

I will always remember the great story of when Mike Keenan came to St. Louis and Chris Pronger wasn't playing well. There were some rumours that he was out a little too late at night, so Mike brought him into his office in St. Louis along with his parents. My office was just outside Mike's. Mike was really giving it to him, really reaming him out. I heard Mike say, "You know, I'm old enough to be your father, and I'm in better shape than you. That guy sitting outside the door (that was me), he's old enough to be your grandfather!" So Pronger comes out and says, "Hi, Gramps." Mike really reamed him out, and he brought his parents in and went through the whole thing with them, and in my opinion that turned Pronger around. Mike deserves a lot of credit there because he did what he had to do with Pronger. He knew Pronger was a bright guy who had a lot of ability.

You've got to know your players and know what will make them respond. The skill in coaching is finding out all about them. I think that's something you've got to look into right away. You've got to talk to other guys who have coached them. **You've really got to know your players to be able to do the best job motivating them.**

How does a coach instill confidence in athletes?

You don't want a guy who gets down too easy, especially if it's pretty obvious to the rest of the team. You've got to try to stay on top of those kinds of things. If you can see the player's confidence is waning, then it's your job to try and build him up. You can do this in different ways. Maybe it's putting him on a new line or with a different defenceman, or sometimes it's having a talk with him and explaining a new role. I think that's where coaching is important.

Do you try to find an angle to motivate the team?

If you can find one that everyone would buy. I remember the mind games or the things that players look at and say, "Come on. You know, some guys might buy that but I'm not going to." You have to be careful, but you should try to come up with some angle.

I remember with the Canucks on our run in 1982 we felt we were the underdogs. We believed that the longer we continued to be in the games and the longer the series went, the more other teams would tighten up. We were really confident going into overtime, and as a result we won four of the overtime games we were involved in. The other teams were too tight. If you can come up with an angle that everyone will buy, sure, it works.

What would be the identity of a Roger Neilson coached team?

The aim is always a hard-working team that plays well together. I've always felt that if a team has reasonable talent, in other words they are in the ballpark, and are sound defensively because that's something every team can be, then you are going to be in most games. You can't always be great offensively, because that depends on your talent. The foundation is to be sound defensively. I don't like my teams to be known as defensive teams, but when the other team has the puck your team should know what to do, for sure. When you've got the puck, then it's more of a skill thing; there's innovation involved. You want guys to use their talents, be creative, and so on, but a hard-working team is what everybody wants.

Have your teams shared any common traits?

I've coached so many different teams. I coached L.A. when they were dead last, and there was no way they were going to be dead last. I've been with a top team like the New York Rangers and then a team like the Florida Panthers, where we didn't have much offence. I don't know if there's been any great common denominator, but I've been able to get all my teams to play pretty well defensively, and we've been able to have decent special teams on most of them. Those are areas you can work on; they're improvable situations. I don't know if I can go any further than that.

How do you keep your players focussed on what's good for the team?

It's more difficult today than it was. Even coaching peewee is more difficult. We used to grab all our guys in the Volkswagen van and go, even though I didn't know half the parents. Now the parents can fire a coach. It's an entirely different set-up. Now they're worried about whether kids in bantam are going to be drafted. When they hit junior it's the same thing about the pro draft. Then as a pro they know they need to get so many goals for their contract next year. Before, all they wanted to do was win, you know, so the whole concept that way is different. What was the statement by John Wooden? "It's amazing how much can be accomplished when nobody cares who gets the credit." In fact that was the motto and has always been the motto of our summer hockey camp. As a coach today it's more of a challenge to get everybody thinking as a team all the time.

Have you done some specific things to enhance team cohesion?

We've always tried to have one or two "fun days" a year. We started in Toronto when we had the Maple Leaf Indoor Games as a one-day competition with the players broken into four teams. In Florida, Craig Ramsey had a golf thing in the dressing room on the carpet where you had to chip onto a target. I had a multiple-choice rule contest and gave four of the players 15 minutes to sit around and try to figure the answers out. Lindy Ruff had kind of a cardboard thing of a referee that he built at home, and you had to run it down with a hockey stick like a javelin, swear, and try to knock the referee's head off. Needless to say, it was front page on the *Miami Herald*. There was some kind of a prize for it. The players appreciate you organizing fun times like that.

How do you develop a tradition of excellence?

I don't talk about it, but I think it comes through. It's a matter of time. You have to have some success. Over the 10 years I was in Peterborough we built up a tradition of excellence. We had good teams, and we probably had more guys attending school than any other major junior team at the time. We were the best-conditioned team because of the early morning runs. Everyone in Ontario knew what the Peterborough Petes stood for. It often takes some years to do that, and it is difficult to do in the NHL with the top guys changing all the time. We had it in New York when I was there for four years, but I don't know if you can do that anymore.

People define success as winning a championship. Do you have a definition of what a successful season looks like?

For a player, success in any game is being able to perform at your best. As a coach you're looking for the team to be its best. Your job is to get the team to play its best. If you do that, then you are successful. We didn't quite make the playoffs my first two years with the Florida Panthers. We missed by a point, I think, both years. Still, I thought we were very successful there because it was a team that played well together, and most of the guys had their best years. You can't ask for much more than that.

What is your most memorable coaching experience or your greatest accomplishment?

Over a season it was probably the first year with the Panthers, which was a great year in every way. We just didn't quite make the playoffs, but we had the best record of any pro team in any sport as a first-year expansion team. I felt that was quite an accomplishment. The best year as a team was the lockout year in 1994. That year with the New York Rangers we were first in almost every special team and points. We had a great team. That was probably my greatest season accomplishment. In the playoffs we had that Lanny McDonald goal my first year in Toronto which eliminated the Islanders, who were heavily favoured. The Canuck run to the Stanley Cup finals was something special. Those are the highlights.

Does the fear of losing motivate you more than the enjoyment of winning?

I don't think you ever are fearful of losing. You don't ever think of that. When you go into a game all you are thinking about is how to get the best out of your team, how to win. You don't even think about losing until it's over and you've lost; then you start wondering why. In my preparation for a game or a series I don't ever think about losing.

Do you win at all costs?

Within the rules. In junior I wasn't opposed to looking for loopholes in the rules. Some of them were fun. I used to read the rule book quite a bit, and one day I thought of something on the bus: It stood out that nothing could stop you from putting a skater in goal. Nothing in the rule book said you couldn't. It just happened that night in a pre-season game that we had a penalty shot called on us, we tried it, and it worked. I put Ron Stackhouse, our defenceman, in goal for the six penalty shots against us that year. It was incredible that we had that many, and he stopped them all. Ron would move out of the net and go halfway toward the shooter. We always thought that some guy might just wind up and the forwards would just go around him, but it never happened. It's not that easy to go around a defensive defenceman. He is such a big guy, and they tried everything, shooting through him and around him. Nobody could get close to scoring, and the next year they changed the rule.

There was another loophole, and I had warned the OHA that there was a bad flaw in the rule book. When there's two minutes to go in the game, if you were to put an extra guy on the ice you couldn't go any shorter than three skaters. When I took over the Petes they were in ninth and last place. We moved up to eighth, I think, during the last two months of the season and just made it into the playoffs. We were playing Hamilton, who finished fourth, in a playoff game. They had us 3–1 in the series back in Hamilton. We were only playing about 10 players and really scrambling to hold on to a 3–2 lead in the third period. Somehow we found ourselves two men short with two minutes to go, so for the faceoff we threw an extra guy on, and as soon as he touched the puck, of course the whistle went and he was sent to the penalty box. When the play resumed we threw another one on, and the referee came over and said I was going to be fined and we were stalling. Anyway, the whole thing was just a stall and I remember sending Mickey Redmond back to ask the ref how much the fine would be, and he came back with $5,000 or something. As soon as the puck dropped we continued to send two players out right to their points. Of course it so upset the other team that finally when the time ran out and the game was over, they went crazy. All the fans in that little Hamilton rink threw stuff, and then all the hockey people came down and everybody really blasted me, said I was ruining the game. I told them that I was following the rules. Of course they later changed the rule and made it a penalty shot if you deliberately put too many men on the ice.

Now, you may say that I was really bending the rules, but I felt that if it wasn't covered in the rule book it was my duty to take advantage of something like that. I don't think it's right to go out and deliberately try to injure a player. I wouldn't consider that. I wouldn't win at all costs that way.

Can you recall your worst moment as a coach?

I have been fired a few times, and the first one is always tough. That was in Toronto. Then there was that time that I was fired and rehired in Toronto—you know that really happened—so at the end of the season when they didn't renew my contract it wasn't a big surprise. Jim Gregory and I were both let go. In Buffalo it was kind of in a disagreement with Scotty, but I knew I could go to Vancouver anyway.

Vancouver was a tough one. We had that early success and then the next year made the playoffs, but lost out in the first round. Halfway through the next year they made the change. I can understand that, you know; it wasn't a great team there. It was never a .500 team to begin with, but it was still difficult because I loved Vancouver so much.

By far the most surprising one was with Florida. We were going down to talk about a contract extension, and all of a sudden they told us they were going in another direction. That was a complete surprise; I never saw that one coming at all. With the Rangers we got into that Messier deal so you could see that one coming a bit, but if I had to pick the most disappointing firing of all, it was probably Vancouver.

I was lucky because three days later I got the job in Los Angeles, so I didn't have time to worry about it. After L.A. I had nothing, and I remember my friend, a lawyer, telling me to go to the draft and see. I said, "I'm not going to the draft to beg for a job." But anyway I did, and sure enough Chicago came by and said they were looking for an assistant coach. I went there and eventually became a co-coach with Bob Pulford. I was with Chicago five years, three in coaching and two as a scout.

How do you handle pressure?

There is always pressure, but to a certain extent you like pressure because it forces you to act. It forces you to make some moves. You need some adversity to become stronger. I mean, that's not only Biblical, it's everything, so that's how you handle it, especially with your team. You explain, "We've got to go through some hard times, and most teams that win the Stanley Cup, or come close, have had some prior heartbreakers that they learned from."

Pressure can be due to slumps. Usually you work harder in slumps. You make sure you are stressing things that have been successful. Other times you have to try something completely new if all else fails. **Adversity is a real test of character, and your team has to know that you work your way through it.**

There are different ways to approach it. You usually just work harder. That's what everybody expects. Sometimes, though, you let up completely and take the day off or get them completely away from the rink for two days. You can go back to things that have been successful, or you can try something completely new. You have to judge, but I don't think you can just let it happen. You have to do something to snap them out of it.

How do you deal with confrontational situations?

I don't think you want to look for them or particularly enjoy them. **I try to avoid public confrontations with players. I don't mind private ones at all. I think it's not bad to go toe to toe when it's an issue with a player.** He knows that if he comes into your room with some ideas that are definitely going to be different, it's going to be a battle. I think that's the way it should be. I don't like public confrontations with players. I don't like them on the bench, and I don't like them in front of the media. I like to keep it on the side burner.

Thomas Jefferson said, "In things of style swim with the current, and in things of substance stand like a rock." If a player is coming into your room for confrontation, what are the issues that are substance for you?

I don't think you can say what they are because every situation is so different, but, oh, yeah, definitely the line has to be drawn. You like players to have their ideas and to come in, and you like to implement them where you can, but sometimes a player comes in to look into something that's going to benefit him more than everybody else. That's where you have to cut it off.

What type of player is most challenging to coach?

The superstar can be the most difficult. Some are really easy to work with, but these are the guys that you have to pay special attention to. I can remember Neil Smith sitting with the coaches in New York, telling us we spend 90 percent of our time talking about Mark Messier, and he was right. It was almost the same in St. Louis. Ninety percent of our time was spent with Brett Hull. Your highly skilled superstars can take a lot of time, and they often take special treatment, but the point is if you don't get along with them it's going to cost you your job. Still, it's always your choice; you're the coach. With other players it could be personalities or whatever; you deal with them as you can, but the superstar is the toughest.

If we were to interview some of your former players, how would they de-scribe their relationship with you?

I hope that they would describe me as being honest in terms of work ethic and my dealings with the team. I'd like the players to think that the team was well prepared, the coaches were well organized, and the players knew what their role was and were therefore able to play at their best. I like players to feel that way.

How close do you like to get to your players?

The further along I went in the NHL, the closer I became to my players. When I got to New York I definitely changed. I'm not sure what prompted the change, but I became friendlier and more accessible, joking around a little more in practice. Prior to that I had remained pretty aloof from players. In New York I made more of an effort to be friendly to play-ers and find out about them and their families. Before, I didn't even know if they were married or not. I probably should have, but I didn't. Previous-ly I had been just all team, everybody's the same, but everything changed when I went to New York.

When you're going into a game and you're looking a guy in the eye, can you read whether a player's "on" and ready to play a great game?

No, I'm not very good at that. I had Ron Smith as assistant for half a season, and he enjoyed doing this. He would write down in the morn-ing skate whether he thought they were up, down, or can't tell, and then for the pre-game skate he did the same thing, and we found there was ab-solutely no correlation whatsoever. He did it for 40 games. We wanted to find out about that because I didn't believe he could tell whether they were up or not. As a goalkeeper in Junior B I found that some nights when I was as sharp as anything in the warm-up I didn't have a good night at all and couldn't stop a beach ball, for some reason. So I'd have to say that I'm not very good at judging, and I'm not sure anybody is.

Do you try to influence the environment in the dressing room?

The dressing room environment belongs to the players, and I don't think a coach can get involved. I never liked slogans. With most teams I go in and take down the slogans. **If the team doesn't have a good feel in**

the dressing room and your chemistry is somehow not right, then you have to make changes and get enough players who can keep things going in the room. I was trying to get Jacques Martin to get Marc Bergevin for Ottawa because he's such a great guy in the room.

How much emphasis would you put on leadership, and how would you describe it?

Everybody is so different. Some guys can lead because they're big, blustery guys; they give that great aura of confidence. General Patton's "Let's go get 'em, boys." Other leaders can be like Doug Jarvis; he was a real leader in junior, and he never said a word. So when Doug said, "Hey, let's get going," to the guys, everybody went, "Wow!"

In Florida we had six guys who could have been or had been captains. It was an incredible situation, and each guy had his own distinct qualities, so I don't know if you can define leadership by specific qualities. Even with coaches, you've got the quiet coach like the Fred Shero type, and you've got the Pat Burns type, and then you've got Scotty Bowman, who's another completely different guy. You've got Mike Keenan and a guy like Andy Murray. **I think for players now, the definition is you've got to get players, without sort of knowing it, to carry out what you want them to do, and at the same time they've got to be convinced that that's what they want too.** Certainly the best captain was Darryl Sittler, with my first team. He was quite able to completely get the confidence of the team. Mark Messier had some great qualities too, but Sittler would be my number one.

What did Darryl Sittler do? Was it his personality, was it his leadership style, or was he just the right guy at the right time?

His personality was excellent. I can remember it was the first game we were playing in Atlanta in the playoffs in my first year, and we had one of those 10 a.m. meetings. I went walking down to the room, and as I got near I could hear Darryl talking to the team. I just stood outside the door and listened, and he was great; after that I had hardly anything to say. He was able to talk to the team, take charge of situations, was one of your hardest workers in practice, and kept himself in top shape. The guys all really respected Darryl. He knew when to just be funny and have a good time with the guys and joke around. I used to room him with a different guy that was coming out of junior every night. I went in one night, and he was with Jimmy Jones. I asked how the two were getting along, and he said, "Great. I'm teaching him how to score. He's teaching me how to check." Sittler was like that; he was perfect. To me he was the perfect leader.

Do you try to teach your players life lessons along with hockey lessons?

I am not a coach who plays mind games. I'm not into many gimmicks like that. I guess as a coach you like to think you are helping build guys' character, but I wouldn't want to be coaching a pro team with that as one of your main objectives. It would be nice if things worked out that way. I do think when you're coaching kids it should be right near the top of the list.

You mentioned that you changed your style in New York. Have you had to adjust to the players coming into the league?

In junior everyone was even. I don't care how many goals you scored; everything was even so everybody got treated exactly the same. Everybody got paid the same; everybody got treated the same. One of the things you have to learn as a coach going into pro is that they're not the same. You've got your superstars. In junior you might treat the players differently in the way you talk to them or something, but when it's in front of the team everything is exactly the same. In the pros it doesn't work that way at all, and so that was something that had to change.

Looking back at over 25 years in the league I don't know how much I've actually changed. There are a lot of things that remain the same. I think you become a better coach, of course, over that time just because of experience.

Do you trust your gut instinct as a leader?

I think some coaches go with it way more than others. I try to go more by the book than my gut.

What do you mean "by the book"?

Well, the way it should be. I was thinking more on the percentages. I'm more if you had the left-handed hitter coming up with a right-handed pitcher and I had a left-handed hitter, I'm not going to think that this guy's going to cork one tonight. I try to stay away from that. I try to go with the game plan. I'll change once in awhile, but I think you can get into trouble if you're always operating like that. Once you do something on a gut feeling, the team all know that that's not the way it's supposed to be. That's fine if it works, but I don't do that much.

How do you cast the vision as a leader/coach?

You always wonder every year how high you should set your sights, and you don't want to set them too high, that's for sure. That's something that coaches have to take into consideration. I'm not a guy for saying, "OK, we need to get 25 points in the first half." I'm much more general than that: "If things fall into place this year we've got a chance. We work hard enough, we could be there." I'm more that kind of a coach than stating specific goals. I think you are better off that way because sometimes you can be way off and that team is trying all year long to live up to the fact that they're not nearly as good as they thought they were.

One mistake coaches make at times is telling their players that they are a better team than the opponent and should win that game or series. That's not something I would like to hear. I think that you might sometimes say, "Look, this is a pretty skilled team we're playing, but I think we've got more character. I think we're the kind of guys that when the chips are down …" but to say, "Hey, we're a better team than them. We're better in every way. We're better at power play. We're better at this," you know, I think that puts the pressure on you. Some coaches think that is the kind of pressure you want. I don't like that, and I don't think it's necessary. I think there are times, with the way you handle video and things, that you can get across that your team is good without constantly telling them. You can say, "Hey, we had a really good segment here, we did a good job, but the next one's going to be tough," not "Look at all these easy teams we're playing. The next time we should be able to do it again."

So many coaches come and go each year, and you've worked for 10 organizations. There must be a secret to your success.

Well, I've sort of been able to fool them for 26 years. I've been really lucky that way, I guess. There is a huge turnover in hockey, more so, it seems, than other sports. It seems like guys get one chance and they're out. I certainly haven't burned any bridges wherever I've been. There is no question that through all the hockey camps and clinics we run every year, we know a lot of people, and that helps.

How do you handle the responsibilities that you have as a head coach? Do you like to be hands-on, or do you like to delegate?

When I first started, of course, I was the only coach with the Leafs. I had talked Ron Smith into helping by giving him $25 gas money to come down from Cambridge for practice and assist me out on the ice. Usually you were completely by yourself. On the road I had the airline tickets, the tickets for the game, the bus schedule … I did absolutely everything. I remember we had a very successful road trip and were like five wins and one loss at the start of the season, and we ended up coming back from the West right to Montreal to play before we came home. It was a Saturday night in Montreal, and 10 minutes before the game I was upstairs trying to teach some kid from Concordia University how to work the video camera, and you know, I never really did get down to give the pep talk. That's the way it was in those days.

Now, of course, it has changed. I like to have a coach do the defence, I like to change the forwards, and I like it when a guy looks after the power play and another guy does the penalty killing. In Philly, Craig Ramsay used to give a pep talk every game. Some nights I added something, and some nights I didn't. Nowadays in the NHL there is so much more delegation.

I came from being a guy who did everything to a guy who now likes to delegate, but you can delegate too much. I think that the team has to feel that you're in charge. Jacques Martin did a pretty good job that way in Ottawa. They all know he's running things, but he still delegates. I think that's the key.

Are you happy as an assistant coach (in Ottawa) after being a head coach for so long? Do you ever think you will be a head coach again?

Well, a lot of that has to do with my health. I would much rather be a head coach, but I think that through my experience I am able to do both. I'm happy in Ottawa, but I don't think I'll ever be a head coach again, because of my health. The kinds of cancer that I have are not ones that are going to get better. They keep them under control for as long as they can. The chances of being a head coach at this time are not good.

Roger, do you still dabble with the video aspect of hockey, even though most teams have a video coach?

We all do it now because it's become an important aspect of the game, the power play and penalty killing, the forecheck and defensive zone coverage. These video technicians put everything on the hard drive now. I haven't got a clue how to work the machines. I might have been "Captain Video" at one time but it has passed me by long ago. It's pretty high-tech these days, but I enjoy watching video and coming up with things to help the players.

How do you relax as a coach? How do you get away?

Aside from the ice, I love reading. I've read every one of Wilbur Smith's books. They are books about Africa and pirates and certainly take me away from the game. And I like Leon Uris's stuff on Israel.

Where do you get your advice?

There was no one in my early career when I was in Toronto coaching all the youth teams in baseball and hockey. I was also on my own in Peterborough. When I got to Toronto my first manager was Jim Gregory, and since that time we've remained pretty good friends. When I've had different problems in the NHL or gotten fired or whatever, I've often called Jim and he's been really good. I played with Scotty Bowman and we had some differences, but we're very good friends and I like to phone Scotty on stuff. There are different people I'm quite happy to do that with, but if there was one guy, it was my first manager, Jim Gregory.

Have there been people in general who have shaped you as a leader and as a person?

No, but I like John Wooden. Apparently he was an excellent coach, and I just liked his quotes and the things he said and the way he ran a team. In that way you could say he's been an influence. I certainly read all of his stuff.

Is it important for a young coach to have a mentor?

I think it's nice if you can have a mentor, but I think in most cases you just find your way. It's great if you happen to know somebody who can help you out. So many times, though, you just don't have one so you have to find your own way.

Let's talk about how you became a Christian and how it has affected you.

I was in a Christian family. Dad was president of the Gideons. When I was about 12 years old we used to go over to this church on Friday nights and play basketball and hockey in the basement, and then afterward we would go up with the youth guy, and he would give us about a four- or five-minute talk and some Cokes. That was our Friday-night routine. One of those Friday nights I guess I happened to be listening, and I can remember he asked whether anyone wanted to stay around after and talk. Another kid and I stayed, and he explained Christianity the way we could understand it, that Jesus loved us and wanted to be our friend and wanted to help us out, and then explained what we had to do. I turned my life over to the Lord that night as a 12-year-old kid. I remember I went home and told my mom and dad, and of course they were really happy. It didn't seem much at the time, but looking back it was probably the greatest influence in my life.

What keeps you close to your faith?

At first it was probably just going to church on Sunday and saying my prayers every night. Eventually it became reading the Bible every day, and now, of course, it's a couple of Christian publications and a little other Christian book I always have going and the Bible. It's not a lot, but it's probably a 20-minute to half-hour deal every day. I have a prayer book that's evolved over the years, and you get a real appreciation for the Lord. I think when you have the hardships and the jackpots we all get ourselves into, that always draws you closer.